IMAGES
of America

MESQUITE

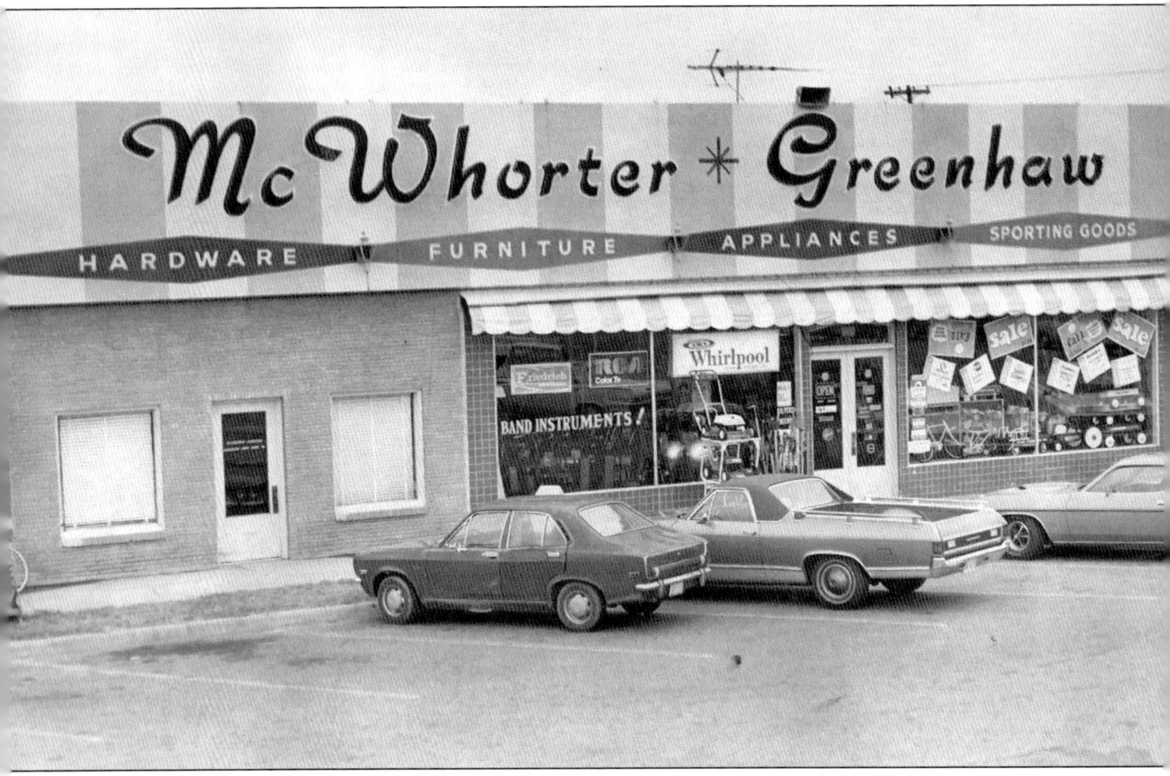

A landmark sign attached to a landmark building housing a landmark family business is pictured here in all its neon and porcelain-on-steel glory. Designed from a sketch by Frank W. Greenhaw and erected in 1964—at a then substantial purchase price of $3,748—the famous sign still welcomes customers today to the building's dance and recording enterprises. (Courtesy of the Holley-McWhorter-Greenhaw Collection/Frank W. Greenhaw Archives/Texas-Dallas History and Archives, Dallas Public Library.)

On the Cover: The Holleys sold groceries from this frame building on the south side of Main Street, located near the Mesquite Heritage Square and what is now a Wells Fargo Bank property, before constructing and moving into their final brick building in 1932. It still stands at 117 West Main Street. Joining Nathaniel "N.A." Holley for this photograph are his wife, Adell, and his sons Anson (back left) and Raymond (back right). As demonstrated by the Holley family, it often took the resources of all willing family members to operate a successful small business in early-20th-century Mesquite. (Courtesy of the Holley-McWhorter-Greenhaw Collection/Frank W. Greenhaw Archives/Texas-Dallas History and Archives, Dallas Public Library.)

IMAGES
of America

MESQUITE

Art Greenhaw

ARCADIA
PUBLISHING

ISBN 978-1-4671-3357-9

Published by Arcadia Publishing
Charleston, South Carolina

Printed in the United States of America

Library of Congress Control Number: 2015930465

For all general information, please contact Arcadia Publishing:
Telephone 843-853-2070
Fax 843-853-0044
E-mail sales@arcadiapublishing.com
For customer service and orders:
Toll-Free 1-888-313-2665

Visit us on the Internet at www.arcadiapublishing.com

This book is dedicated to 19th-and-20th-century community builder Nathaniel A. Holley, who fought the good fight through it all, including the death of his first wife and son in Mesquite's spotted fever epidemic of 1891; who gave birth to a new family eventually becoming the Holley-Shands-McWhorter-Greenhaw family; and who finished his course and kept the faith.

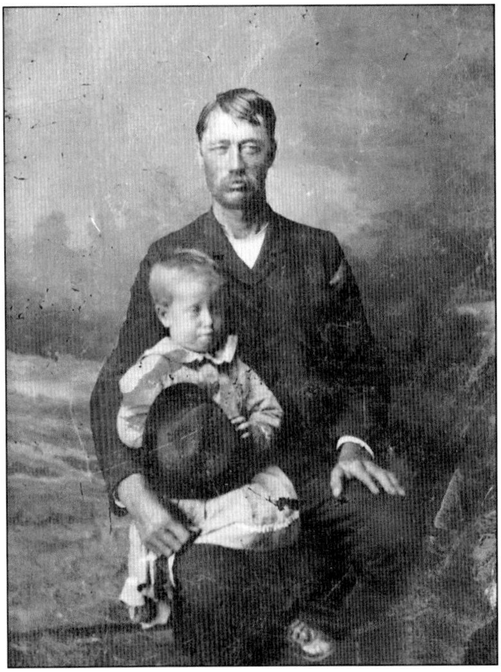

Nathaniel A. Holley is shown with his son Sammie who died in the 1891 epidemic. (Courtesy of the Holley-McWhorter-Greenhaw Collection/Frank W. Greenhaw Archives/Texas-Dallas History and Archives, Dallas Public Library.)

Contents

Acknowledgments

I wish to thank my publishing team at Arcadia Publishing—Michael Kinsella, Matthew Todd, and Jeff Ruetsche—for their support and belief in the direction and content of this book. I am grateful to Jeannie Johnson, Mesquite Public Library, for my original contact with Arcadia Publishing. Highest regards go to Bryan McKinney, Brian Collins, Adrianne Pierce, and the entire Texas/Dallas History and Archive Division, Dallas Public Library. Please visit and access whenever possible the Holley-McWhorter-Greenhaw Collection and the Frank W. Greenhaw Archives of the Dallas Public Library. Also, please visit and access whenever possible the Light Crust Doughboys Archives of Hill College Library, Hillsboro, Texas; thank you, Joe Shaughnessy and Eve Bowen.

For this photograph-rich book, the following photographers have inspired me and have contributed both directly and indirectly to the book's scope: Frank W. Greenhaw, Robert Bradford, Sheila Schindler, and Nathan Shands. Terry Reid was the best possible project manager for this book, aiding me in countless ways. Believers in the power of history who assisted me include Eve Bowen, Daniel Laney, Charlene Orr, John Tilton, Mike Burkett, Cindy Burkett, Dr. Bob Deuell, Misti Pierce, Josh Knight, Coy Poitier, Carrie Gordon, Larry Gordon II, Regina Farris, Patricia Greenhaw, Larry Carlson, Caryl Semmler, Glenda Smith, Stephen Lehew, Chad Bozarth, and Eunice Wheat Futrell.

There are giants of Mesquite history and research who laid a firm foundation for this book, specifically Max McCullough, Suzanne Starling, Weldon Lacy, Marjorie Bays, and the entire committee responsible for the ultimate, extended, 260-page, text-driven history of Mesquite, *A Stake in the Prairie*. A most dedicated supporter and encourager to Mesquite history and me is Frances James. I am grateful for past historical help and research from Charlene Orr and Jean Ann Ponder Flatt. Mesquite City councilman Bruce Archer has provided much-needed leadership dedicated to bringing back prosperity to Mesquite's central business district and family-owned and -operated businesses. And finally, I want to thank the following family members of mine who, through every step, embodied the highest and the best principles of truth, justice, and the American Way: Nathaniel and Adell Holley, Raymond and Anson Holley, Ferd and Eula McWhorter, and Frank and Patricia Greenhaw.

Unless otherwise noted, all images appear courtesy of the Holley-McWhorter-Greenhaw Collection/ Frank W. Greenhaw Archives/Texas-Dallas History and Archives, Dallas Public Library.

INTRODUCTION

Charm is deceptive, and flowers will fade,
Here for a season and then decayed.

—from "Our Wedding Song" by Engelbert Humperdinck

From this town we helped build, we are leaving,
For it's changed from the place we held dear,
But that spot where we lived, loved and labored,
I am sure in our hearts will stay near.

—from "Town in the Valley" by the Light Crust Doughboys

It was a sobering experience. It was the fall of 2012, and I had returned to my 40th Mesquite High School class reunion with a mission to find 11 other people willing to band together to revitalize our hometown of Mesquite, Texas. Not only could I not find 11 (for a good total Biblical number of 12, along with me), I could not find even one. The following reasons were unanimously given: "Too late," "too much socioeconomic decline," "too much cultural decay," and "too much of a transient, apathetic, nonowner/noninvestor population."

What on earth had happened in such a relatively short amount of time to cause this much malaise and pessimism amongst Mesquite's former class favorites, honor students, most-likely-to-succeeds? As I ask myself this question, I ask you readers to do the same. But I also ask you to remember an optimist's creed, that it is always darkest right before the dawn. Might Mesquite, Texas, be right on the verge of new leadership and a new morning time that will bring back the Boomtown USA years covered by this book? If this book that you are holding, Images of America: *Mesquite*, helps in any way to return our town to its once highly ranked, suburban prosperity, then all our efforts have been worthwhile. As the words of "Town in the Valley" state:

Come and be by my side as we're leaving,
Take my hand as we hold back the tears,
We'll remember our stake in the prairie,
That we'll love for the rest of our years.

Some New Day we'll come back to this city,
To a city that once was so bright,
And we'll build once again homes and businesses,
And we'll fight one more day the Good Fight.

There are hundreds of men and women who built Mesquite and carved out a stake in the prairie. These real, true heroes of Mesquite were not in the back rooms making the insider land deals; they were not bowing down low to the public sector for favors, fame, and fortune. They were quietly, year in and year out, standing up for home, family, private-sector job creation, free enterprise, and limited government. When I was asked to write and compile this book, these individuals, these true heroes of Mesquite, were foremost in my mind and thoughts. To borrow a technique from Mesquite native Walter Hailey's book, *Breaking the No Barrier*, the following is a partial listing of my mentors and heroes who lived and/or worked in Mesquite, Texas:

Algia Allen
Elland Archer
Virginia Armstrong
David and Marjorie Bays
Frank Berry
Solly and Marcy Berwald
Bill Blackwood
Peggy Bowdoin
Sue Braden
C.D. Brimer
Corrine Cook
Waco Crane
Joe and Donna Crook
Ben Cross
Leon and Katie Crouch
Ruth Davis
Homer DeMoss
Billie Durand
Vernie and Betty Erwin
E.K. "Big-Un" Franklin
Jeannette Franklin
Eunice Wheat Futrell
Carolyn Gilbreath
Dr. Glenn Green
Frank and Patricia Greenhaw
Fred and Evelyn Gregory
E.H. and Dona Hanby
Robert Lee and Billie Hanby
Walter "Bitsy" Hailey
Rev. Earl and Vivian Harvey
M.E. and Bernice Hamm
Joe and Joyce Hicks
Raymond Holley
Anson Holley
William and Mildred Hooper
Rev. Hulon Hood
Eula Humphreys
Kellie Kauitzsch
Rev. Earl and Georgia Kifer
Flossie Kilpatrick
A.B. and Anita Kyle
David and Hilda Joseph
Robert and Ima Lawson
Stephen Lehew
Ted Lyon
Barbara McCarley
Max McCullough
T.H. and Era McDonald
J.J. and Minelle McGlothlin
Ferd and Eula McWhorter
Lana Miller
Tut and Tommie Morris
Dr. Jack Nelson
Mike Newsom
Brunhilde Nystrom
Herbert Oyler
L.G. and Zenna Phillips
Gil and Elma Porter
Mac and Martha Range
Rex and Lorene Range
Amelia Reilly
Walter and Elizabeth Robinson
Bob and Maurine Robinson
Bert Sandlin
George and Mary Liz Schrader
Gene and Sara Lee Shands
N.E. Shands
Nan Smartt
Opal Smith
Dr. John and Jean Stack
Jack Toby
Joe and Josephine Tosch
Rev. J.V. Thomas
Glenn Thurman
Hobart and Martha Treece
Julius and Wanda Vassallo
Hub Waddill
Inez Wallace
Eva Watson
Tommy Whitlock
Sara Beth Wilcox
Joe F. Wood

One

COMMERCE

PRIVATE SECTOR AND COMMERCIAL BUSINESSES

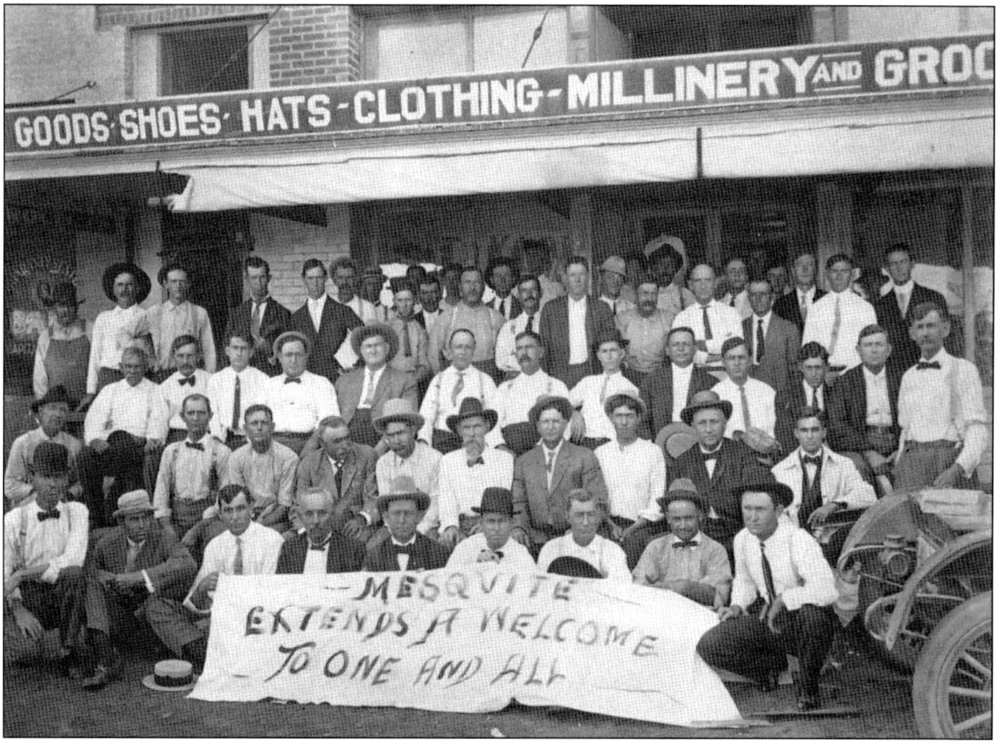

This photograph should be alternately captioned "Men Who Built Early, 20th-Century Mesquite." Businessmen from the downtown business district pose before McCullough's Store in 1911 as they are about to embark upon an automobile excursion to neighboring towns to promote "doing business" in Mesquite. Over 100 years later, it is unlikely that there would be enough "name-above-the-door" downtown business owners in the city of Mesquite to form a Mesquite trade excursion that would even fill one row of a photograph like this.

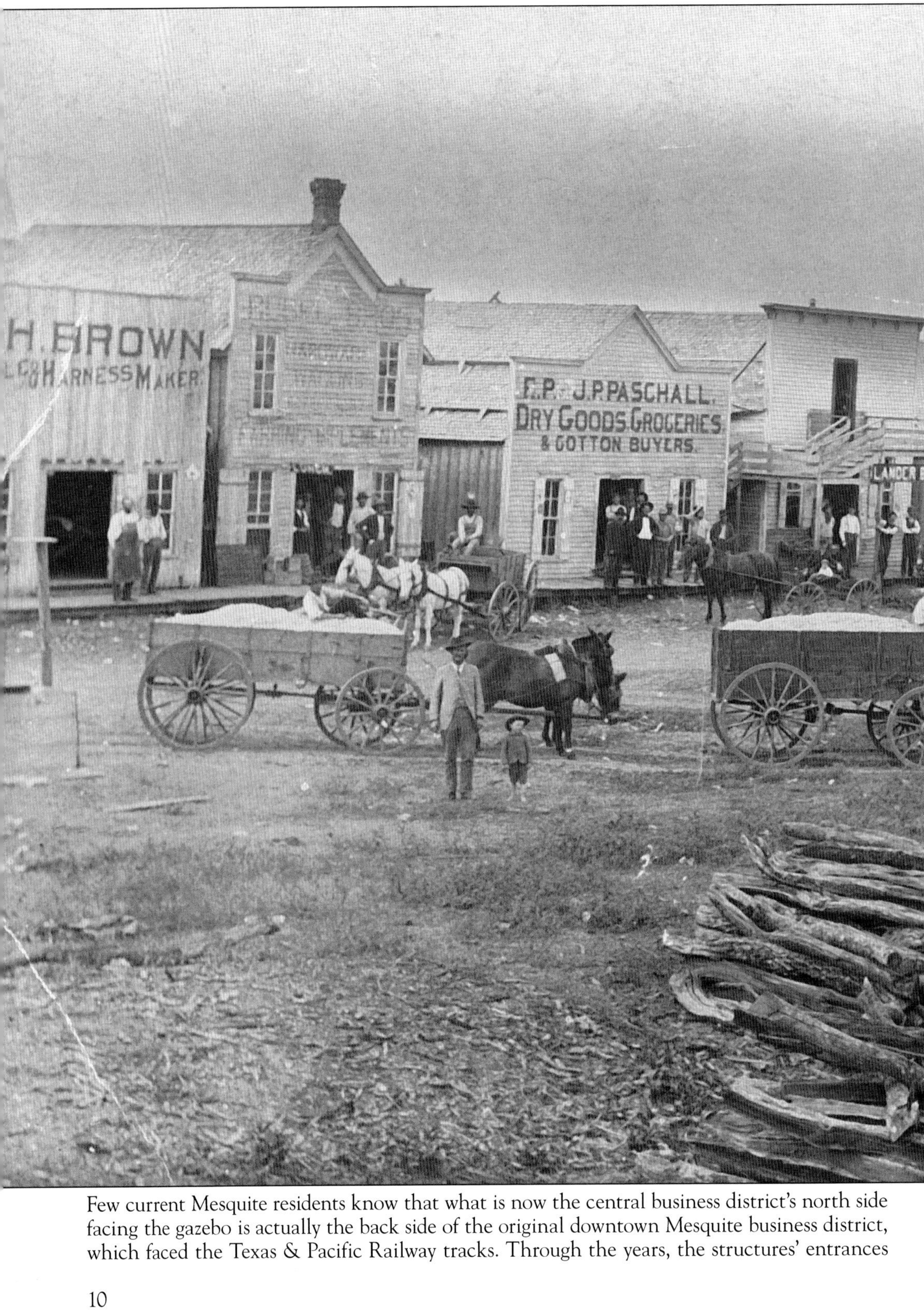

Few current Mesquite residents know that what is now the central business district's north side facing the gazebo is actually the back side of the original downtown Mesquite business district, which faced the Texas & Pacific Railway tracks. Through the years, the structures' entrances

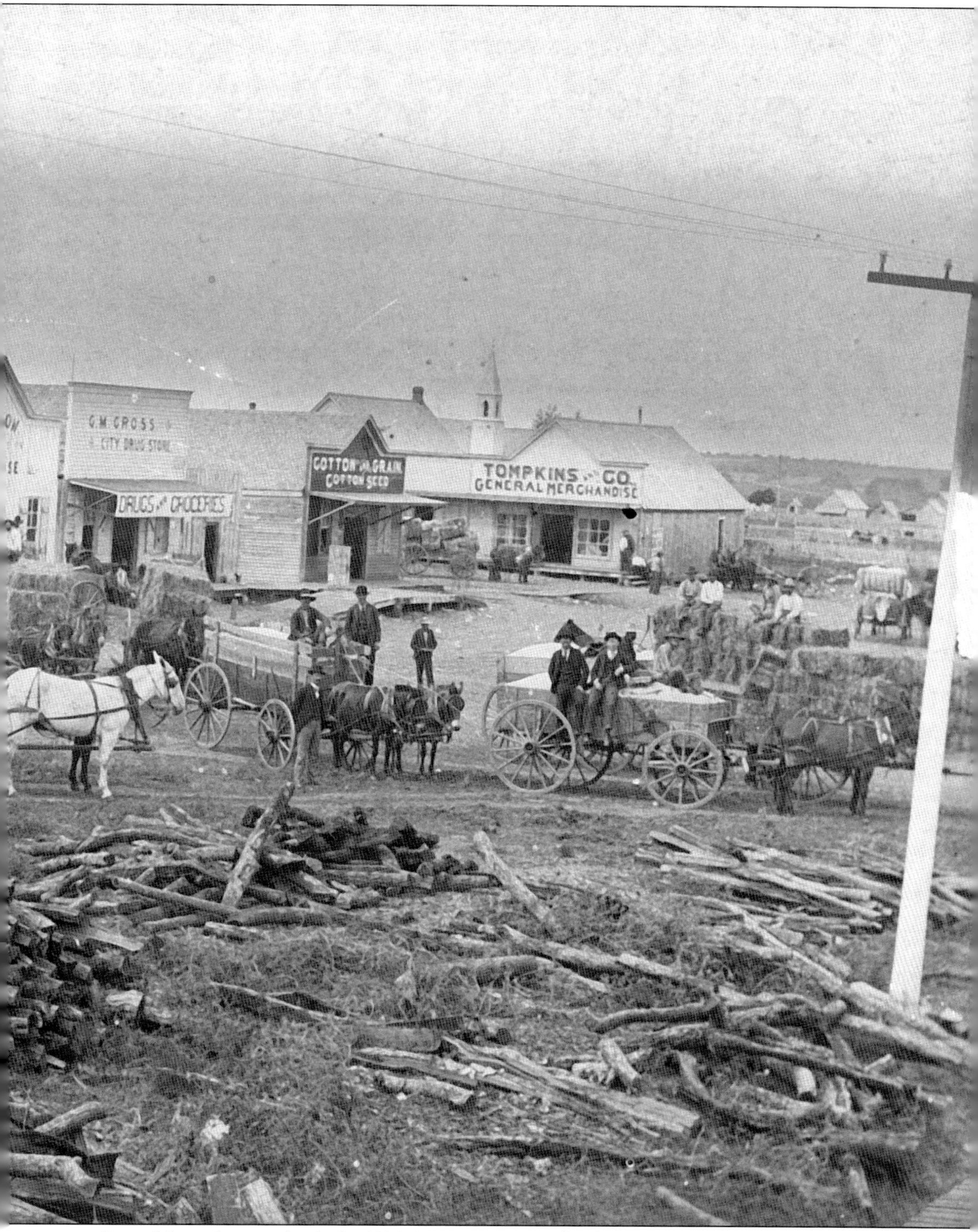

were flipped from front to back. In 1890, Mesquite was still a horse-and-buggy town, and stores provided harness making, cotton buying, dry goods and groceries, general merchandise, and drugs (medicines).

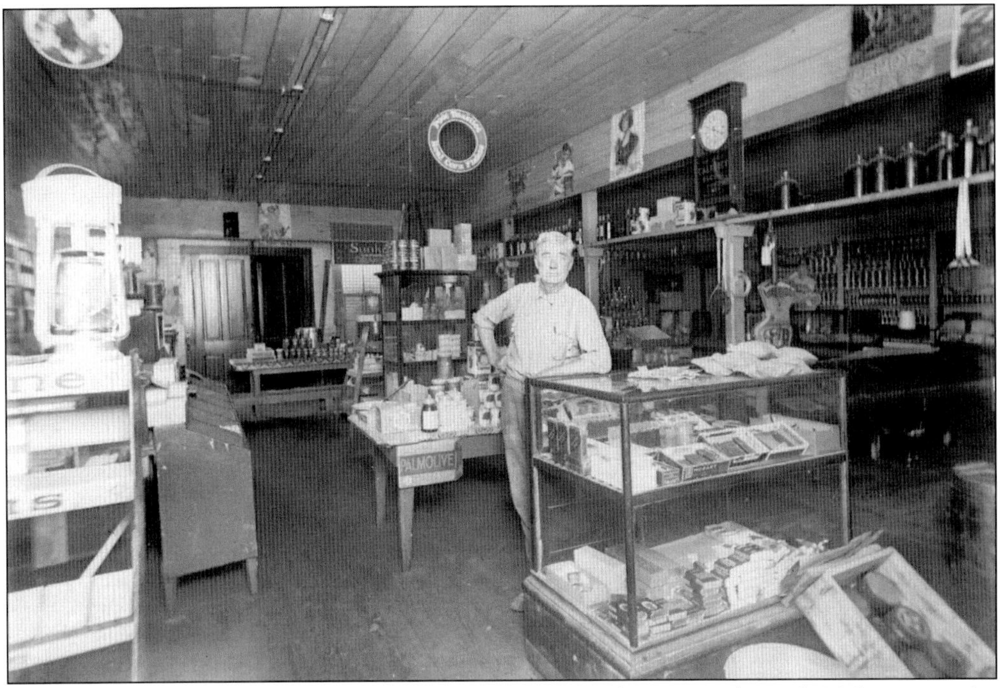

In a scene that was familiar to Texans in small towns across the state in the early 20th century, the interior of N.A. Holley and Sons Grocery in August 1923 beckons shoppers with its well-stocked merchandise display. Patriarch N.A. Holley is depicted minding the store.

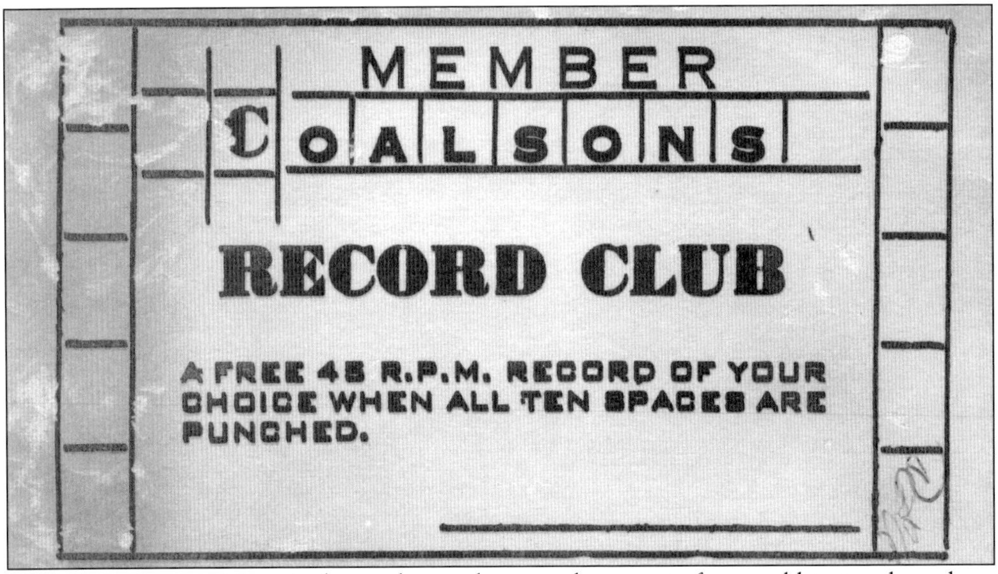

In 1964, Downtown Mesquite boasted several stores where music fans could test and purchase musical instruments; record players; and 45 rpm single records, 45 rpm extended plays, and 33 1/3 rpm vinyl albums. Coalson's TV and Record Shop issued record club punch cards for free goods and was located just off the downtown square in a strip center across from the 1960s Minyard's Food Store. The strip center is still standing today with the original Rutherford Building signage intact.

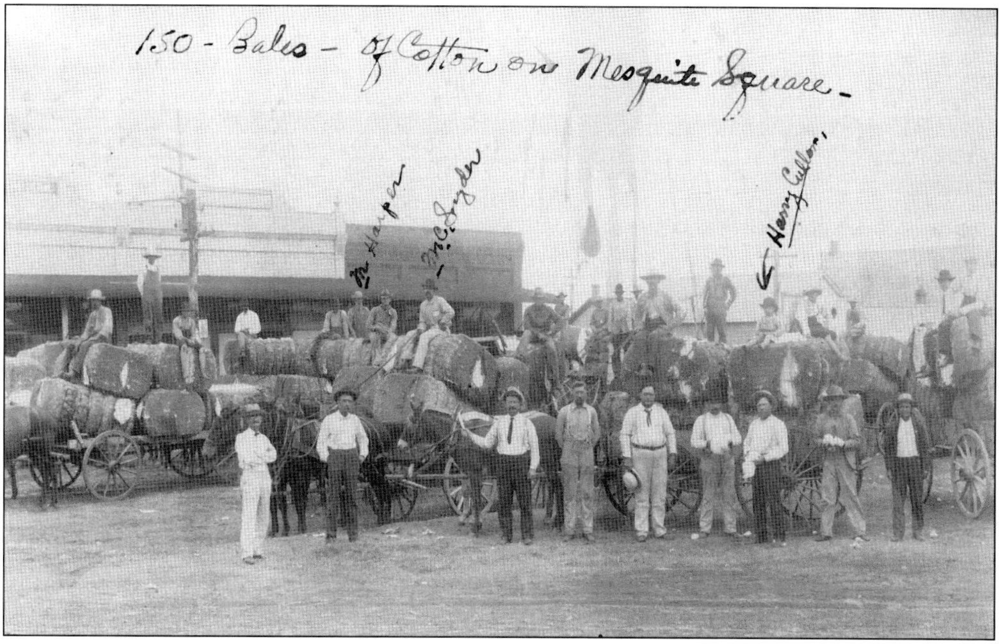

From the time of the establishment of Mesquite as a town built beside a railroad, cotton was the king commodity driver of the Mesquite economy until Mesquite's agricultural and rural decline in the 1940s. In 1924, Mesquite businessman N.A. Holley was issued one share of capital stock in the Mesquite Cotton Warehouse Company. L.C. Ebrite, president, and John S. Lawrence, secretary-treasurer, signed the stock certificate. Ebrite was one of Mesquite's earliest, most influential leaders, and his layout and design of the existing Mesquite Cemetery is still intact. Three years after the signing of this stock certificate, Lawrence gunned down and killed a man on the Mesquite downtown square. Lawrence later received a full pardon from Texas governor Miriam "Ma" Ferguson. At the time of the shooting, Lawrence was mayor of Mesquite. Ebrite was a former mayor of Mesquite, elected in 1888 and reelected in 1890 according to a Dallas County history report.

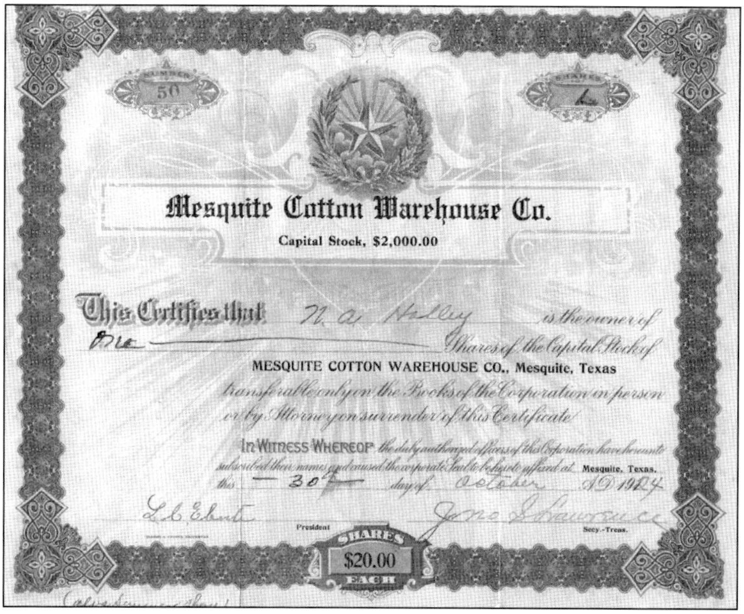
50

1

Mesquite Cotton Warehouse Co.

Capital Stock, $2,000.00

This Certifies that N. A. Holley is the owner of One Shares of the Capital Stock of MESQUITE COTTON WAREHOUSE CO., Mesquite, Texas transferable only on the Books of the Corporation in person or by Attorney on surrender of this Certificate.

In Witness Whereof the duly authorized officers of this Corporation have hereunto subscribed their names and caused the corporate Seal to be hereto affixed at Mesquite, Texas, this 30th day of October A.D. 1924

L. C. Ebrite, President

Jno S Lawrence, Secy.-Treas.

SHARES $20.00 EACH

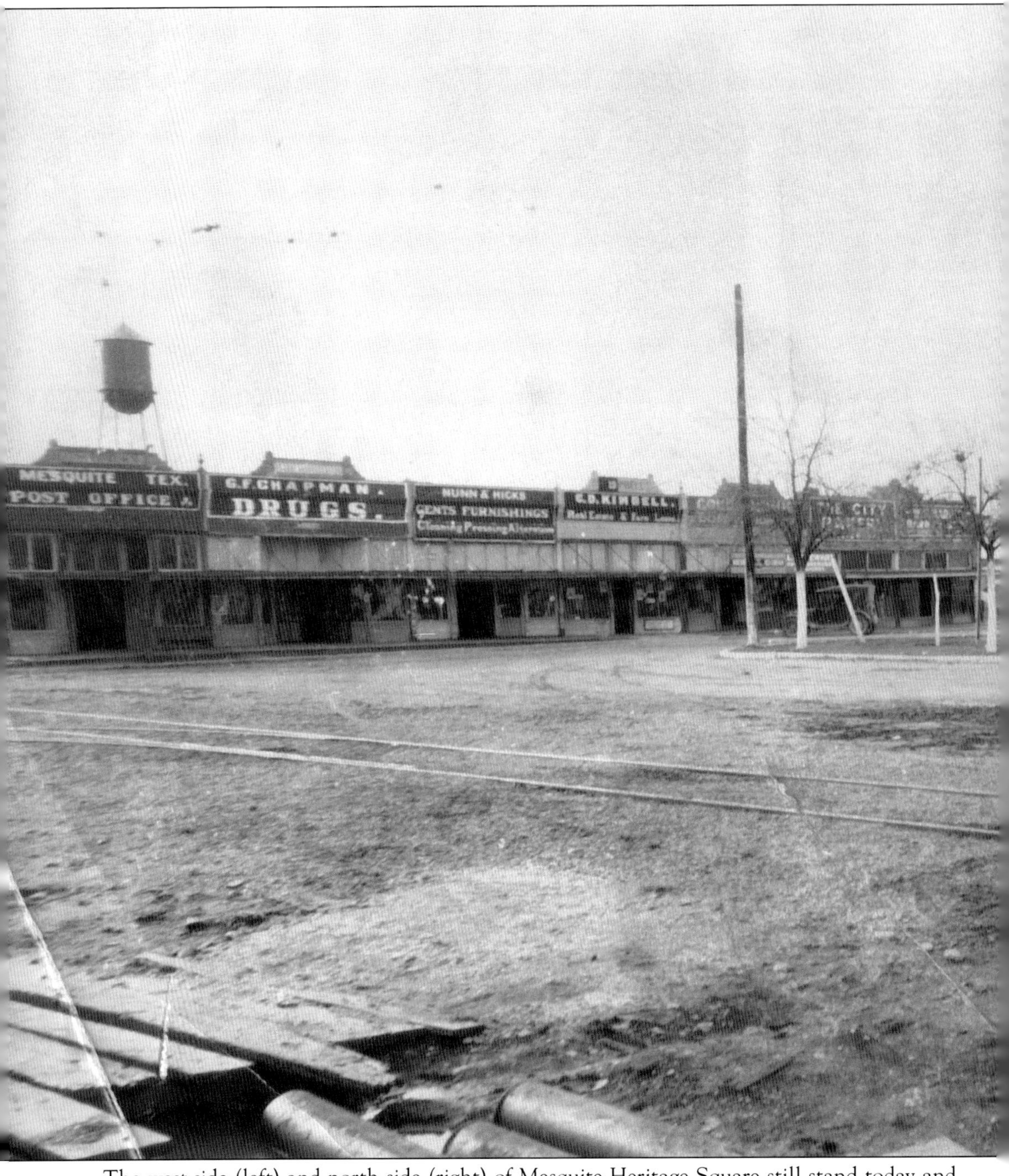

The west side (left) and north side (right) of Mesquite Heritage Square still stand today and virtually cry out for revitalization, which would usher in a variety of businesses to rival the number found in this photograph around the mid-1920s. Note Nunn and Hicks, Gents Furnishings, which offered, until the store closed in 1927, the latest, trendiest styles of ties, shirts, hosiery, gloves, and underwear in addition to made-to-order suits and overcoats and, later, ready-to-wear suits and Dobbs and Stetson hats. Nunn and Hicks became Mesquite's first fashionable clothing store with forward-looking colors, fabrics, and styles. The store was a bit too "hip" for the community, and

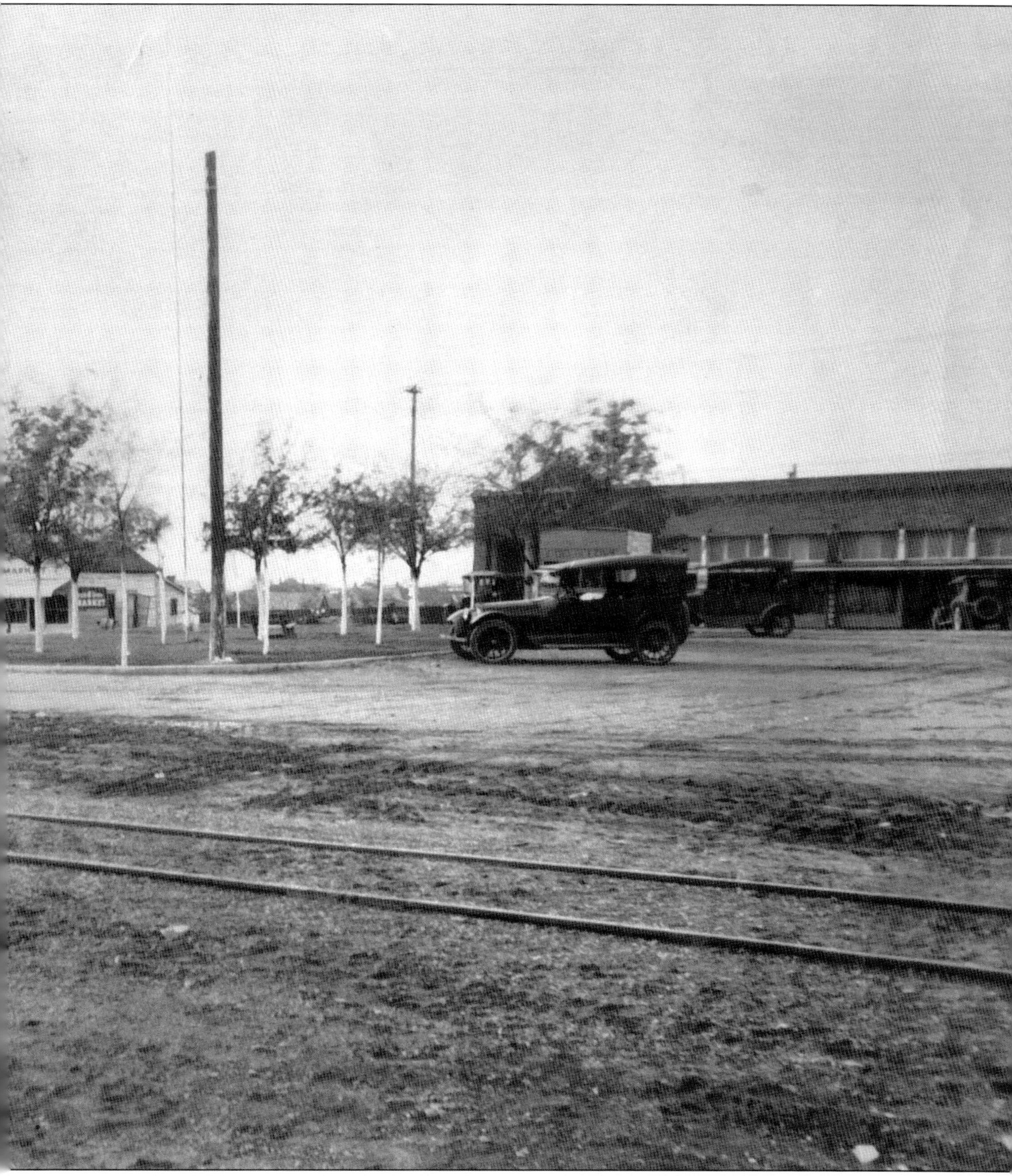

proprietor Grady Nunn moved to the E.M. Kahn store in Dallas, and many of his stylish Mesquite customers moved their shopping to him in Dallas after 1928. This remarkable photograph depicts store names including Mesquite Post Office, Chapman Drugs, Nunn and Hicks, Kimbell, and City Bakery. The landmark, 75,000-gallon Mesquite water tower rises above the square's buildings as a somewhat recent construction at the time of this photograph. The water tower stood for 36 years until its demolition in 1959, when it was sold for salvage parts for $500 to Pioneer Contractors.

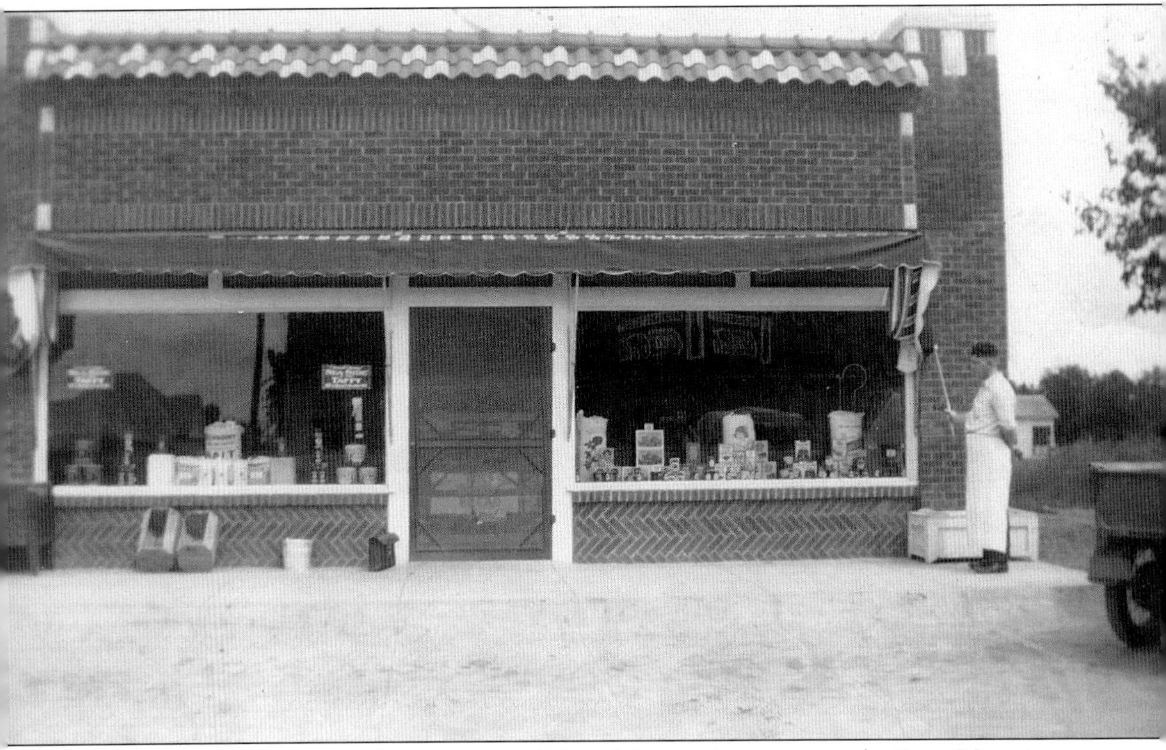

The only time in history that an entire edition of the town's newspaper, the *Texas Mesquiter*, was devoted to a business and a business family was when this building was open to the public in 1932 as the freestanding and modern Holley & Sons Grocery Store. The building and its adjacent parking lot are still there today at 117 West Main Street, directly to the north of Wells Fargo Bank. Here, grocer and merchant Ferd McWhorter stands to the right of the building.

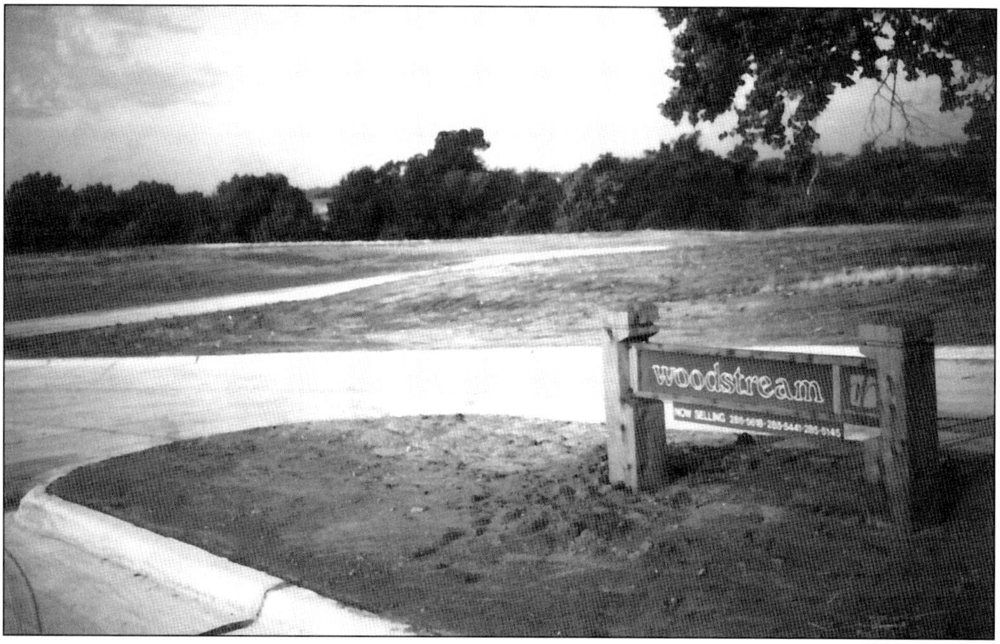

In 1980, the Woodstream Estates monument sign was erected to welcome residents and guests to the last large-lot subdivision developed in Mesquite.

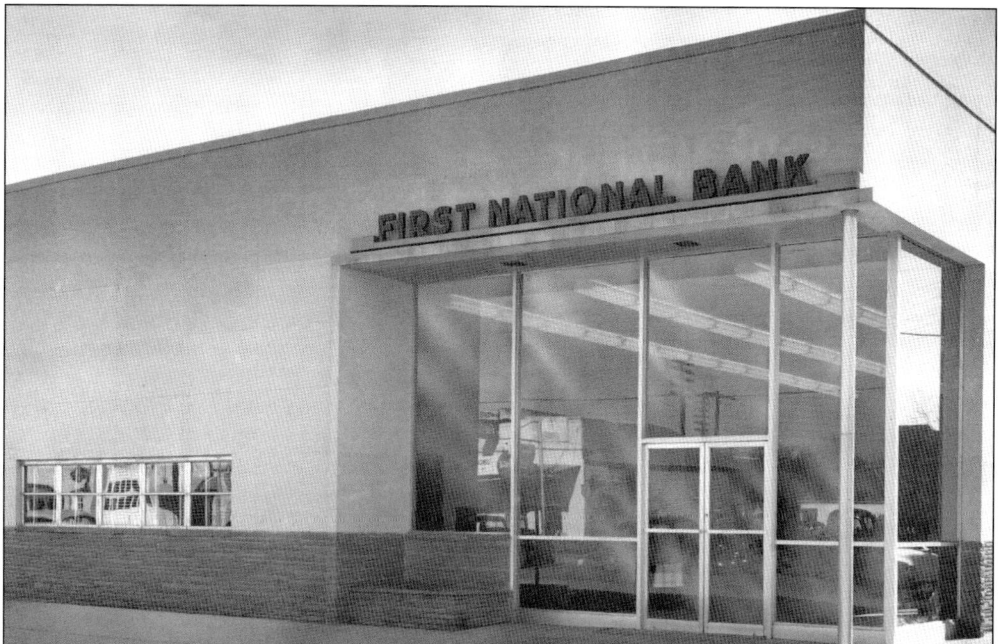

The landmark First National Bank Building is shown here shortly after its formal opening in January 1952. The bank advertised the $100,000 structure as "the city's largest and most attractive building," and it replaced the bank's former small headquarters on the northwest corner of the square. During the boomtown years of the 1960s, the bank operated a unique and atmospheric cafeteria on the second floor. The eatery was open on Fridays to bank employees, customers, and fellow downtown merchants.

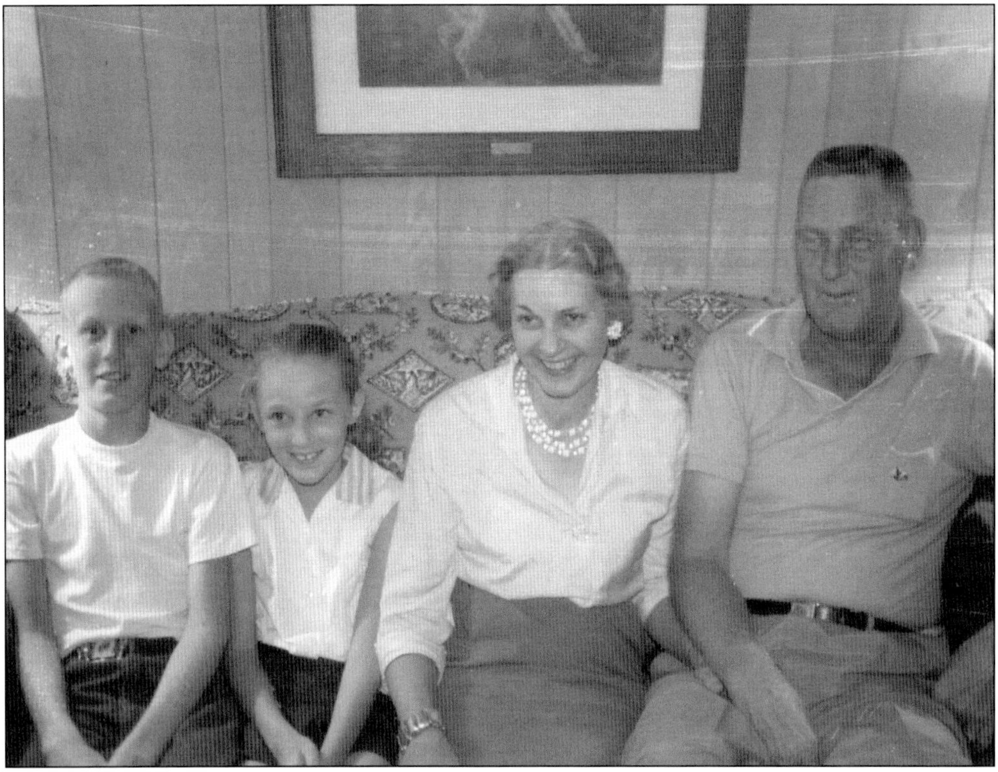

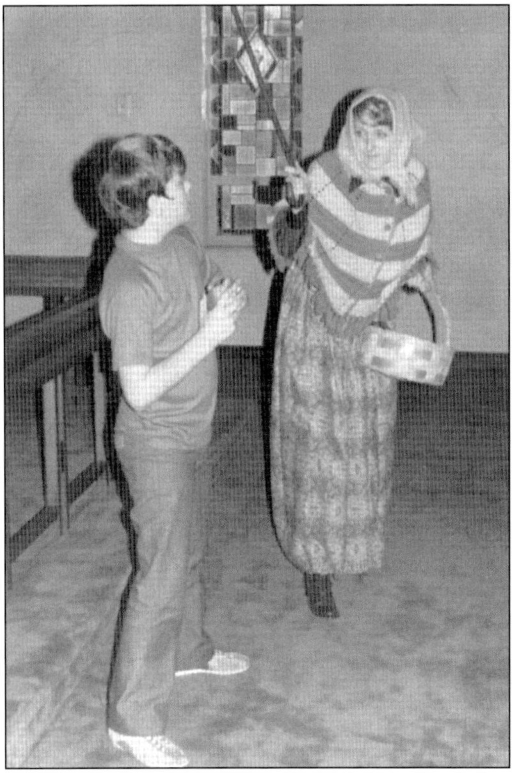

The backbone of the Mesquite community in its best of times is the family. Pictured here in 1960 are the McGlothlins—from left to right, John, Missy, Minelle, and Mack—at the Greenhaw home place. Mack McGlothlin served on both the Mesquite City Council and Mesquite School Board. His successful company, J.J. McGlothlin, pioneered innovative wood flooring–care products and services. Minelle served as organist for First Methodist Church. Twelve years later (in the photograph at left), Missy costars in the musical production *Once Upon a Christmas*. She is a successful author of several books on aging and faith. John McGlothlin, PhD, CFP, founded his own firm, Plan Data, Inc., and is a lecturer at the University of Texas at Austin.

fficers

N. E. SHANDS
Chairman of the Board

GENE SHANDS
President

E. R. (TUT) MORRIS
Executive Vice President

R. L. HANBY
Senior Vice President

KENNETH PACE
Vice President

DELBERT REED
Vice President & Cashier

WANDA BEASLEY
Vice President

BEN HATCHER
Vice President

ELIZABETH DAUGHERTY
Assistant Vice President

MARGARET GOOD
Assistant Vice President

ROSS WILCOX
Assistant Vice President

LILA WARE
Assistant Cashier

LORENE LANDER
Assistant Cashier

JOHN SHOBE
Assistant Cashier

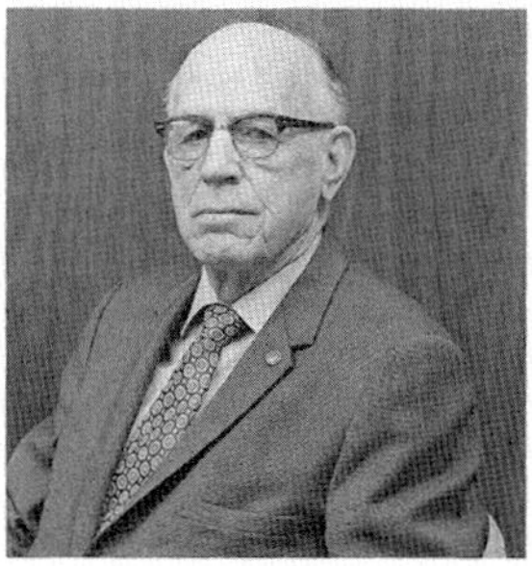

N. E. SHANDS — *Chairman of the Board*

irectors

J. B. GALLOWAY
R. L. HANBY
RAYMOND HOLLEY
LONCY LEAKE
E. R. MORRIS
DR. J. M. PIRRUNG
GENE SHANDS
N. E. SHANDS

GENE SHANDS — *President - Chief Executive Officer*

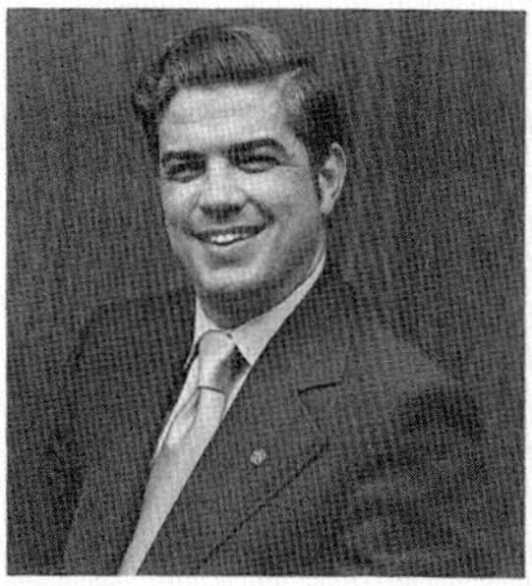

Throughout much of the 20th century and until today, the anchor for the central business district has been First National Bank, which became Allied Bank, then First Interstate Bank, and lastly, Wells Fargo Bank. This 1972 bank brochure lists officers and directors. Chairman of the board N.E. Shands and his son Gene Shands, president and chief executive officer, are depicted in the brochure.

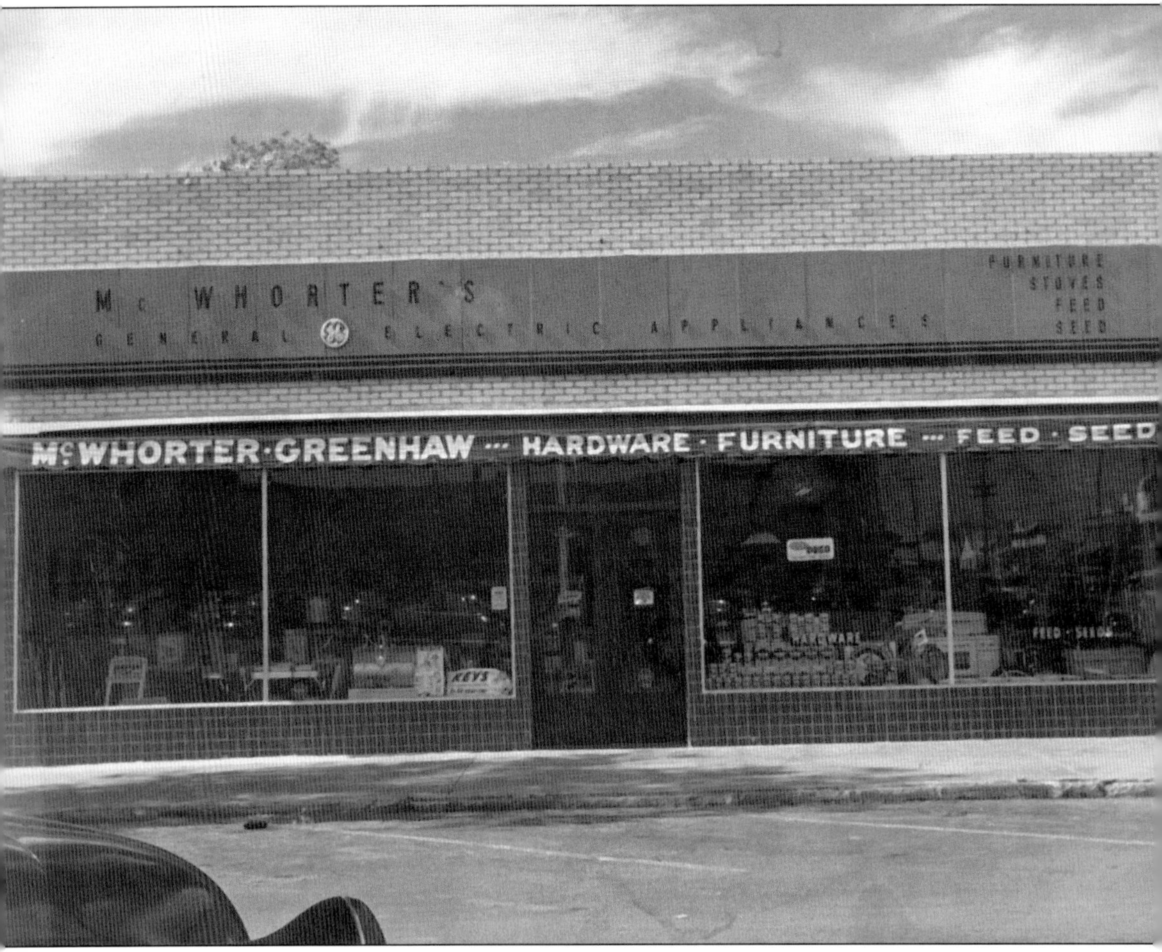

Pictured around 1955, the McWhorter-Greenhaw Building was located on the west side of the Mesquite Downtown Square prior to the installation of the McWhorter-Greenhaw landmark neon sign. Architectural elements include the decorative tiling and vintage hand-cranked rollup awning emblazoned with the store name and product categories sold. During this period of store history, some of the items most in demand were room space heaters, farm animal feed, garden vegetable seeds, furniture, mattresses, carpet, linoleum, and General Electric brand appliances.

Stylish gentlemen of Mesquite, Raymond and Anson Holley escort their beautiful protégé to the 1936 Texas Centennial Celebration at Fair Park in Dallas, Texas. Citizens enjoying Mesquite's first public park, City Lake Park, located downtown, have these two brothers to thank. The Holley brothers and N.E. Shands donated the entire 12-acre City Lake Park in August 1947, for the betterment of the town.

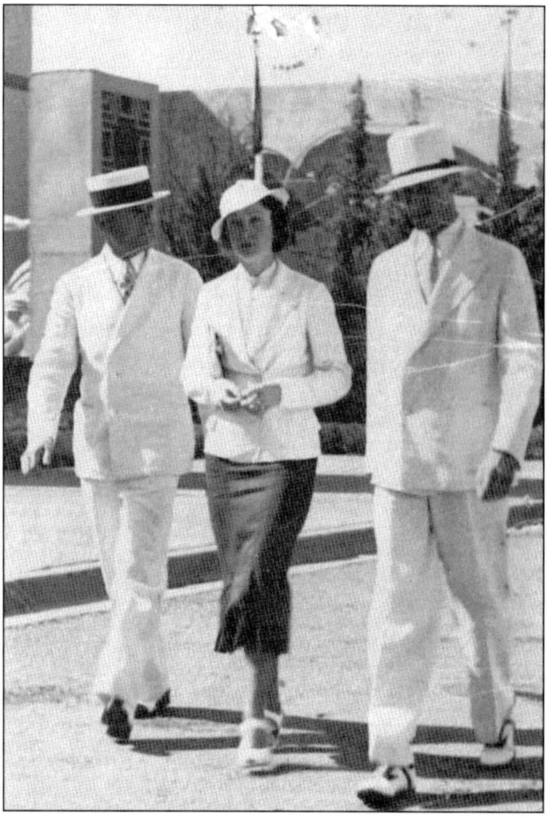

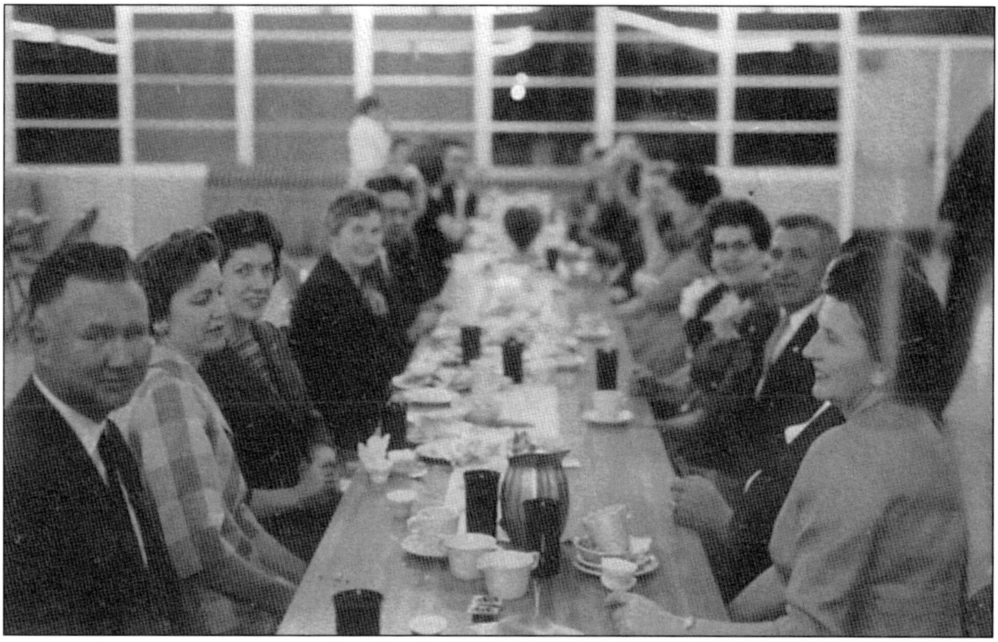

Service clubs such as Kiwanis, Rotary, Lions, Optimist, and others played an important part in the best of Mesquite times. The public schools of the day often hosted banquets, such as this early-1960s Mesquite Kiwanis Club Valentine's Banquet, in school cafetoriums.

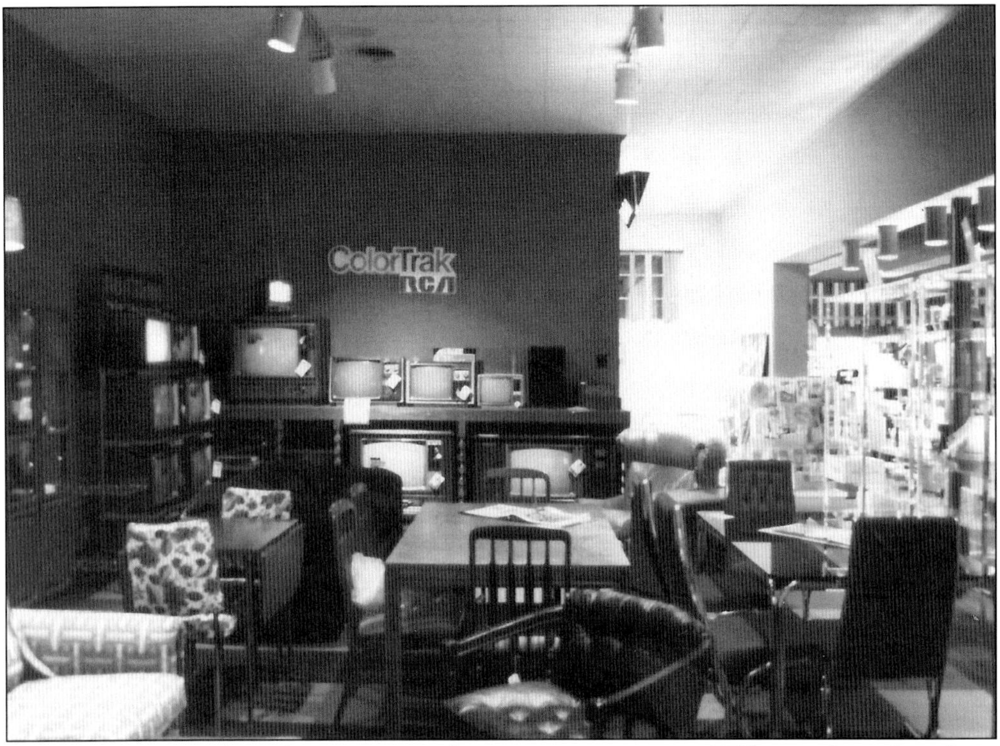

Paving the way for the early-1980s major downtown renovation, McWhorter Greenhaw Store established a high-end boutique style for its furniture and television departments in 1977.

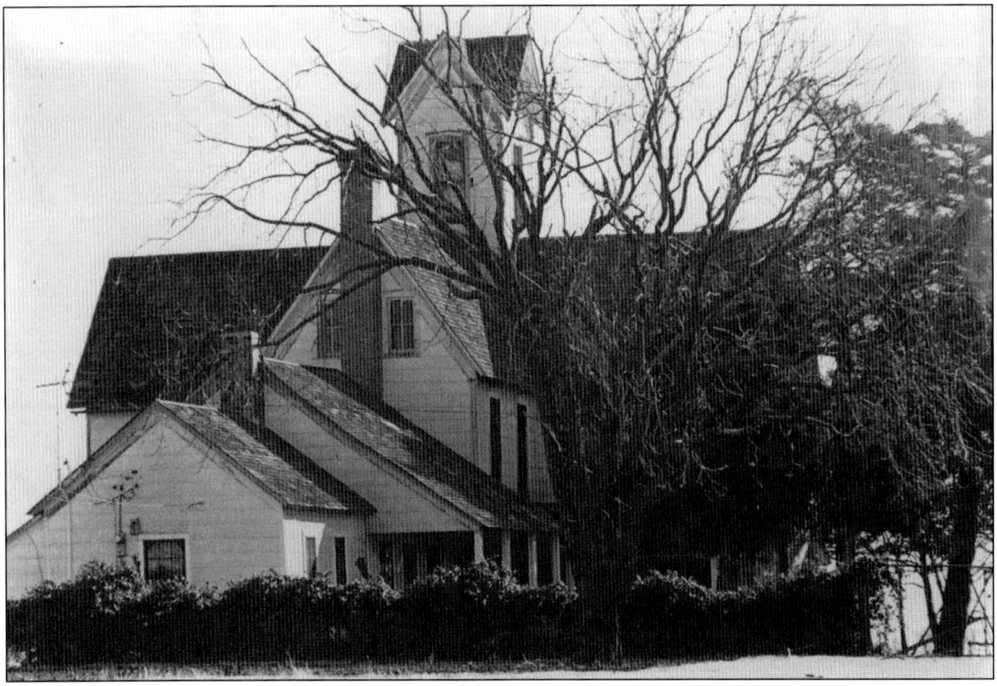

The Stephen D. Lawrence home is pictured around 1900. Today, the 4,000-square-foot house is part of Opal Lawrence Historical Park. (Courtesy of Historic Mesquite, Inc.)

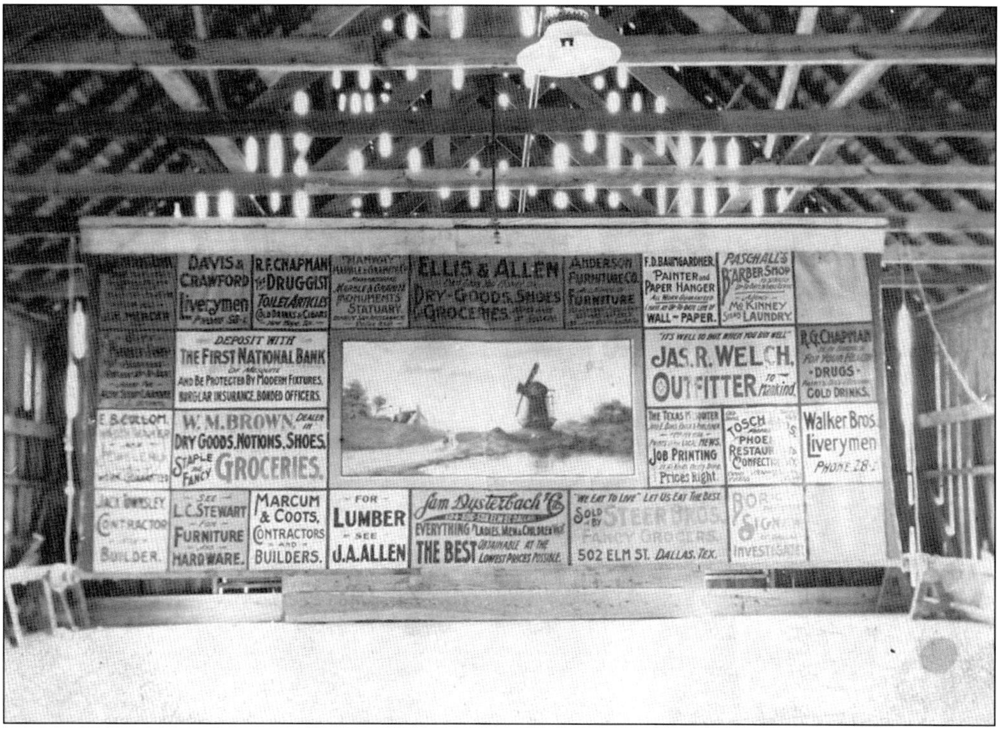

The Mesquite Auditorium was located above James R. Welch Outfitters on the east side of the square. The backdrop for the stage shows advertisements for Mesquite businesses prior to 1907. (Courtesy of the Mesquite Public Library System.)

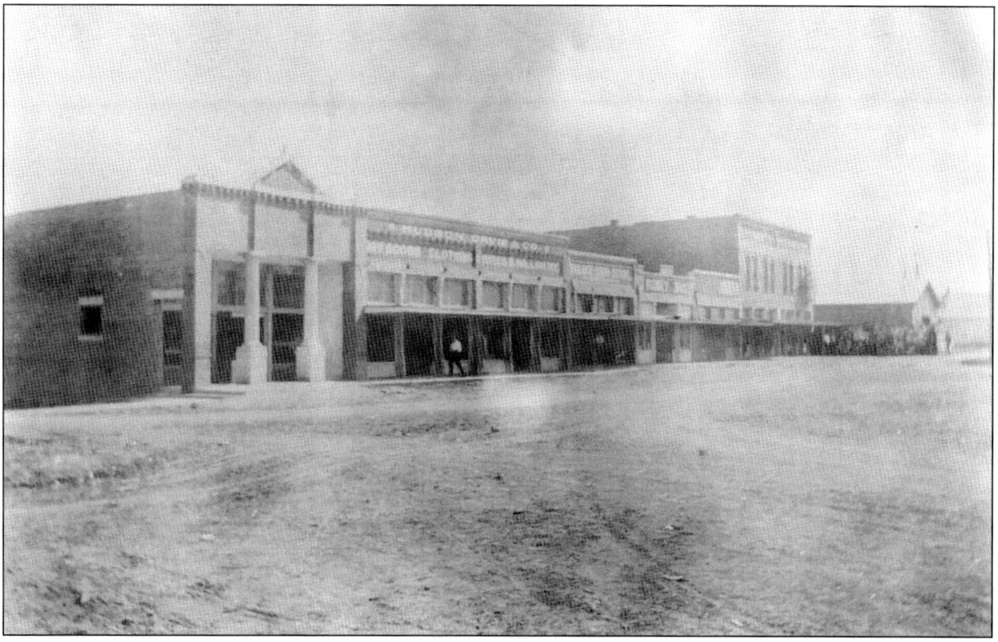

Stores in downtown Mesquite, including A. Hudson Davis & Co., Palace Drugstore, and McKinney Bros., are shown between 1900 and 1910. (Courtesy of Historic Mesquite, Inc.)

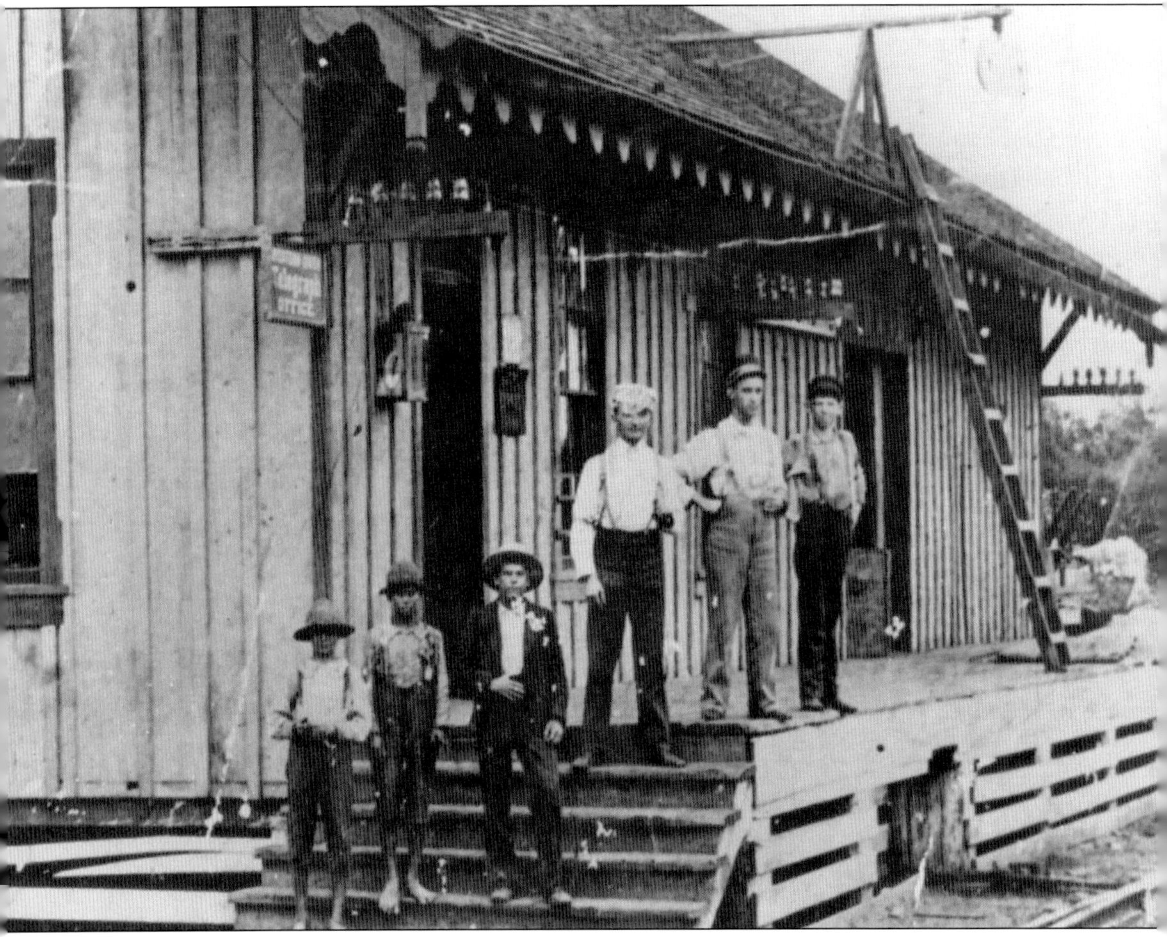

Here, six boys are standing on the station platform of the original wood-frame Mesquite train depot constructed in 1873. (Courtesy of Historic Mesquite, Inc.)

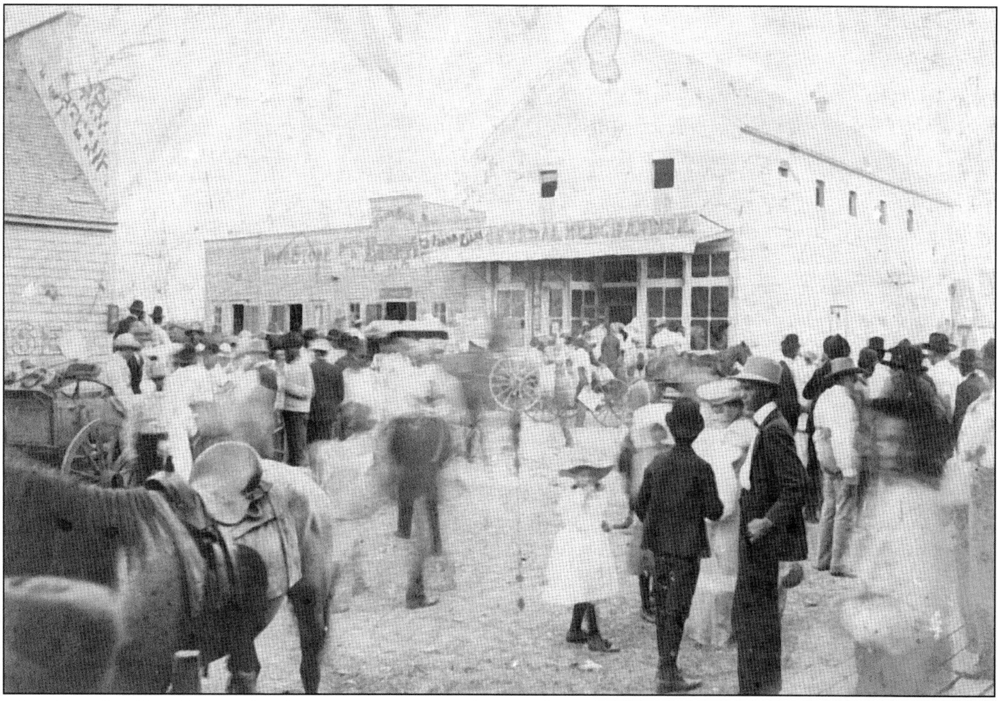

The Frank Ellis General Merchandise Store located at the intersection of Belt Line and Town East Roads is shown sometime before 1919, when it burned down. Kearney's Store is now located near the spot depicted in this image. (Courtesy of the Mesquite Public Library System.)

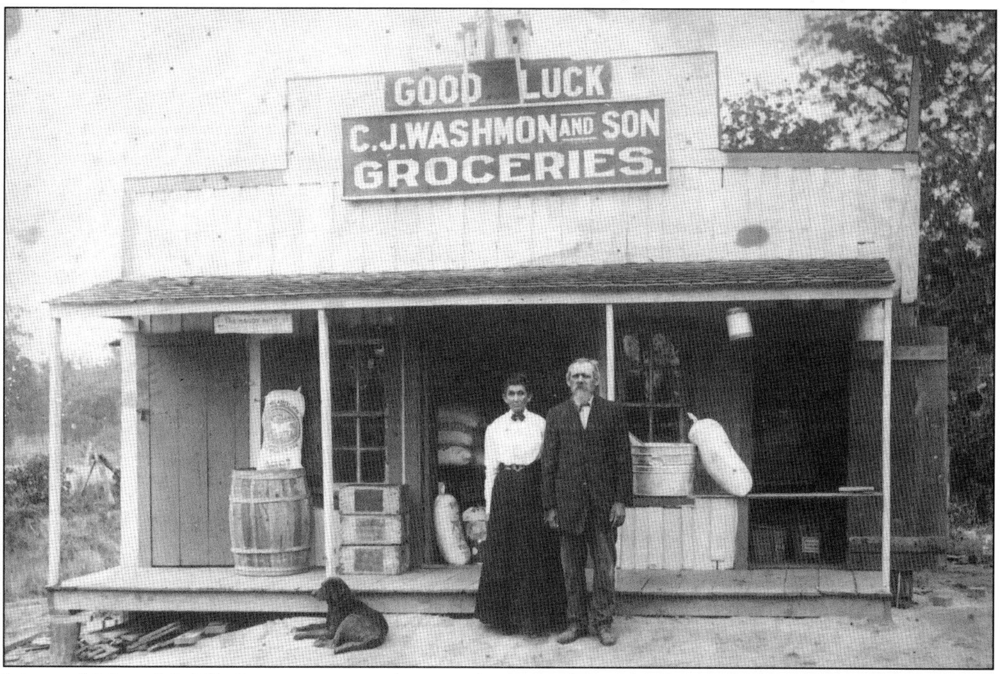

Mr. and Mrs. C.J. Washmon are standing in front of their grocery store located near Tripp and Collins Roads. Legend has it that a beloved dog named Tripp inspired the naming of Tripp Road. The dog in this photograph might be Tripp. (Courtesy of the Mesquite Public Library System.)

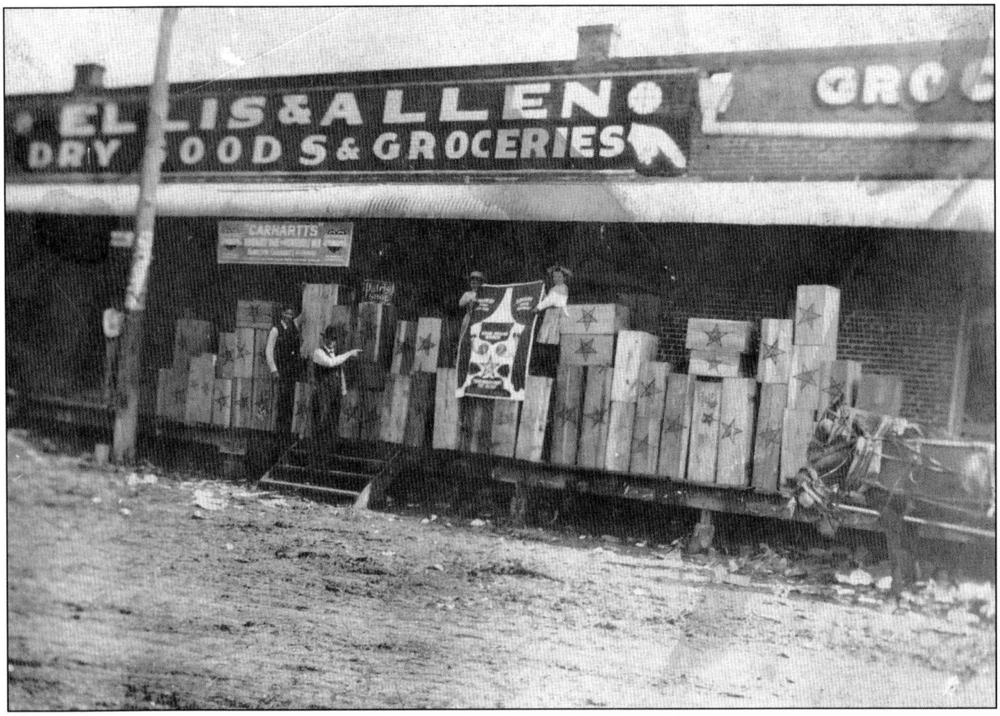

Ellis & Allen Dry Goods and Food store is depicted in the early 20th century displaying dozens of boxes of shoes on the front walkway.

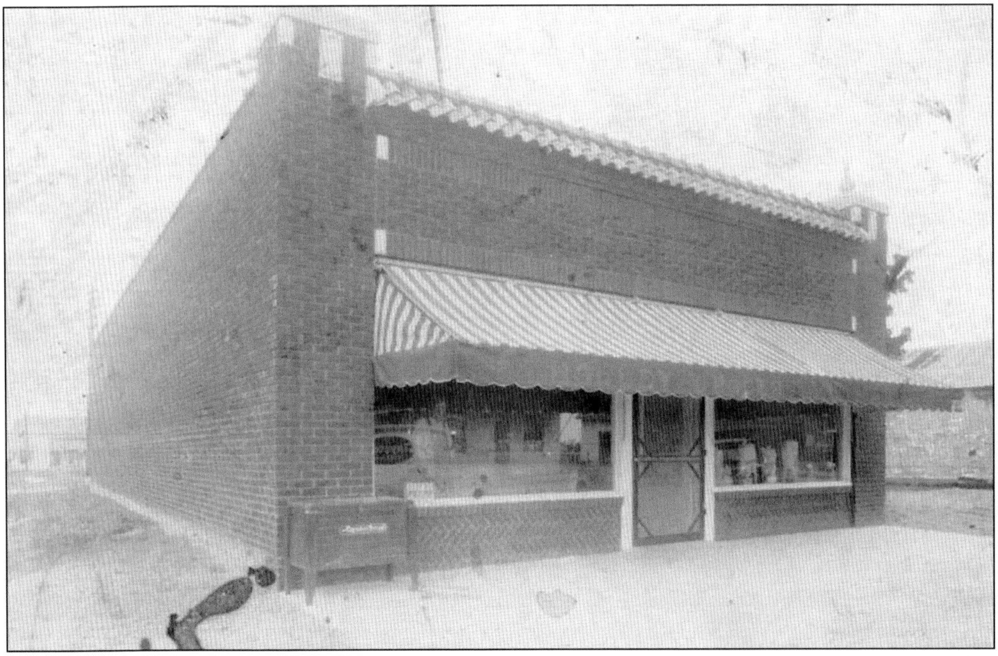

The last great incarnation of N.A. Holley & Sons Grocery Store is pictured here shortly after its construction in 1932. Note the total lack of business signage. Evidently, word of mouth brought customers to N.A. Holley & Sons, since the enterprise in various forms lasted over a half a century.

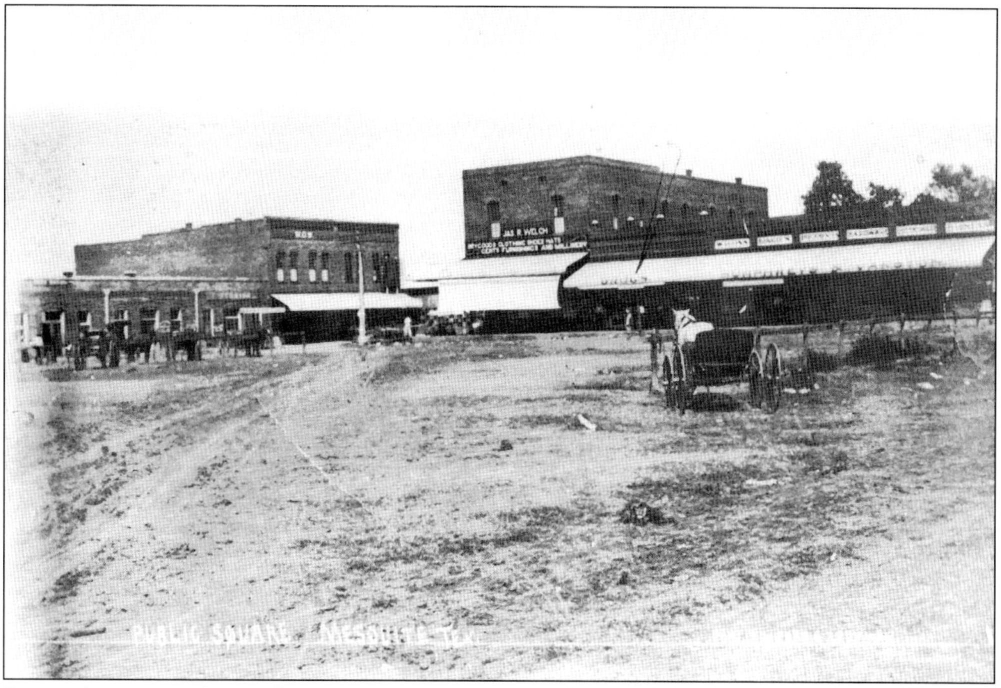

Pictured in 1907 is the northeast corner of downtown Mesquite's square before the Guarantee Bank was built. Several horses and carriages wait at the hitching rails. This photograph also depicts unpaved streets and one lone telephone pole. (Courtesy of the Mesquite Public Library System.)

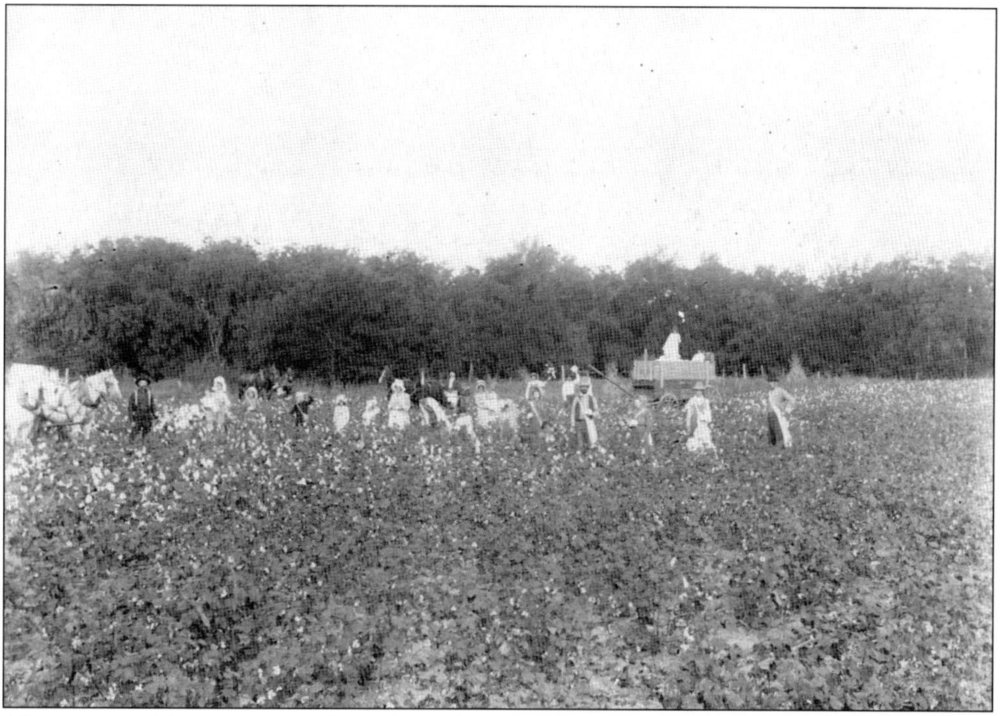

Almost every Mesquite citizen born from 1886 to 1939 experienced firsthand the grueling task of cotton picking, as seen in this photograph.

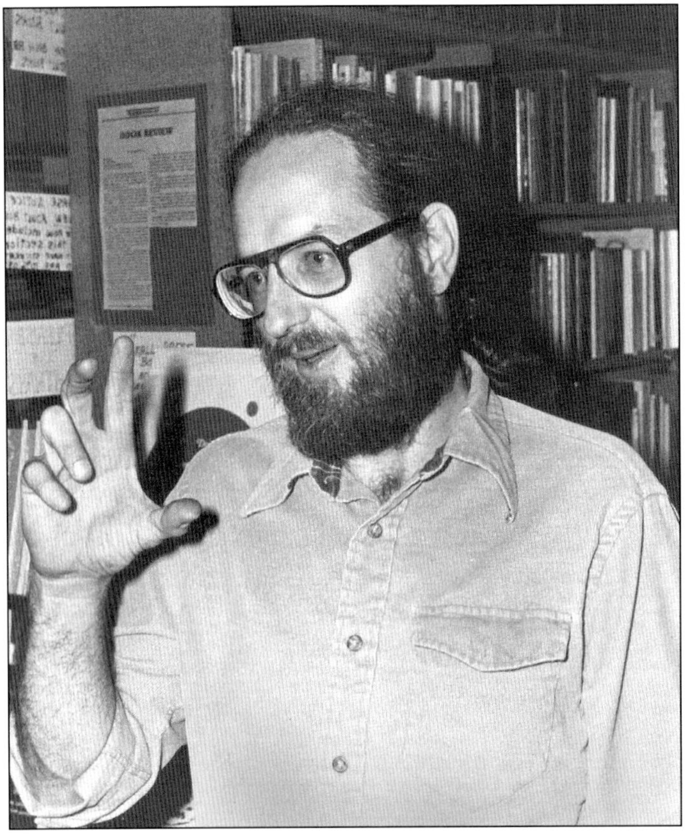

In 1974, John Tilton cofounded Paperbacks Plus-Mesquite with his wife, Marquetta Herring, and he is shown here in a photograph from around 1982. (Courtesy of Ron DeJulius.)

Cofounder Marquetta Herring and her dog Leadbelly are shown around 1979 promoting the store's used paperback books for resale. David Hall, who, like so many over the years, started working at Paperbacks Plus-Mesquite as a student at Mesquite High School (located one block from the bookstore), stands ready to assist customers with their selections. (Courtesy of John Tilton.)

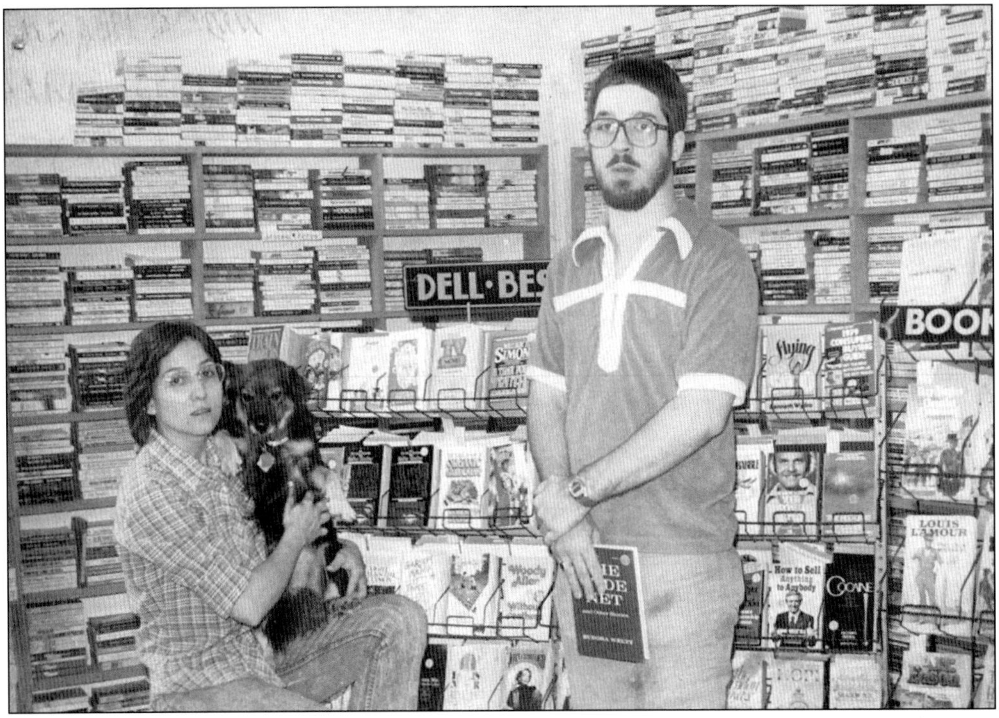

Frank Parman of Point Riders Press in Norman, Oklahoma, is shown here at a reading of his original poetry at Paperbacks Plus-Mesquite, as part of the literary series that ran for several years there, starting in 1979 through the early 1980s. (Courtesy of Ron DeJulius.)

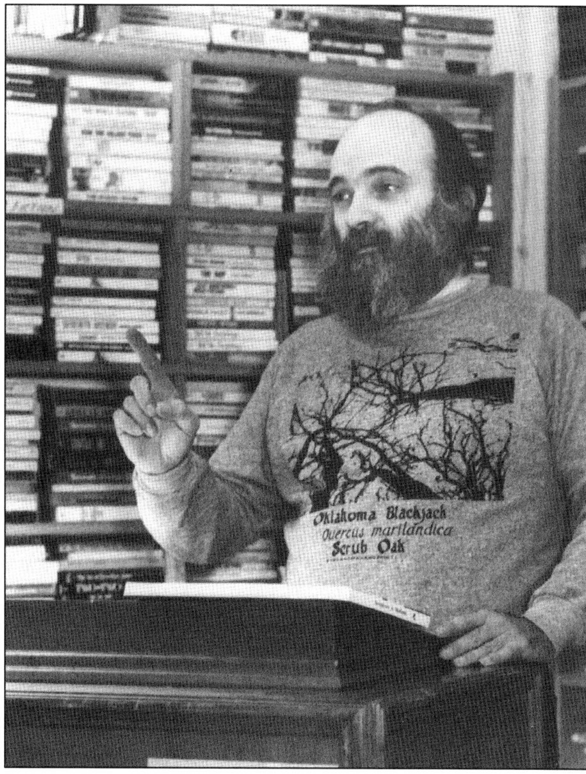

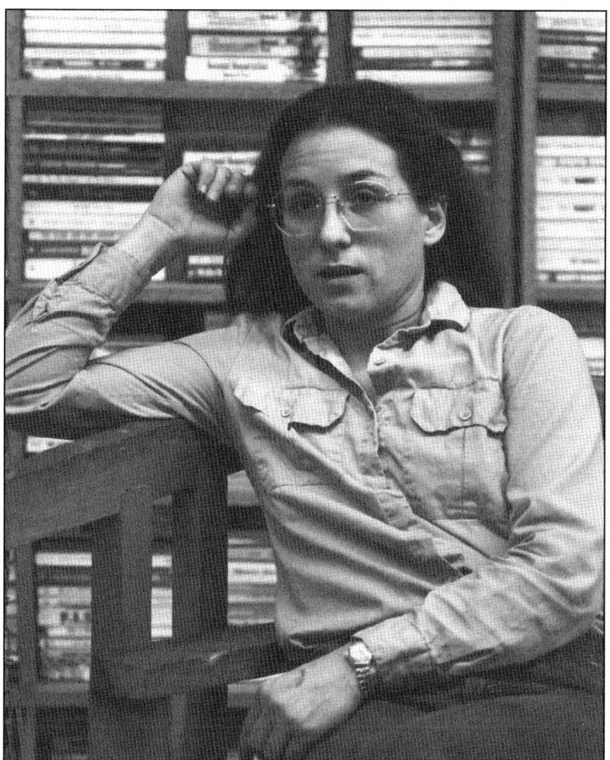

Cofounder of Paperbacks Plus-Mesquite Marquetta Herring is shown at the bookstore in 1982. (Courtesy of Ron DeJulius.)

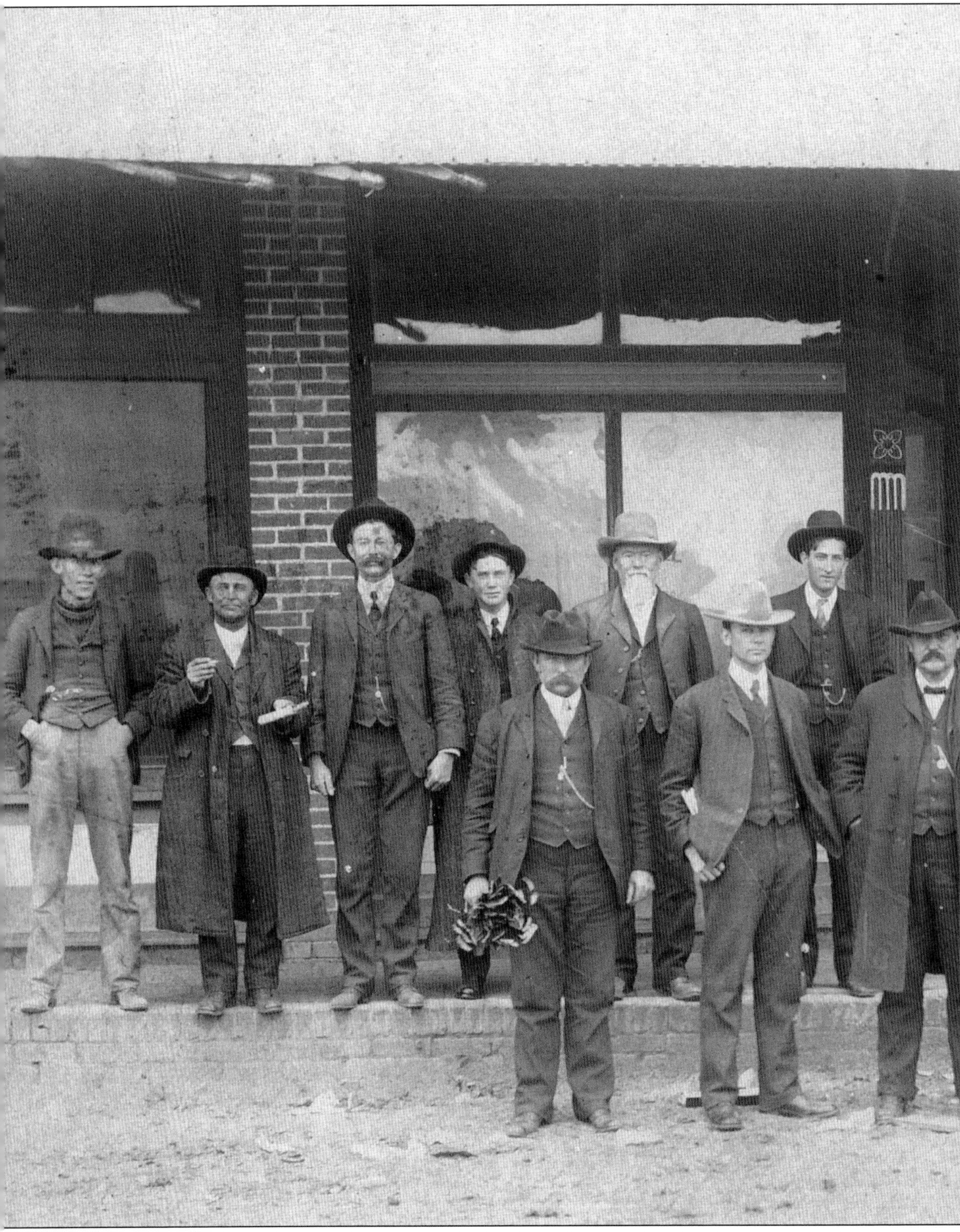

The mustached man front and center is R.S. Kimbrough, one of the leading figures in the town's history. He was a dominant force from the 1870s until his untimely death in 1905. As reported by the *Dallas Morning News*, 2,500 people attended his funeral service at the Baptist Church of

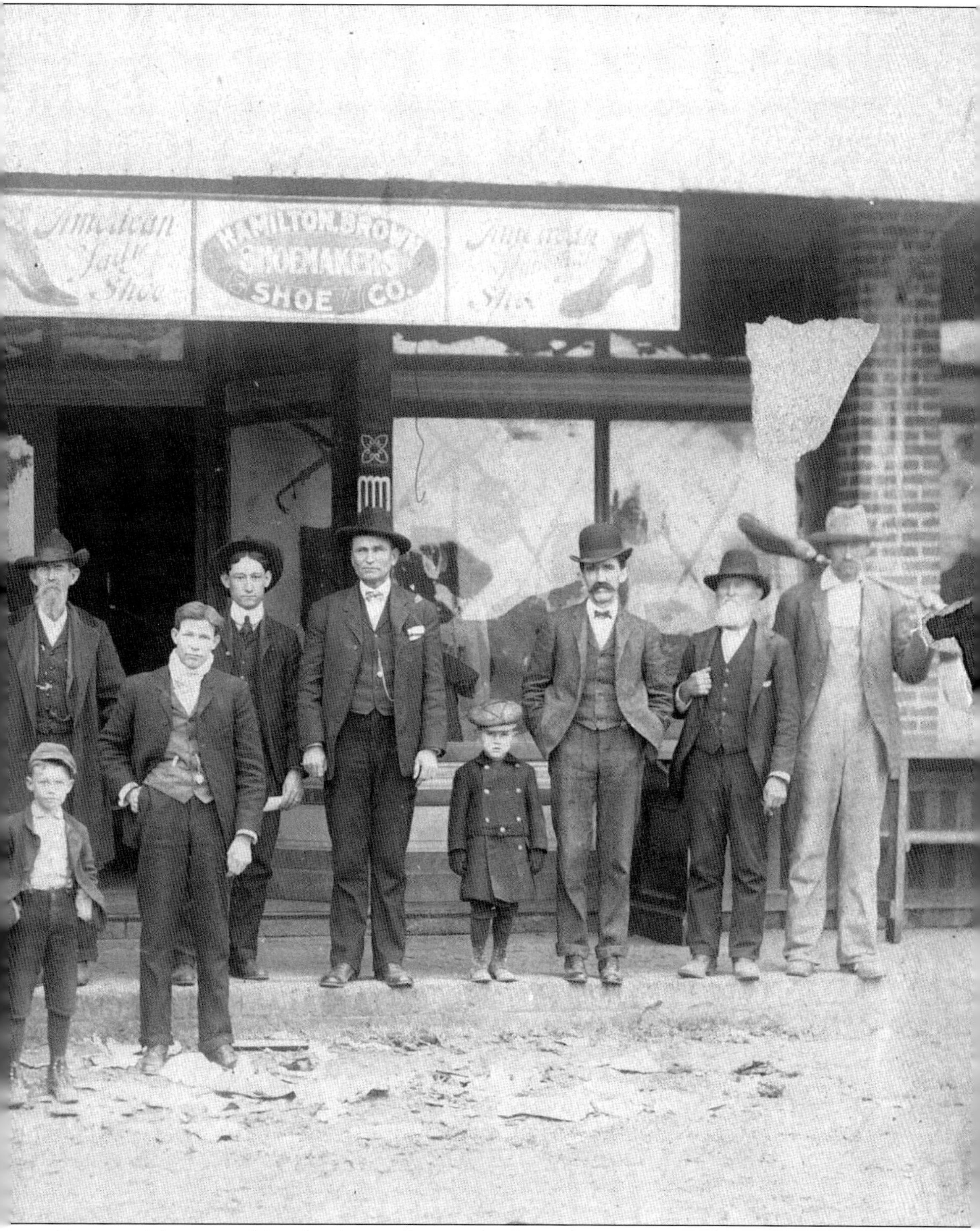

Mesquite. Mesquite public schools were dismissed to honor his memory, and a special train from Dallas brought sister cities' leading businessmen to pay their final respects.

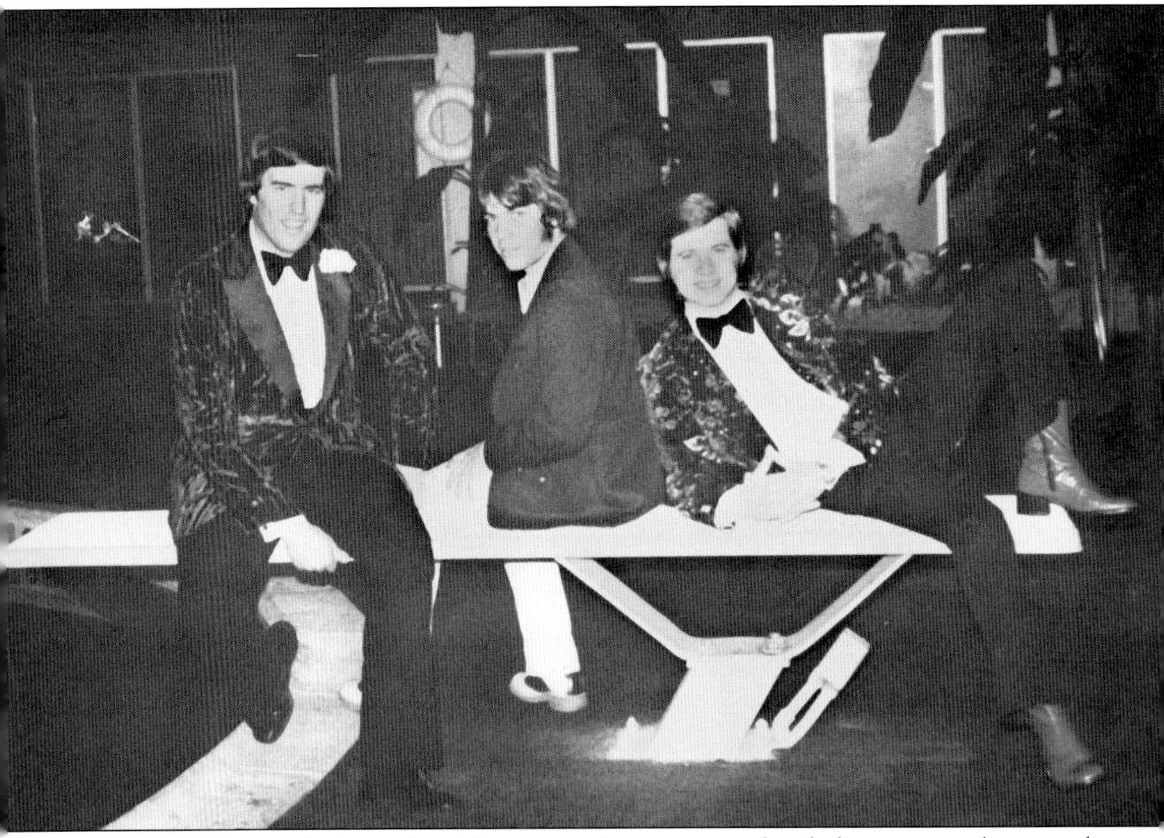

Difficult as it may be for modern Mesquite residents to comprehend, there were quality, upscale motels along Highway 80 during the 1970s. One of the most popular was the Villa Inn, which was the site of wedding receptions and civic banquets. The Villa Inn sported its own indoor swimming pool, with the diving board seen here. A musical combo comprised of, from left to right, Terry Tosch, Rik Murray, and the author is set to entertain in 1974.

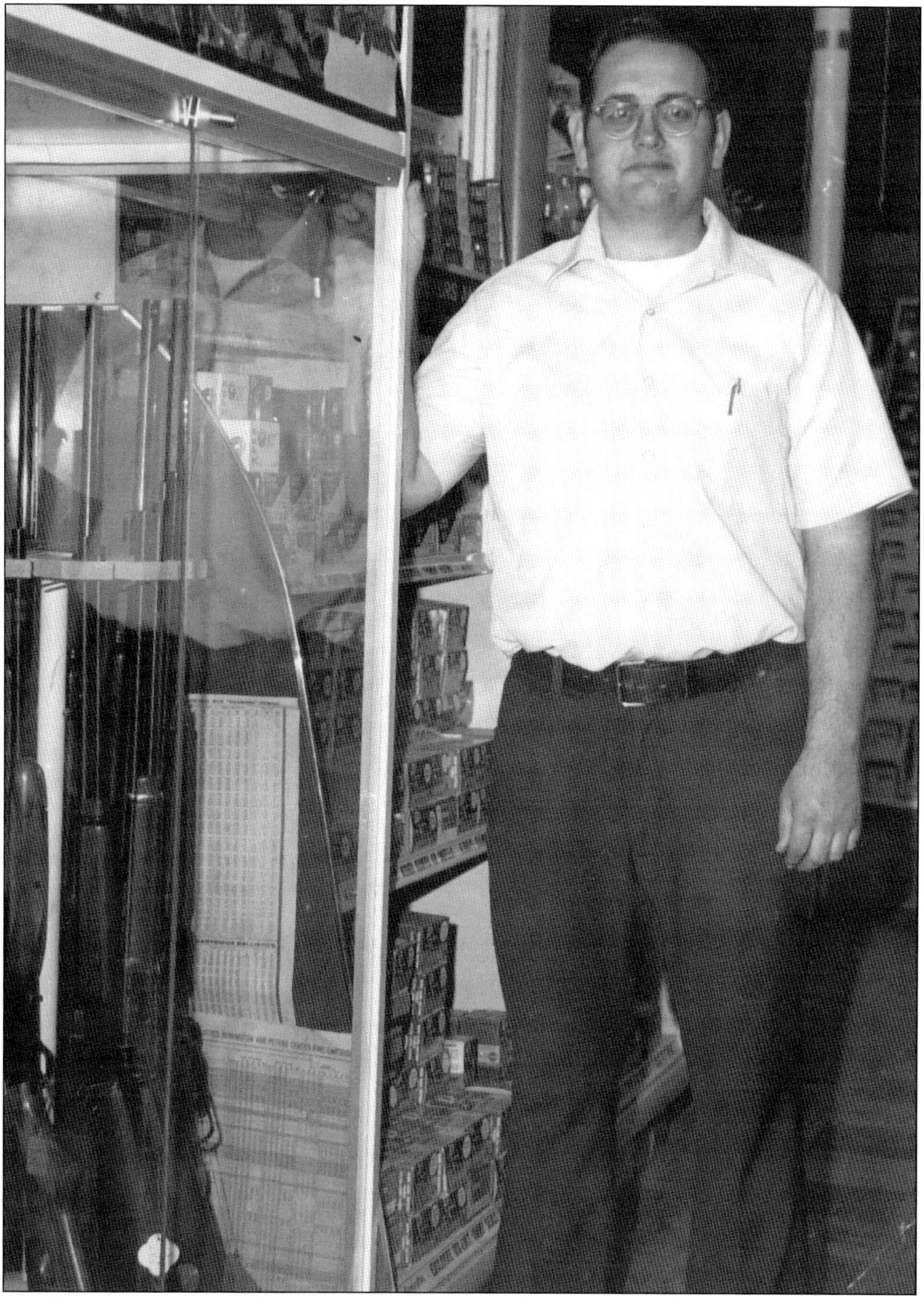

Standing next to the long-gun inventory at McWhorter Greenhaw downtown Mesquite is employee David West, who was also known as the projectionist of the iconic Texan Theater on the town square's south side. Constructed in 1946, the brick theater building originally cost $30,000 and seated 600. The well-known proprietors of the Texan Theater during Mesquite's boom years were M.E. and Bernice Hamm.

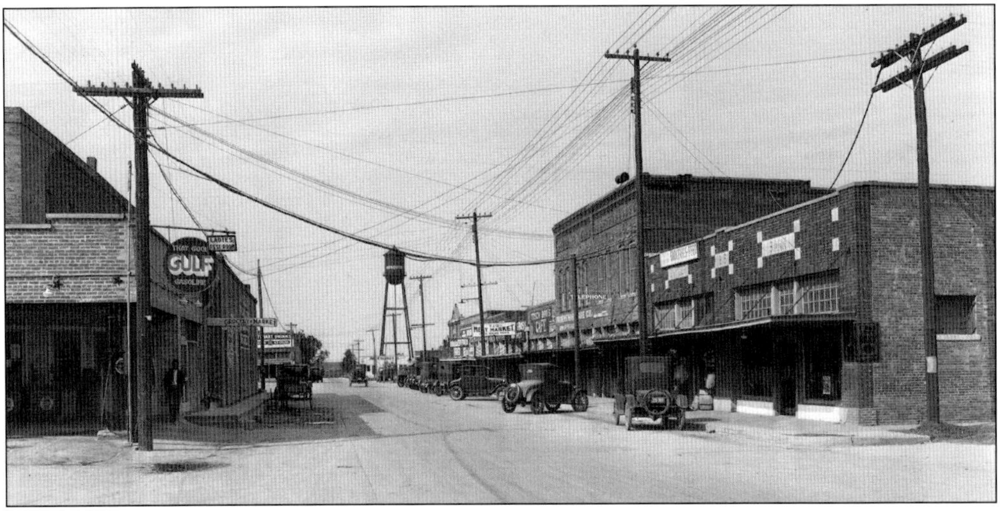

The name-above-the-door stores and businesses that contributed so much to the Mesquite's builder and boomtown days of yesteryear were impossible to separate from their proprietors, as is the case of Porter's Drug. A customer of Porter's Drug could be assured that his prescription would be filled any time of day or night in an emergency. G.R. "Gil" Porter was no relation to the original Porter—Elma Porter's stepfather, William "Bill" Jackson Porter. Gil married Elma, and they continued operating the store. Quiet by nature, but with great resolve, school board president Gil was truly a citizen's representative and voice in government. Everyday, no-nonsense Elma could be found minding the store behind the classiest costume jewelry counter in town. Even late in her life, Elma was not afraid to take a stand for what she believed. When a Mesquite policeman stopped the car in which she and several elderly citizens were riding to a charity meeting for traveling about three miles over the speed limit, she lectured the officer and asked, "Why can't you concentrate on the real criminals creating so much havoc in Mesquite?"

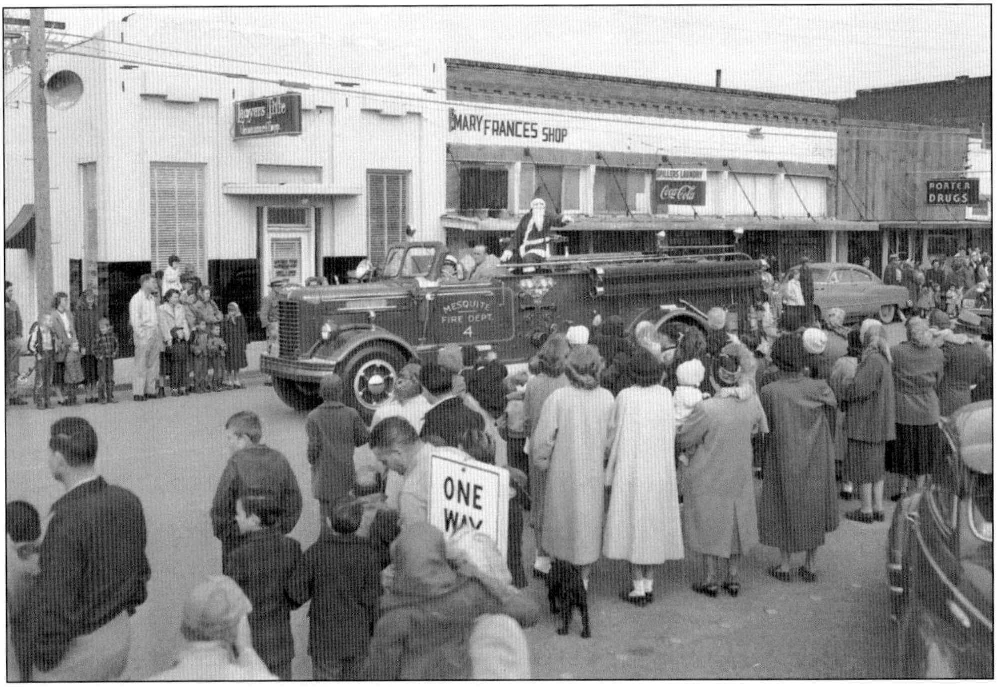

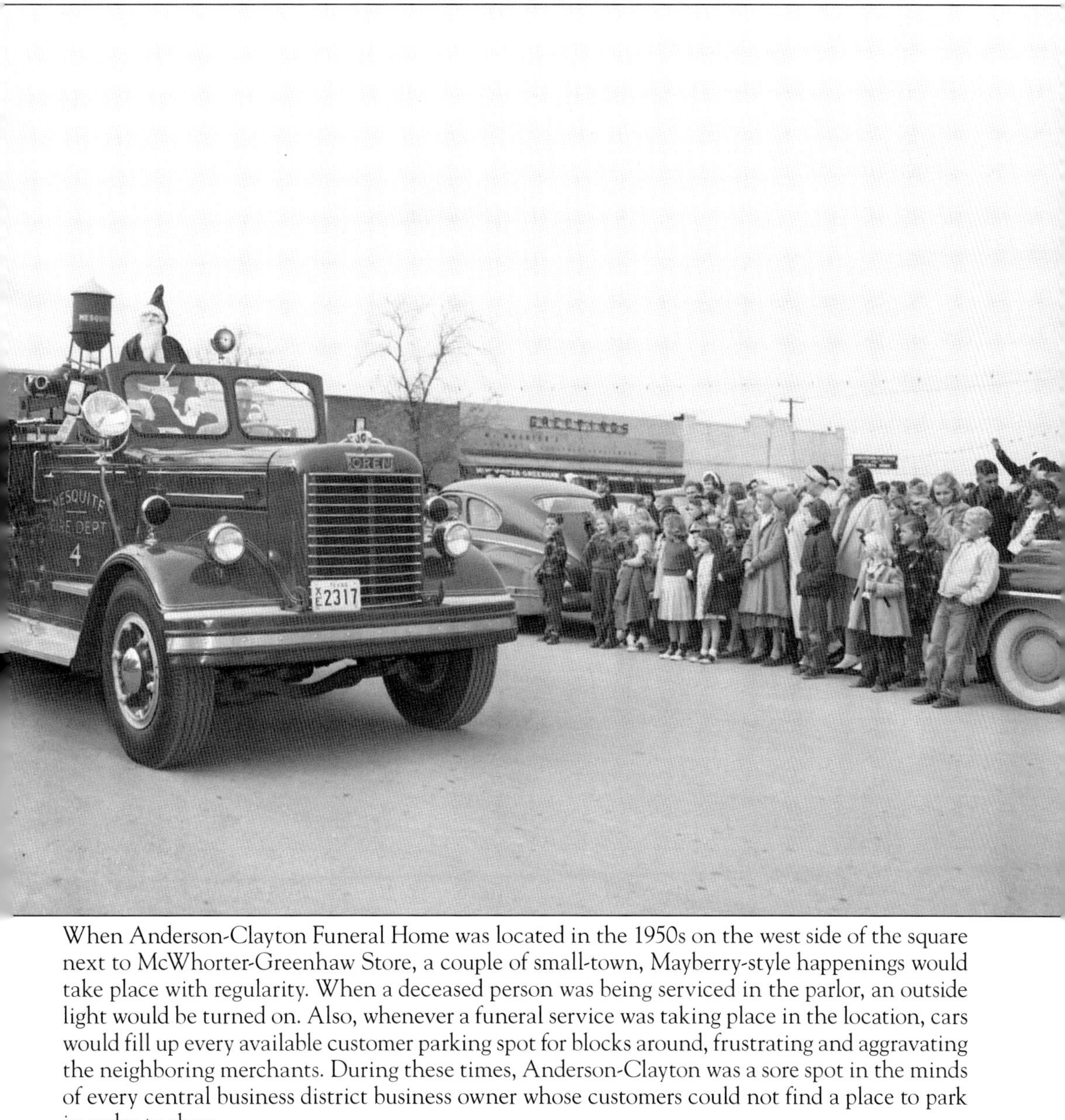

When Anderson-Clayton Funeral Home was located in the 1950s on the west side of the square next to McWhorter-Greenhaw Store, a couple of small-town, Mayberry-style happenings would take place with regularity. When a deceased person was being serviced in the parlor, an outside light would be turned on. Also, whenever a funeral service was taking place in the location, cars would fill up every available customer parking spot for blocks around, frustrating and aggravating the neighboring merchants. During these times, Anderson-Clayton was a sore spot in the minds of every central business district business owner whose customers could not find a place to park in order to shop.

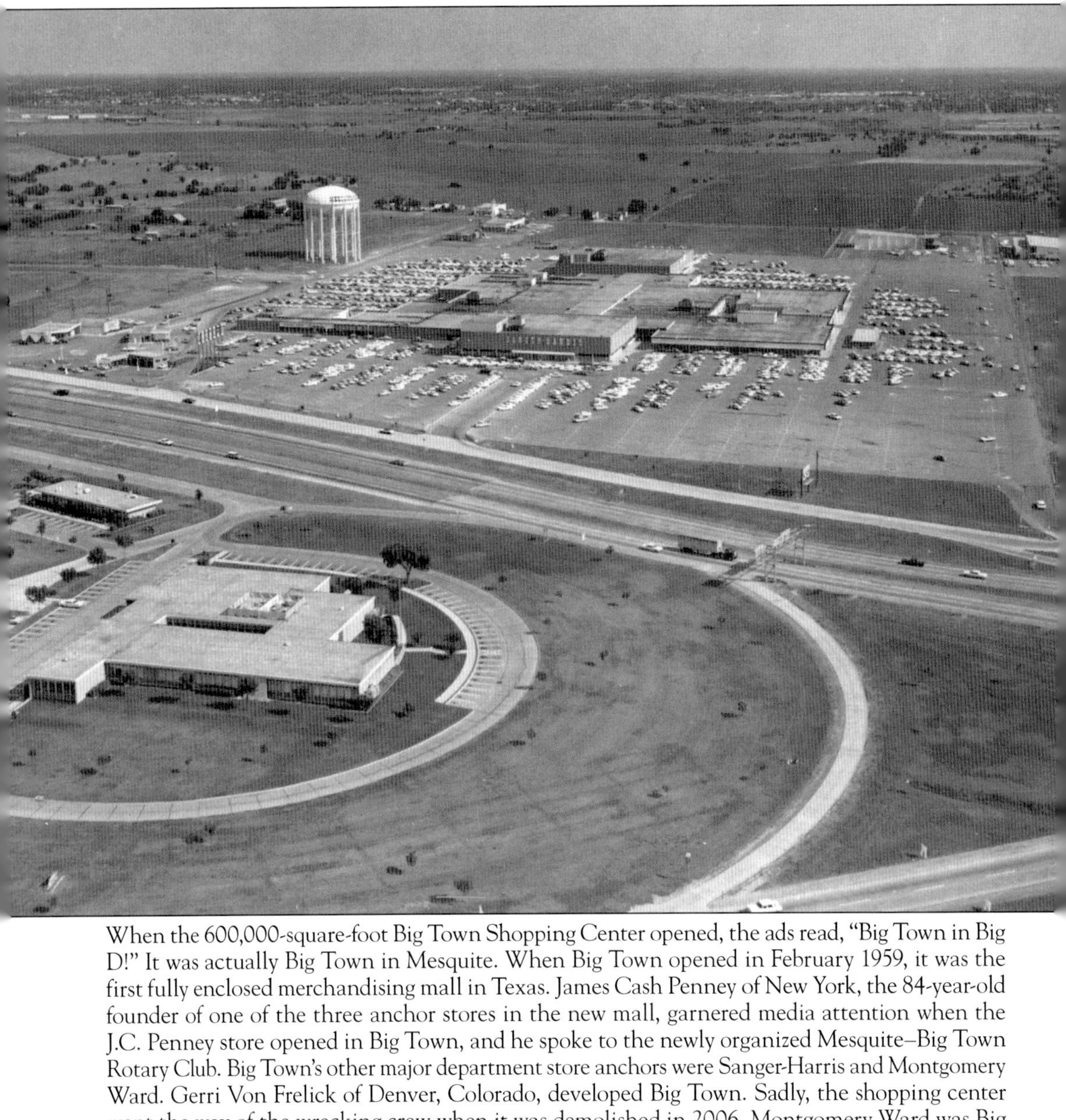

When the 600,000-square-foot Big Town Shopping Center opened, the ads read, "Big Town in Big D!" It was actually Big Town in Mesquite. When Big Town opened in February 1959, it was the first fully enclosed merchandising mall in Texas. James Cash Penney of New York, the 84-year-old founder of one of the three anchor stores in the new mall, garnered media attention when the J.C. Penney store opened in Big Town, and he spoke to the newly organized Mesquite–Big Town Rotary Club. Big Town's other major department store anchors were Sanger-Harris and Montgomery Ward. Gerri Von Frelick of Denver, Colorado, developed Big Town. Sadly, the shopping center went the way of the wrecking crew when it was demolished in 2006. Montgomery Ward was Big Town's last surviving anchor store, valiantly carrying on its retail service until 2001.

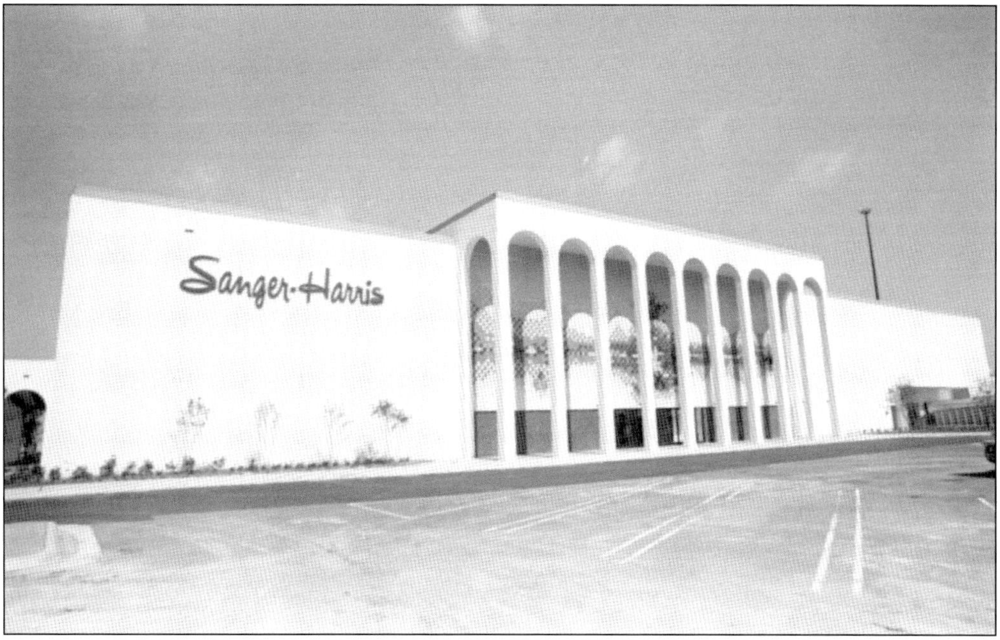

Not only was Sanger-Harris department store a Big Town Shopping Center anchor store, it was also a Town East Mall anchor store. In 1972, these majestic columns and mosaic features were the height of exterior architecture for stores. At that time, the Sanger-Harris at Town East Mall had an innovative marketing and promotional staff and hired the author to help "officially open" this store with his singing and guitar playing while strolling in the women's lingerie department (but far away, of course, from the dressing rooms in the essence of manners and good taste). For an 18-year-old singing guitarist, it was one of the most memorable music gigs of his teen years. This Sanger-Harris location later became Foley's and is now a Macy's store.

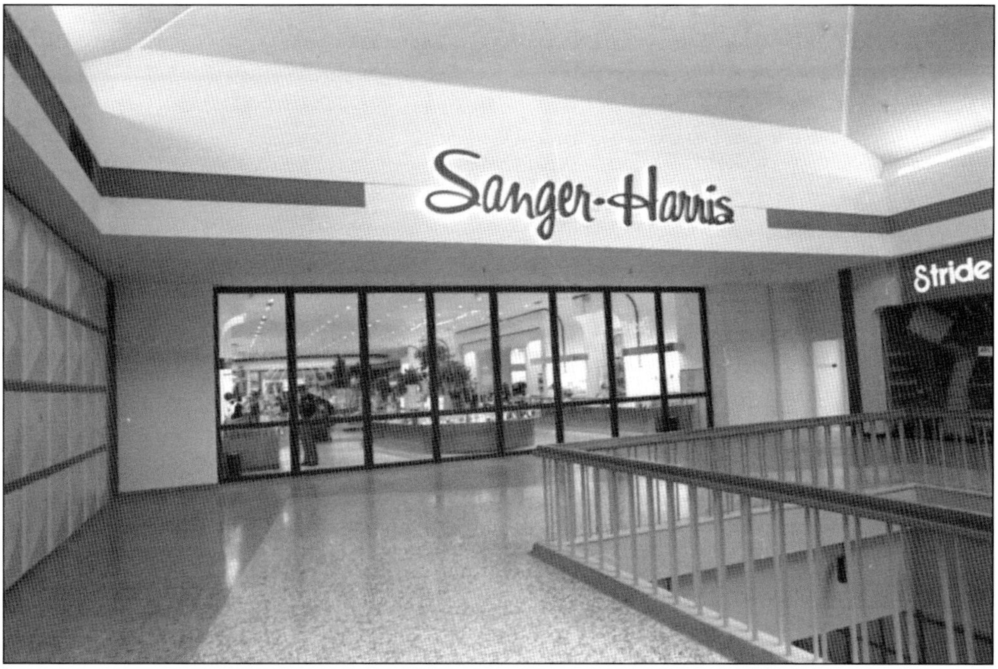

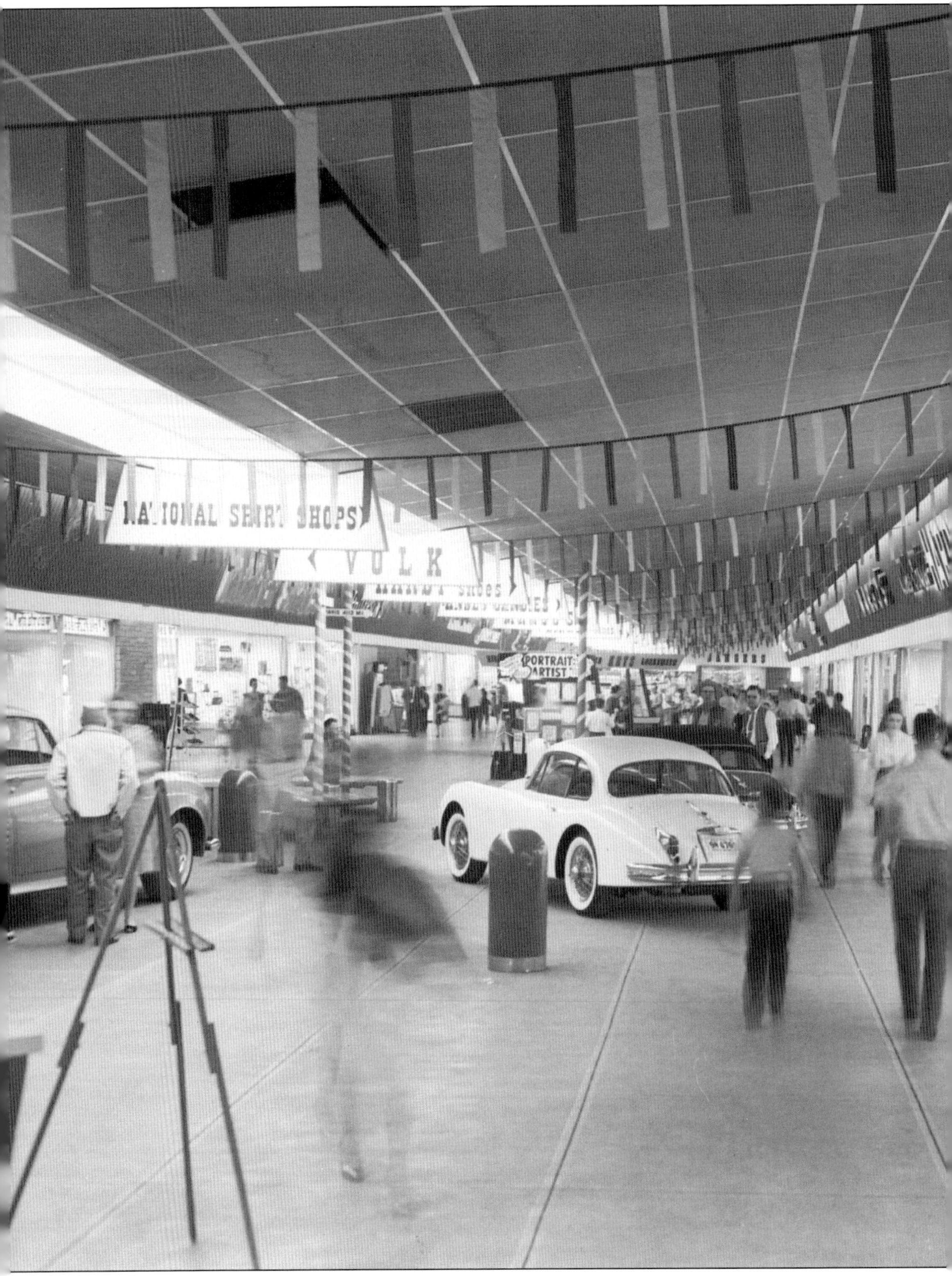
NATIONAL SHIRT SHOPS
VOLK
PORTRAIT ARTIST

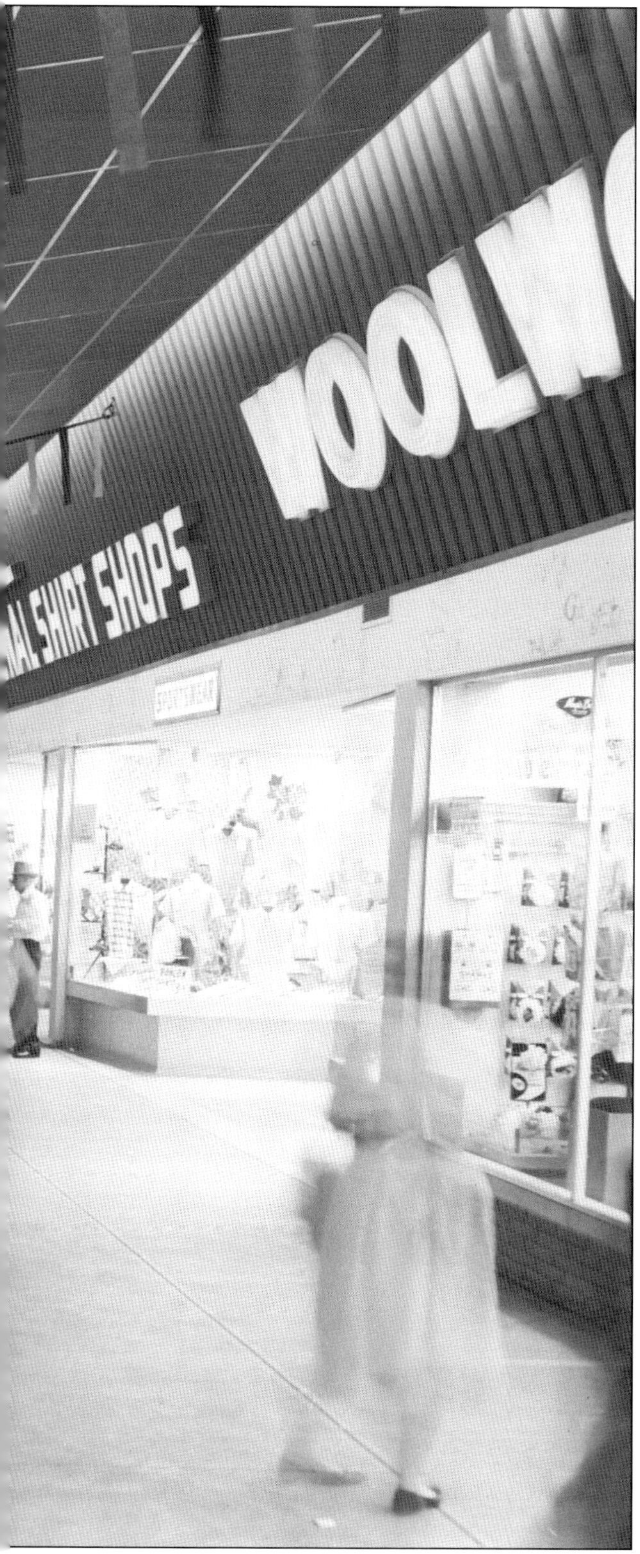

Along with the three department store anchors in Big Town Shopping Center, there were other important powerhouse shops in the mall, as seen in the photograph. Volk Brothers (Volk's) specialty shop sold men's and women's clothing with some of the finest fashions and particularly trendy shoes. Volk's was one of the first fine clothiers in Texas to embrace the mod Carnaby Street fashions of the 1960s and also the "hep cat" fashions of Beale Street and other music-rich regions. Woolworth's was a variety store that reigned supreme in what it sold throughout the 1960s and 1970s. Departments favored by locals featured tropical fish/pets, bulk candy sold by the pound, and a well-stocked record shop of vinyl albums, EPs, and singles. The author first discovered the gospel music of James Blackwood and the Blackwood Brothers in Woolworth's record department, purchasing the RCA Victor album titled *The Best of the Blackwood Brothers.* Three-and-a-half decades later, the author's independent record label and artists would win the Grammy Award for the album *We Called Him Mr. Gospel Music: The James Blackwood Tribute Album* in 2003. It all started at the Big Town Mesquite record department of Woolworth's.

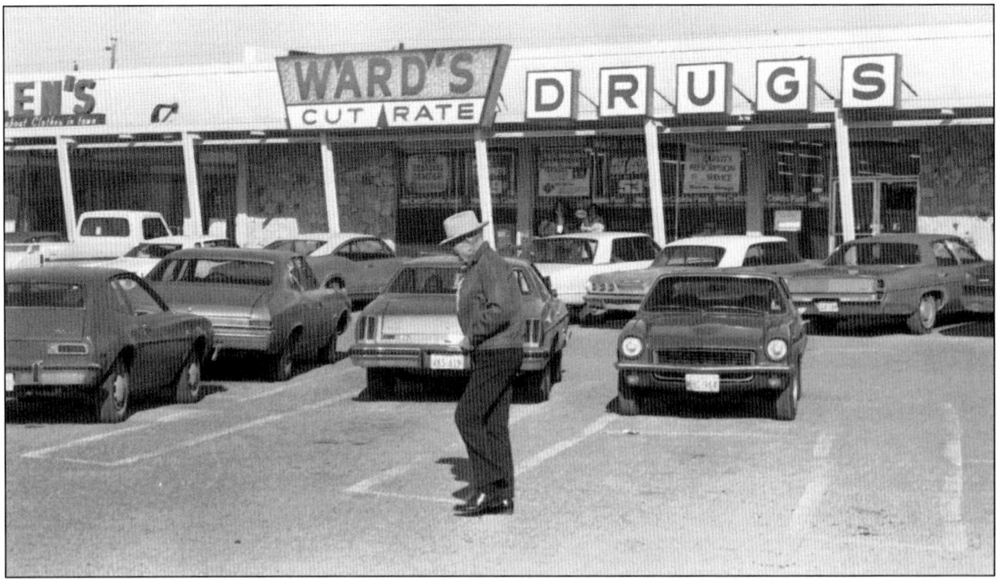

In May 1964, an eclectic strip shopping center, Mesquite Central Shopping Center, was erected next to Fire Station No. 1 on South Galloway Avenue. Through the years, it housed businesses such as cafeterias, Ashburn Ice Cream, Pizza Spa, Levine's, M.E. Moses 5 & 10, Sears Catalog Sales Stores, Kroger, and the center's south end shops seen here around 1975. Future mayor Brunhilde Nystrom voiced the opinion at the time that Mesquite would have been better served by more downtown square expansion as opposed to the construction of both this strip center and also Broadmoor Plaza Shopping Center so close by the downtown square. She was probably right, since in the year of this writing, 2015, Mesquite Central Shopping Center is, and has been for years, demolished, the grounds vacant, and the Mesquite Heritage Square is in desperate need of revitalization and redevelopment.

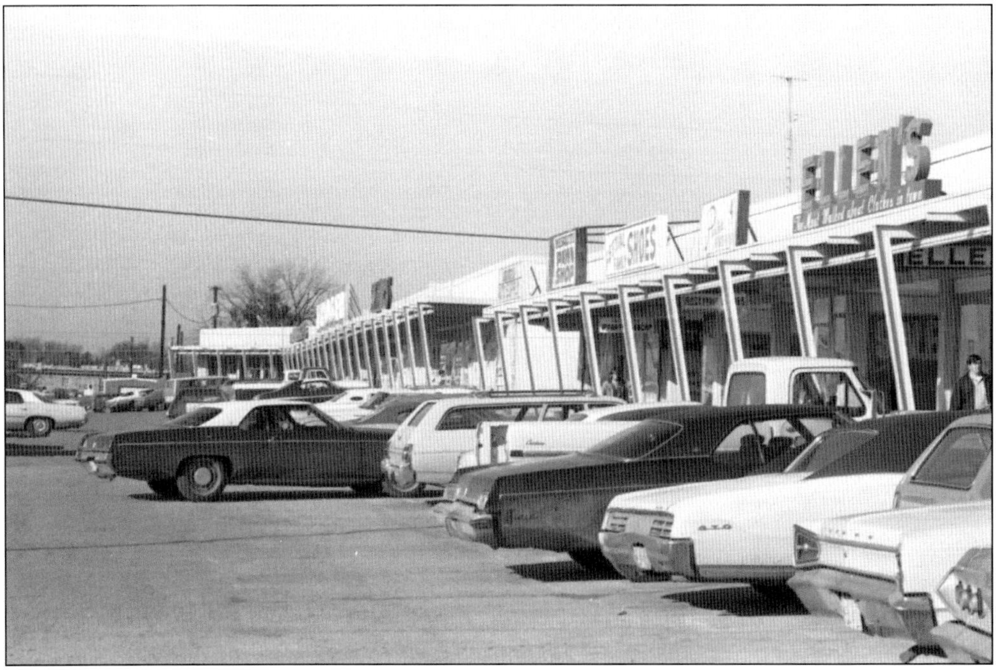

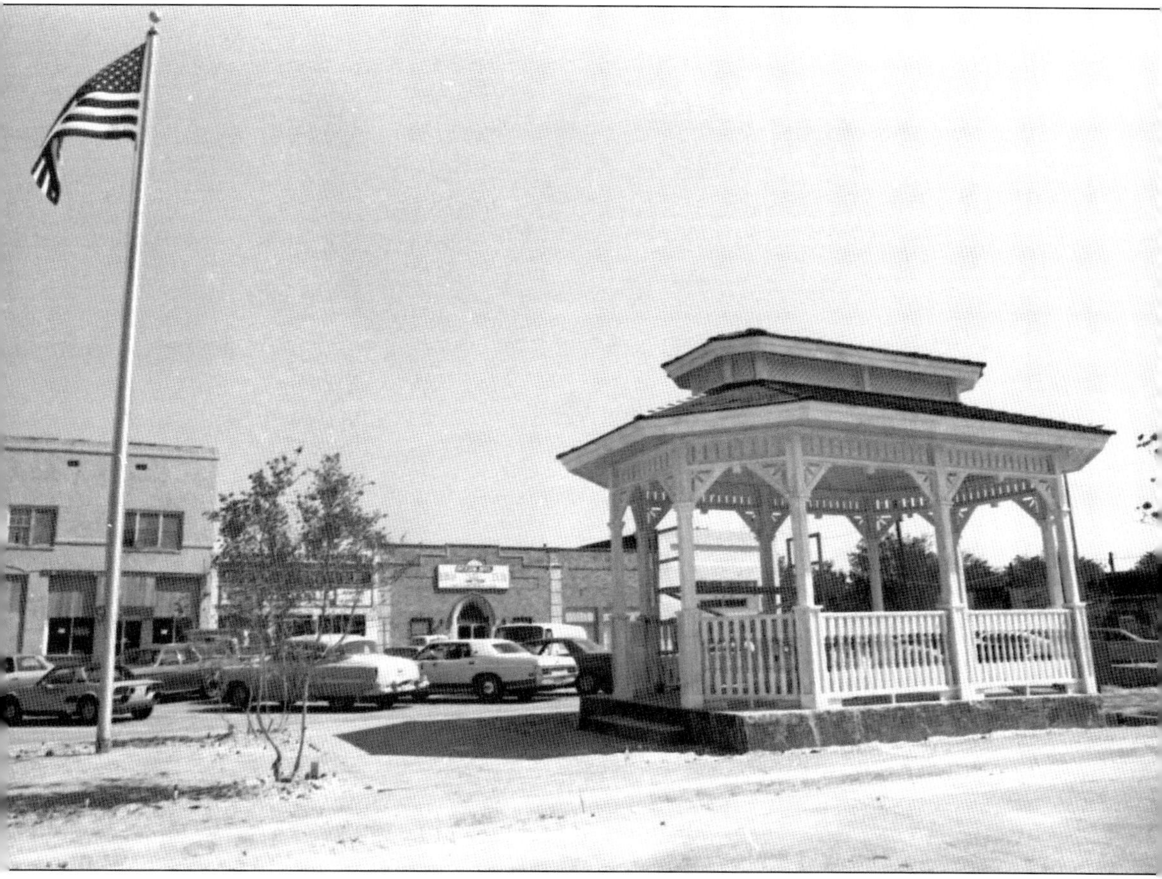

As the once-thriving and prosperous retail operations like bookstores and record shops fade away from the town square, new specialty stores that reflect the wants and needs of the public take their place. Dickson Bros. was two years old when this photograph was taken in 1975. The store is a Mesquite success story with its mix of pool and water supplies along with other sales and services having to do with water landscaping.

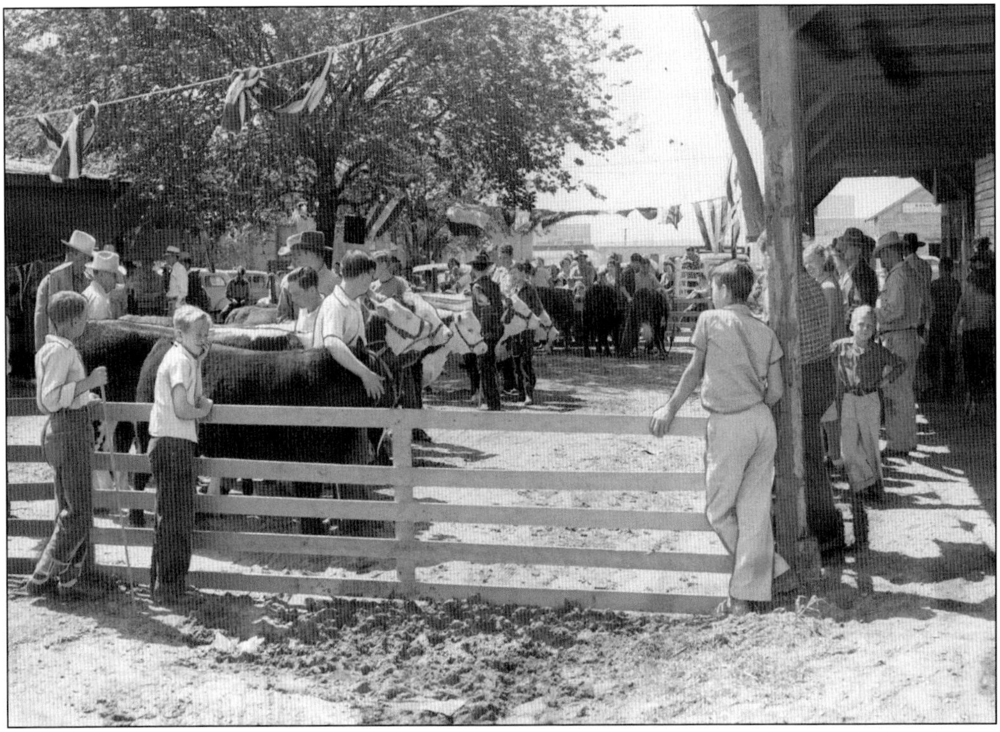

The Mesquite Fair (in later years known as Dallas County Fair) was begun in 1922 and continued through 1959 as a celebration of the community's agricultural business and heritage. This photograph from 1947 depicts the important livestock aspect of the fair. Several Dallas County communities had local fairs, but by 1952 Mesquite's was the last community fair in annual operation.

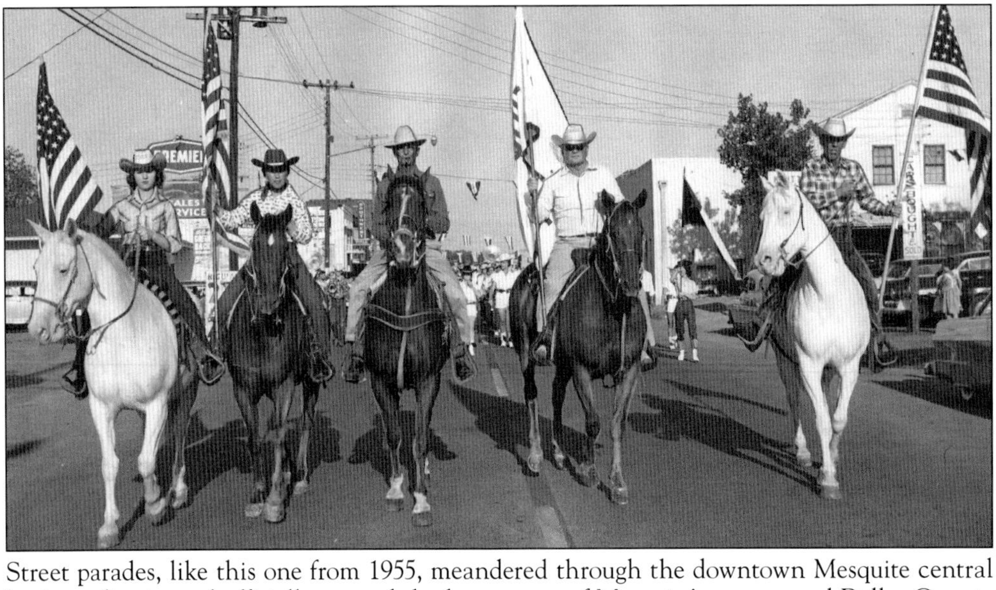

Street parades, like this one from 1955, meandered through the downtown Mesquite central business district and officially opened the latter years of Mesquite's now-named Dallas County Fair. By this fair year, a midway, carnival rides, and automobile exhibits had been added to the traditional farm products displays, and the annual, three-day event (expanded to five days and 7.1 acres by 1958) was now staged at a site east of Mesquite High School.

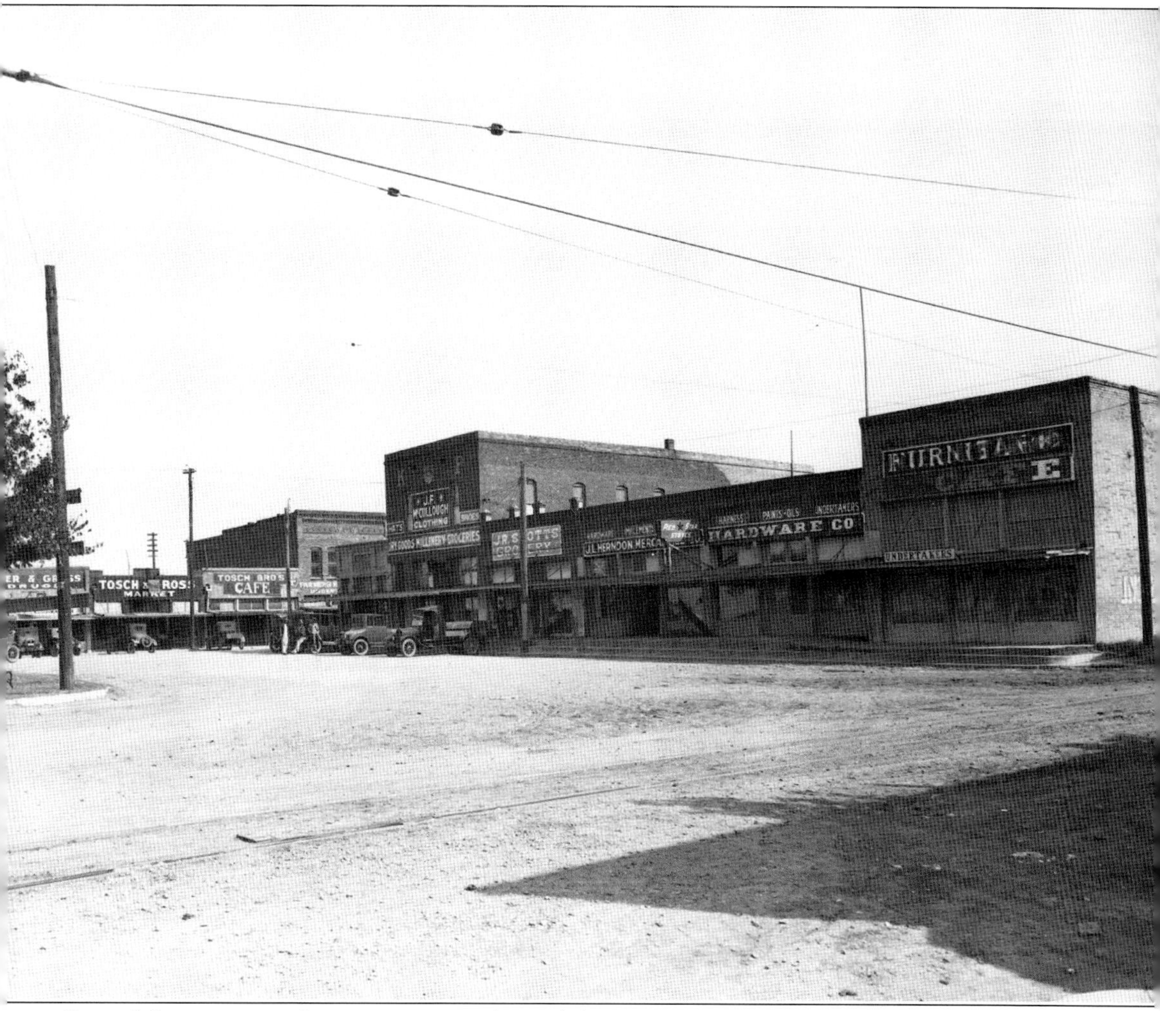

One of the greatest achievements in industrial design in 1920s and 1930s Mesquite was the Dallas-Mesquite-Terrell line of the Texas Interurban Railway. Just imagine a light rail, rapid transit system speeding through eastern Dallas County as early as 1923 and powered by electricity with more speed, comfort, luxury, and interior space than other modes of transportation of the period. This photograph shows portions of the 31-mile line, its tracks, and its power cable rising above the downtown square's stores. Interurban organizing directors from Mesquite were J.C. Rugel and Schuyler Marshall. On March 19, 1932, a notice appeared on the Mesquite interurban depot announcing the end of service. The age of the automobile had caused the eventual financial failure of this thrilling venture, a Mesquite source of pride for its nine years of transportation service to its riders.

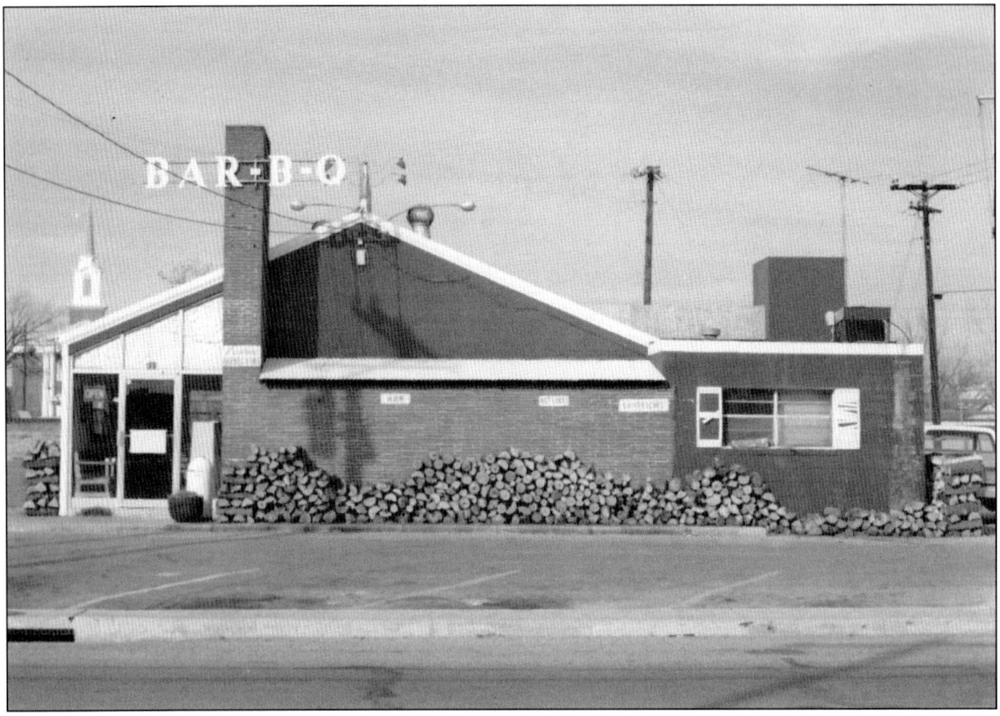

Herbert Oyler, inventor of an entirely new method of cooking barbecue—via a patented automatic wood-burning pit—established Mesquite Barbecue on June 15, 1959, on East Main Street adjacent to Minyard's Food Store. Leon Crouch joined Oyler in operations two months after Mesquite Barbecue opened its doors, and he became owner after Oyler was killed in a tragic train-automobile crash at one of downtown Mesquite's railroad crossings. After Crouch's passing in 1983, his wife, Katy, and son Kent successfully continued the family business along with Kent's wife, Lisa, and were later joined by third-generation Dustin and Melanie. The photograph above depicts the landmark East Main Street downtown location, and the photograph below depicts the business as it stands today on Davis Street across from Mesquite High School. (Both, courtesy of Kent Crouch.)

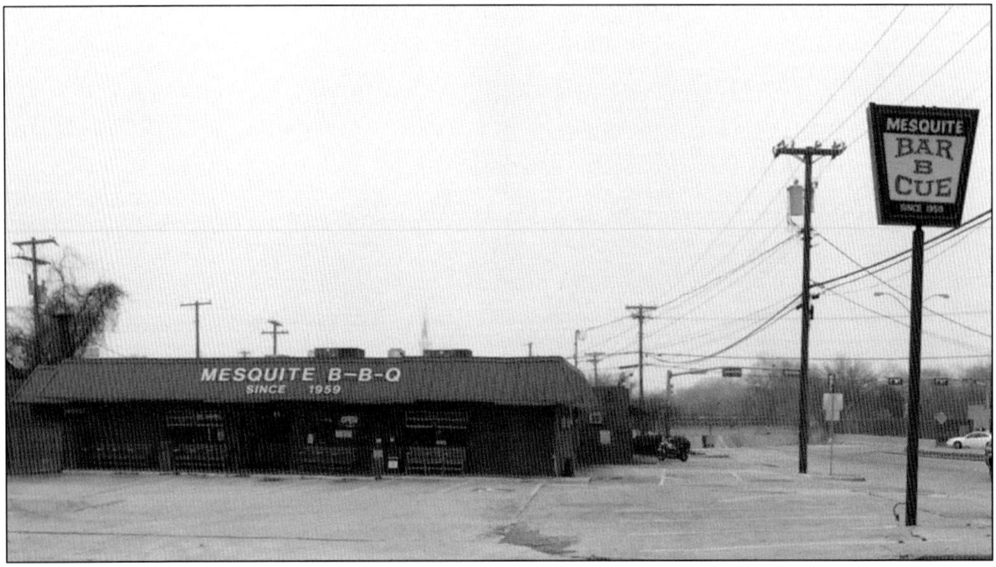

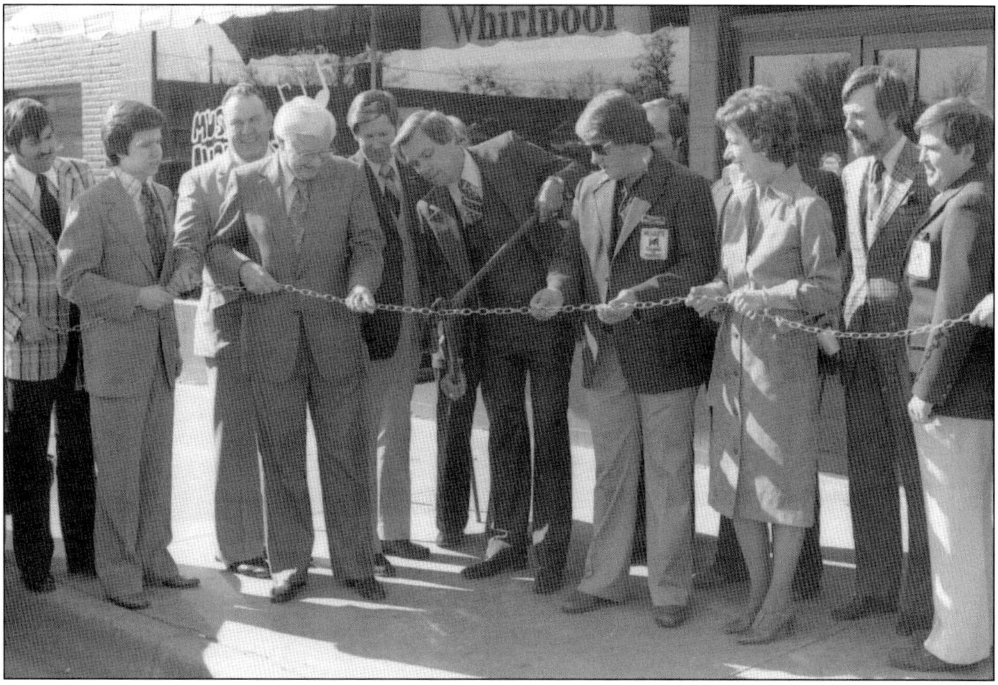

In 1977, business and civic leaders gather around Mesquite mayor B.J. Smith to celebrate the grand reopening and 34th anniversary of the newly remodeled McWhorter-Greenhaw Emporium on Mesquite's downtown square. Chain and bolt cutter cleverly replace traditional ribbon and scissors, commemorating hardware products traditionally sold in the store.

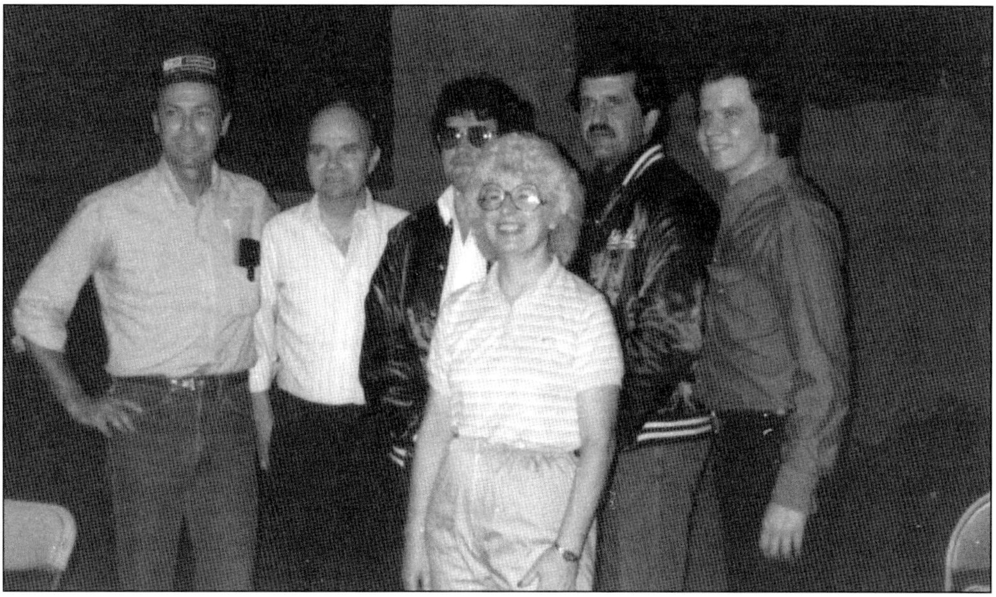

During periods of time when Mesquite was home to more small businesses and family-owned retail, specialty stores like Norris Family Music had their areas of expertise. This music store was known for its concentration in steel guitar. Gathered for a Norris Family Music and Texas Steel Guitar Association showcase concert are, from left to right, Tom Brumley, Bud Carter, Earl Briggs, Janet McBride, Junior Knight, and the author.

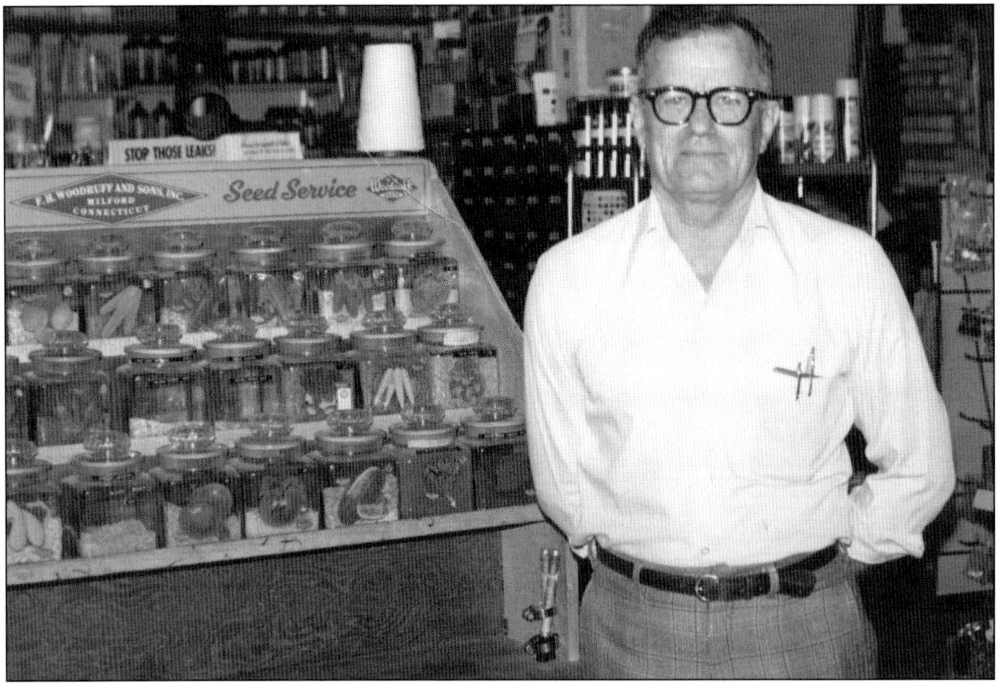

As late as the 1970s, a customer could purchase bulk garden seed from this iconic display for 10¢ per dip at McWhorter-Greenhaw Emporium, located on the square. Faithful employee Woodson Dean stands minding the seed counter.

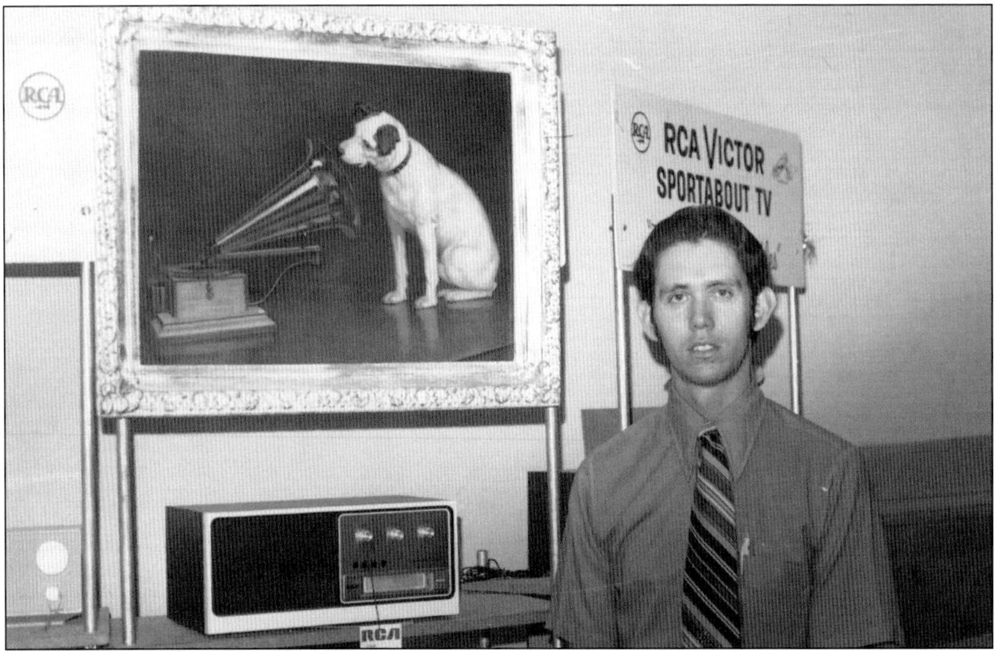

McWhorter-Greenhaw enjoyed a long franchise association with RCA Victor and was the first store in Mesquite to sell televisions and other RCA products including radios and recorders. Store manager Dwayne Richman was a top award-winning Mesquite High School Distributive Education Club of America student taught by faculty member Wendell Ferguson.

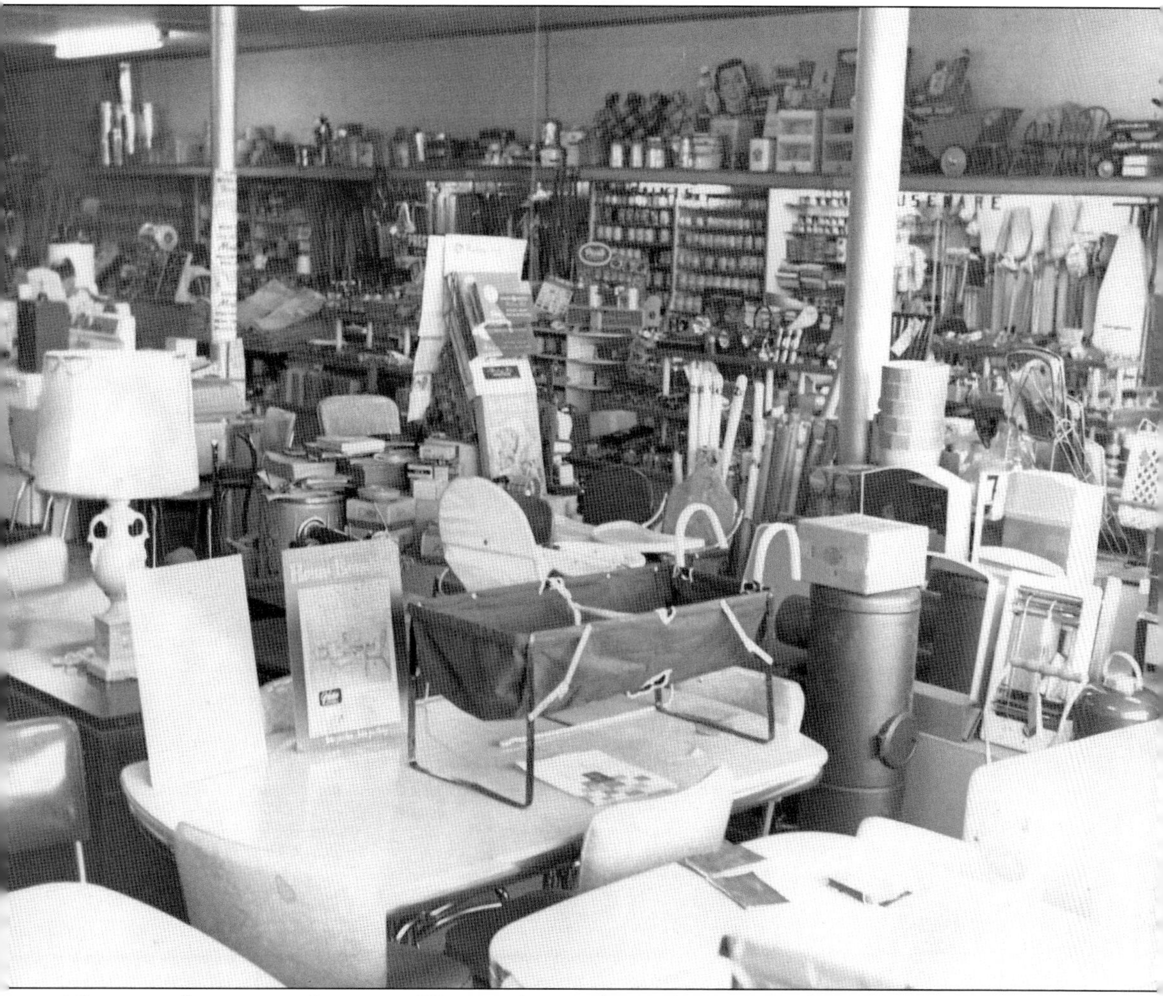

The west-side stores on the square, Western Auto and McWhorter-Greenhaw, provided customers with an extended selection of general merchandise. This mid-20th-century photograph reveals an extensive inventory including a tin heater and little red wagons (on the top shelf).

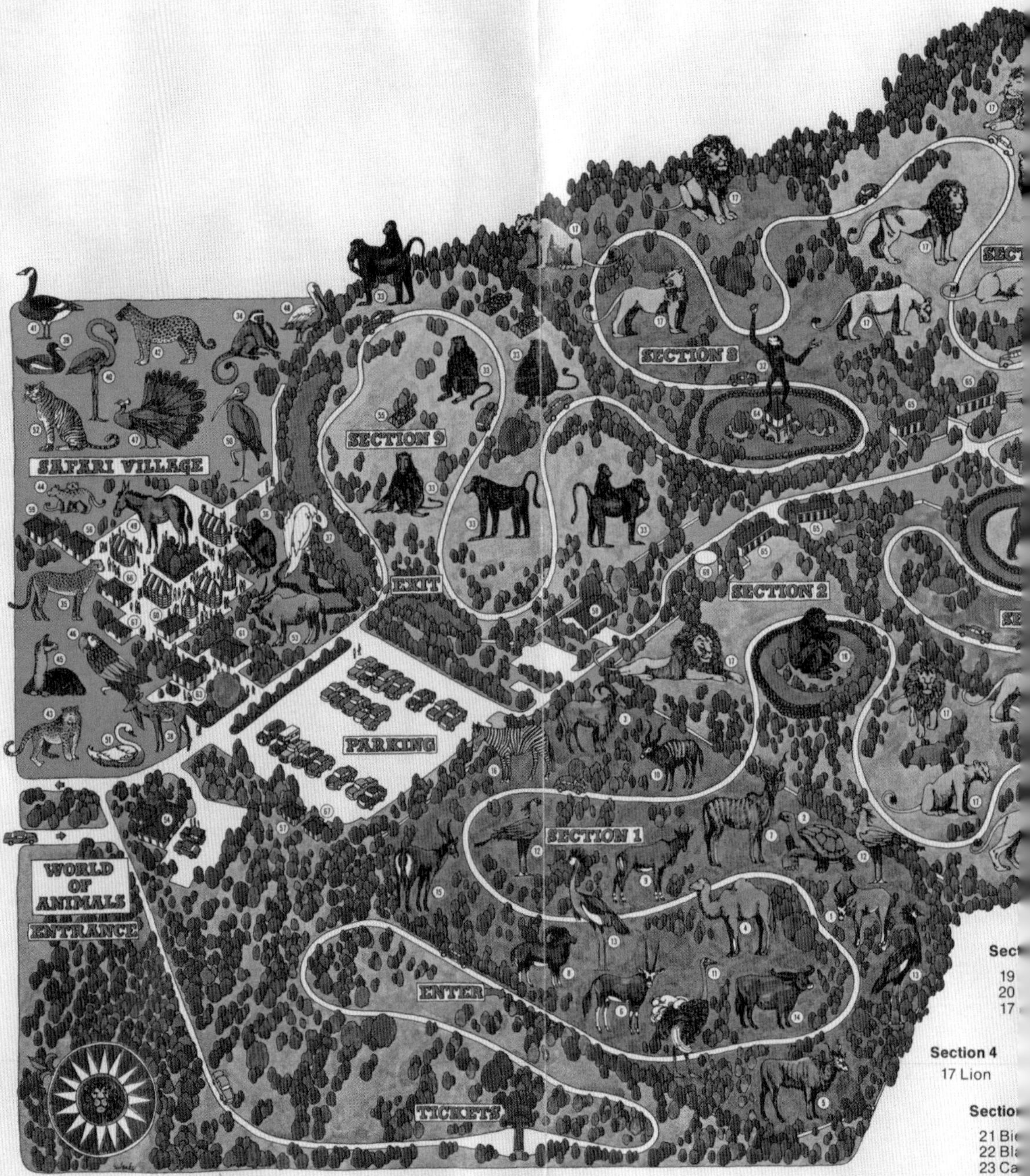

Section 1

1 Addax
2 Aldabra Tortoise
3 Auodad
4 Camel
5 Eland
6 Gemsbok
7 Greater Kudu
8 Mouflon
9 Nilghai
10 Nyala
11 Ostrich
12 Secretary Bird
13 W.A. Crowned Crane
14 Water Buffalo
15 Waterbuck
16 Zebra
plus other animals

Section 2

17 Lion
18 Chimpanzee

Section 4

17 Lion

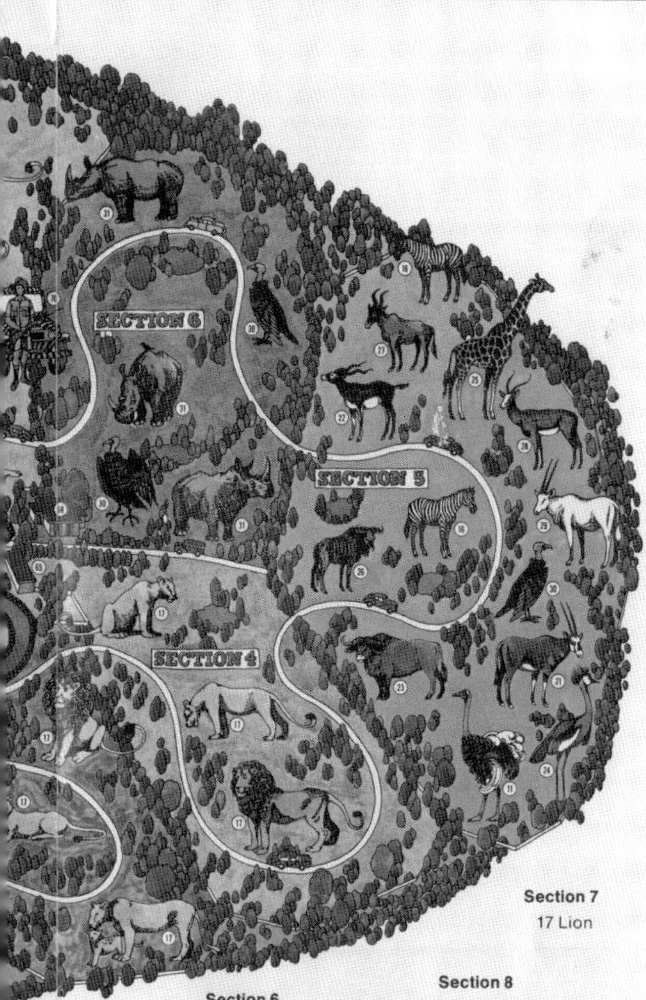

Section 6

30 Vulture
31 White Rhinoceros

Section 7

17 Lion

Section 8

32 Gibbon Ape
17 Lion

Section 9

33 Baboon

Safari Village

34 African Green Monkey
35 Cheetah
36 Chimpanzee
37 Cockatoo
38 Deer Fawn
39 Duck
40 Flamingo
41 Geese
42 Jaguar
43 Leopard
44 Lion cubs
45 Llama
46 Macaw
47 Pea Fowl
48 Pelican
49 Pygmy Donkey
50 Scarlet Ibis
51 Swan
52 Tiger
53 Zebu
plus domestic animals

Structures

54 Administration building
55 Baboon House
56 Barn
57 Camera & Car Rental
58 Commissary (animal food center)
59 Clinic
60 Curio Shop
61 Dining Pavilion
62 Elephant House
63 Food Center (for humans)
64 Gibbon House
65 Lion den
66 Nursery
67 Restrooms (2 locations)
68 Rhino House
69 Water Tank

70 World of Animals Ranger
& Toyota Rescue Vehicle

This rare historical illustrated guide from Mesquite's World of Animals theme park depicts the entire park layout section by section. The map depicts the nine sections of the park, plus various structures, and the Safari Village. Admission was $3 for adults and $1.50 for children under 12, and part of the admission fee was directed toward animal survival research and breeding programs.

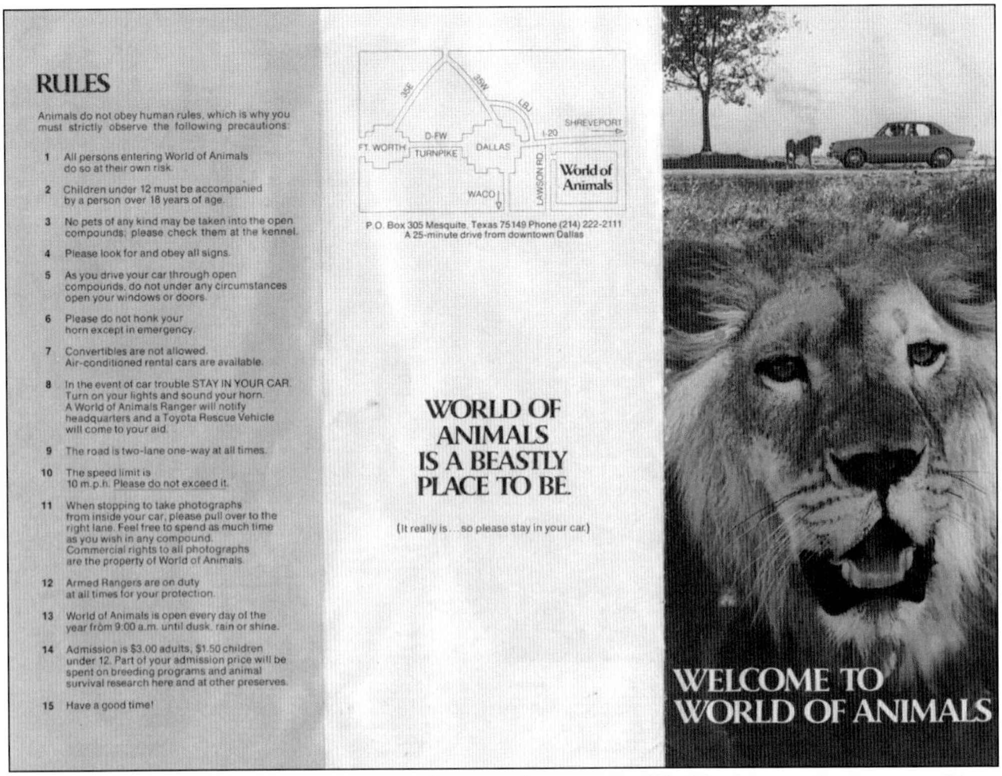

RULES

Animals do not obey human rules, which is why you must strictly observe the following precautions:

1 All persons entering World of Animals do so at their own risk.

2 Children under 12 must be accompanied by a person over 18 years of age.

3 No pets of any kind may be taken into the open compounds; please check them at the kennel.

4 Please look for and obey all signs.

5 As you drive your car through open compounds, do not under any circumstances open your windows or doors.

6 Please do not honk your horn except in emergency.

7 Convertibles are not allowed. Air-conditioned rental cars are available.

8 In the event of car trouble STAY IN YOUR CAR. Turn on your lights and sound your horn. A World of Animals Ranger will notify headquarters and a Toyota Rescue Vehicle will come to your aid.

9 The road is two-lane one-way at all times.

10 The speed limit is 10 m.p.h. Please do not exceed it.

11 When stopping to take photographs from inside your car, please pull over to the right lane. Feel free to spend as much time as you wish in any compound. Commercial rights to all photographs are the property of World of Animals.

12 Armed Rangers are on duty at all times for your protection.

13 World of Animals is open every day of the year from 9:00 a.m. until dusk, rain or shine.

14 Admission is $3.00 adults, $1.50 children under 12. Part of your admission price will be spent on breeding programs and animal survival research here and at other preserves.

15 Have a good time!

35E
35W
LBJ
SHREVEPORT
I-20
D-FW
FT. WORTH
TURNPIKE
DALLAS
LAWSON RD.
WACO
World of Animals

P.O. Box 305 Mesquite, Texas 75149 Phone (214) 222-2111
A 25-minute drive from downtown Dallas

WORLD OF ANIMALS IS A BEASTLY PLACE TO BE.

(It really is... so please stay in your car.)

WELCOME TO WORLD OF ANIMALS

This outside cover for World of Animals theme park's illustrated guide describes the "beastly" facility filled with wild, exotic animals. World of Animals was quite possibly the most ambitious and thrilling tourist attraction to ever set up shop in Mesquite. Selling points of the 1970s theme park included being "open every day of the year from 9:00 a.m. until dusk" and "armed rangers on duty at all times for guest protection."

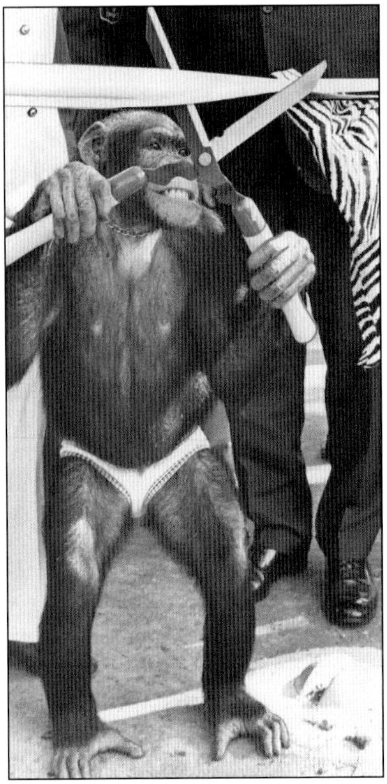

A personable chimpanzee from World of Animals officially opens the theme park by cutting the ceremonial ribbon.

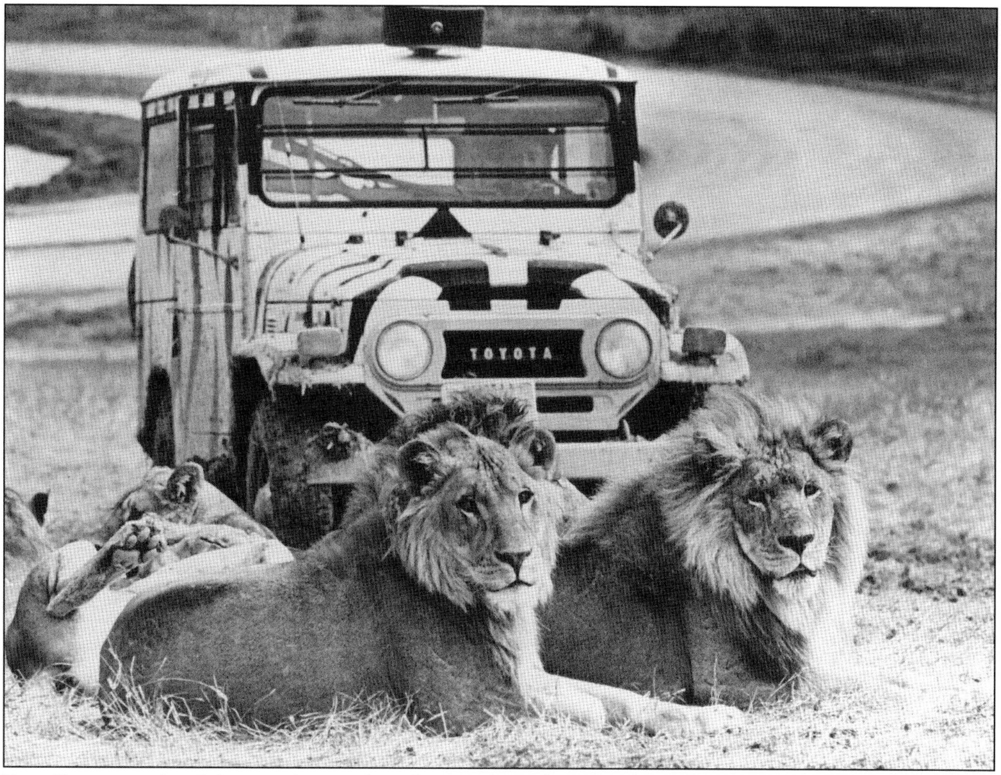

Regally situated as Mesquite's own lion kings, these beautiful creatures observe the guests at the World of Animals theme park.

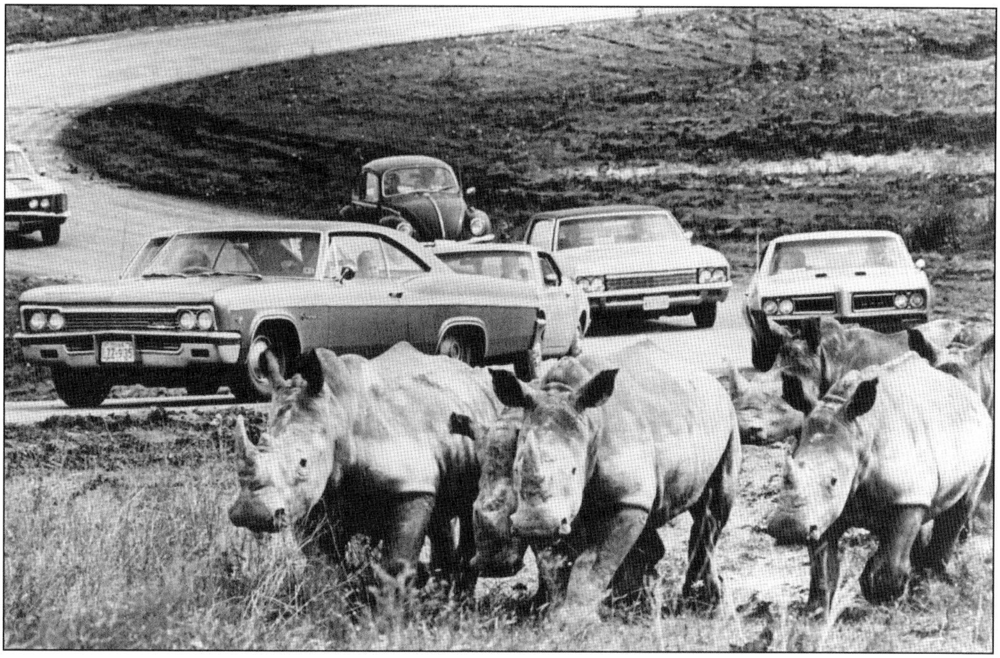

A crash of rhinoceroses gallops alongside the traffic as theme park visitors enjoy the opportunity to see these exotic animals from Africa at World of Animals theme park in Mesquite.

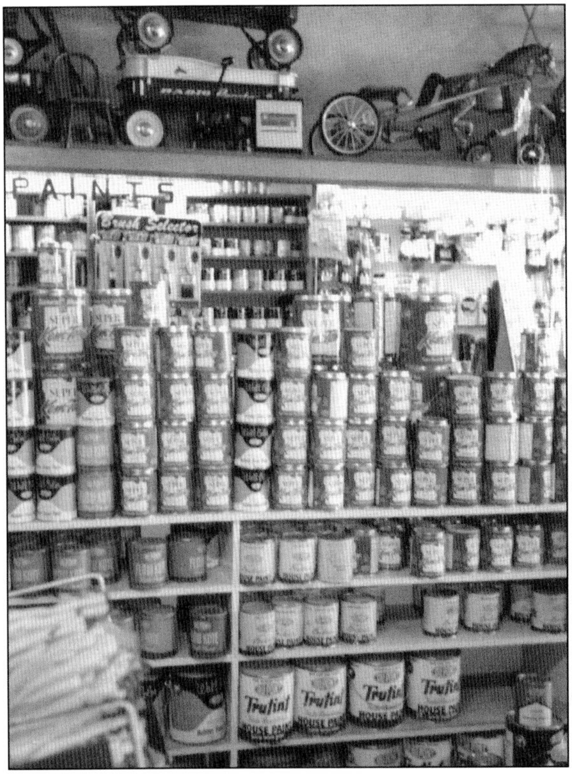

In downtown Mesquite in 1960, there were still retail emporiums packed to the ceiling with general merchandise, much as it had been in downtown Mesquite 50 years prior. Note the high storage of hardware and household items near the ceiling in the bird's-eye view below of the interior of McWhorter-Greenhaw Store. In the photograph at left, there is a full selection of DuPont paints, including DuPont's Lucite line of goods advertised during the period by none other than Lucy herself, Lucille Ball.

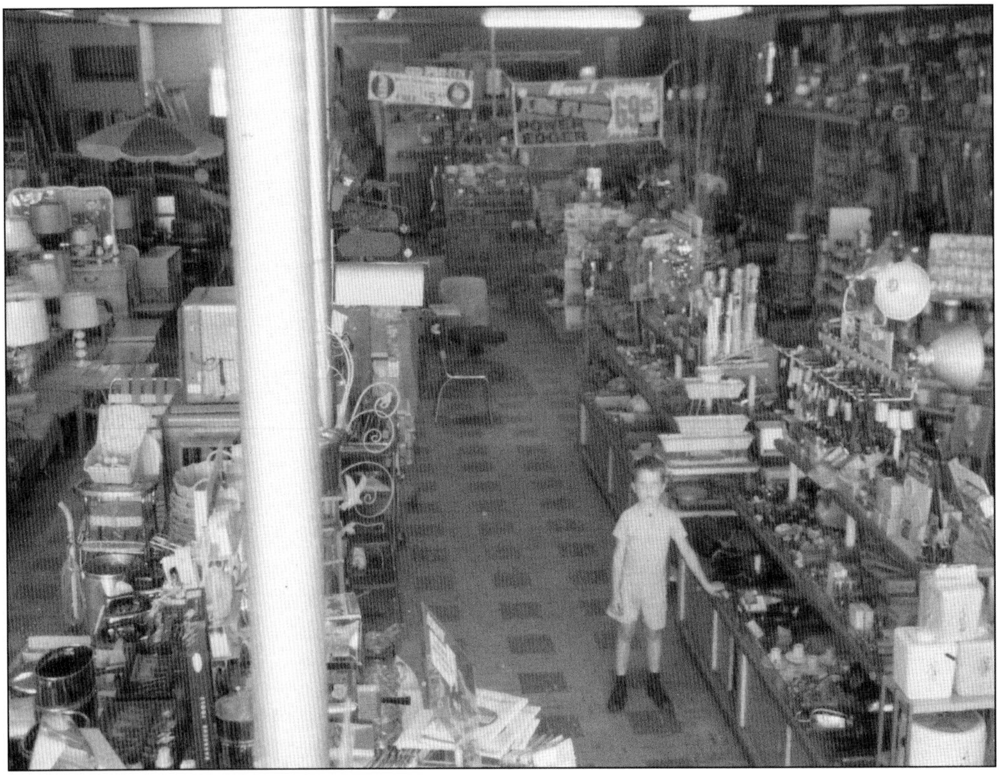

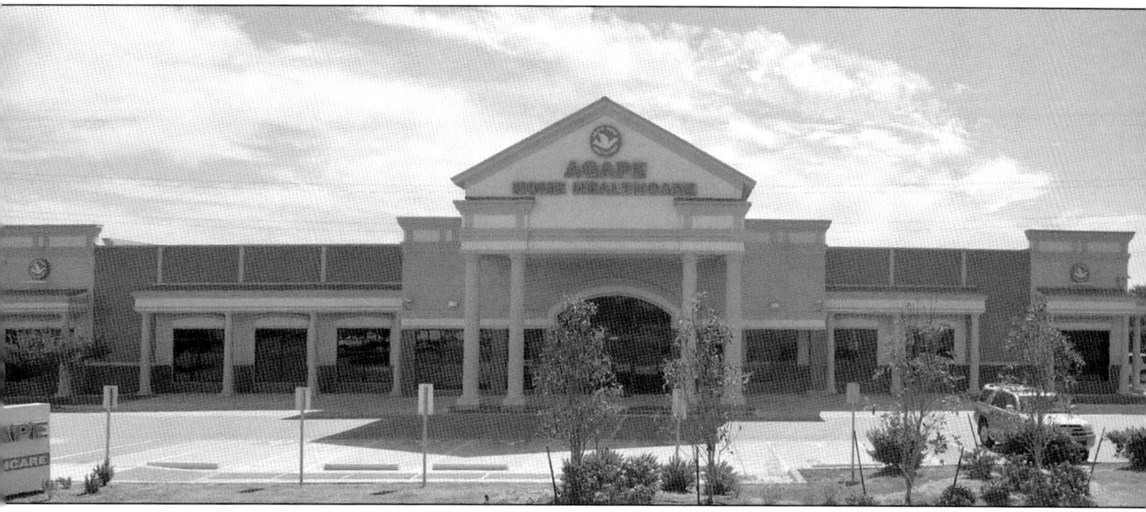

The North Mesquite High School 1987 salutatorian, Shiney Cherian Daniel, would form Agape Group, Inc., with her husband, Shaji Daniel, in 1994. A faith-based health care company, which provides home health and hospice services throughout the Dallas–Fort Worth metroplex, Agape is one of the largest private sector employers in Mesquite. Agape Group, Inc., ushers in a brand-new day on the horizon for the Mesquite economy and continues the local legacy of successful family businesses.

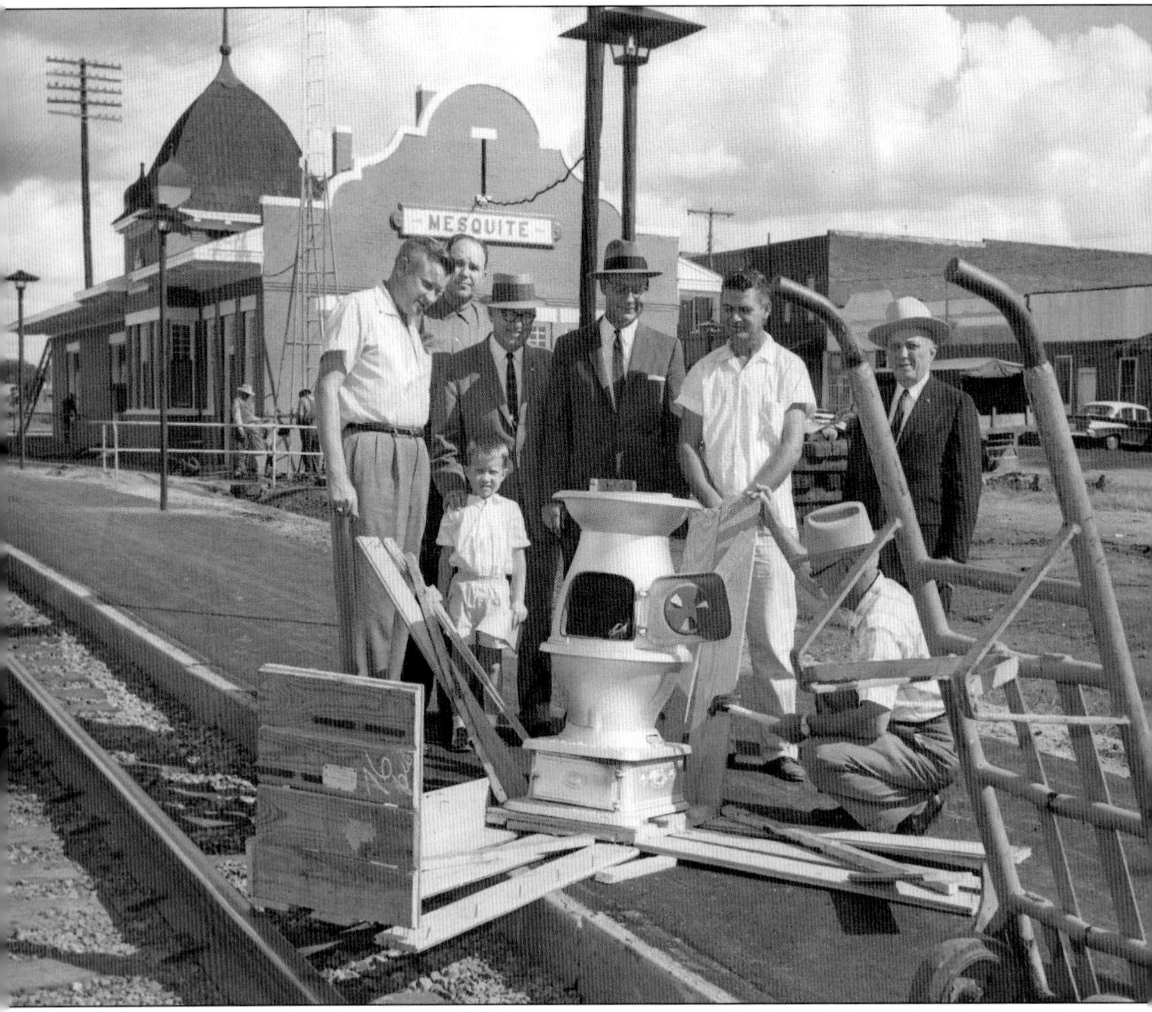

All towns have tales of intrigue, which happen sometimes in the heat of the night and change the course of history for that community. The tale of the Mesquite depot demolition in 1971 is a story of missed opportunity and corporate monopoly and of executive, bureaucratic maneuverings and power plays. It is a tale worthy to be explored by new generations of researchers and historians. As explained by the parties who were there and who were eyewitnesses, word reached the Mesquite community of women's club members that the Texas & Pacific Railway Company no longer wanted a Mesquite stop. Just as the concerned women were discussing the saving of the depot with the railroad representatives, the depot was demolished one night by the railroad organization presumably to avoid the hassle of preservation and negotiation. A landmark of downtown Mesquite was gone with the wind, ending a much-loved piece of Mesquite's history that spurred the formation of the town in 1873. This photograph from the late 1950s depicts business leaders in front of the Mesquite depot.

Two

Education and Government

School-City Days and Nights

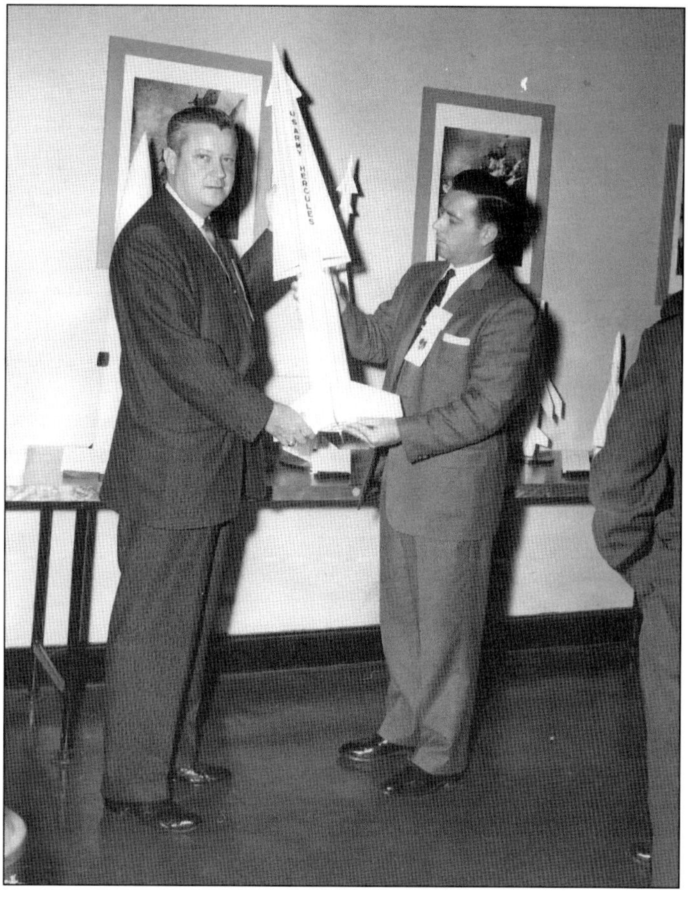

When Mesquite was a Boomtown USA in December 1960, there was a tremendous amount of mutual respect between the business community, the central business district, and the Mesquite city manager. Businessman Frank W. Greenhaw and City Manager George Schrader traveled to Fort Bliss, Texas, in a project called "Operation Understanding" to gain citizen insight into the workings and strategies of the US Army.

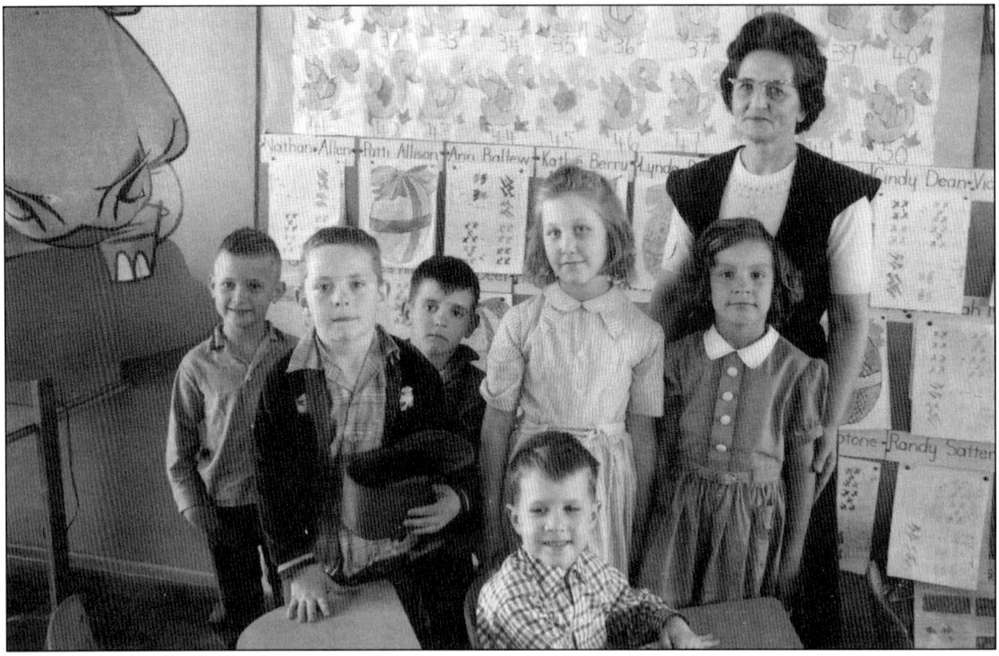

Florence Black Elementary School was formally opened in 1954, under the leadership of the board of trustees and Superintendent McDonald, and was the flagship elementary school of the period. The school was the district's first to occupy a location that was not part of the original central campus, which had been the sole educational site since 1902. Parents and community leaders had complete access to the school campuses of the day, as these photographs taken by a parent attest. Virginia Armstrong was highly respected as a best-of-the-best elementary teacher, and she is shown here in her first-grade classroom at Florence Black Elementary School during the 1960–1961 school year.

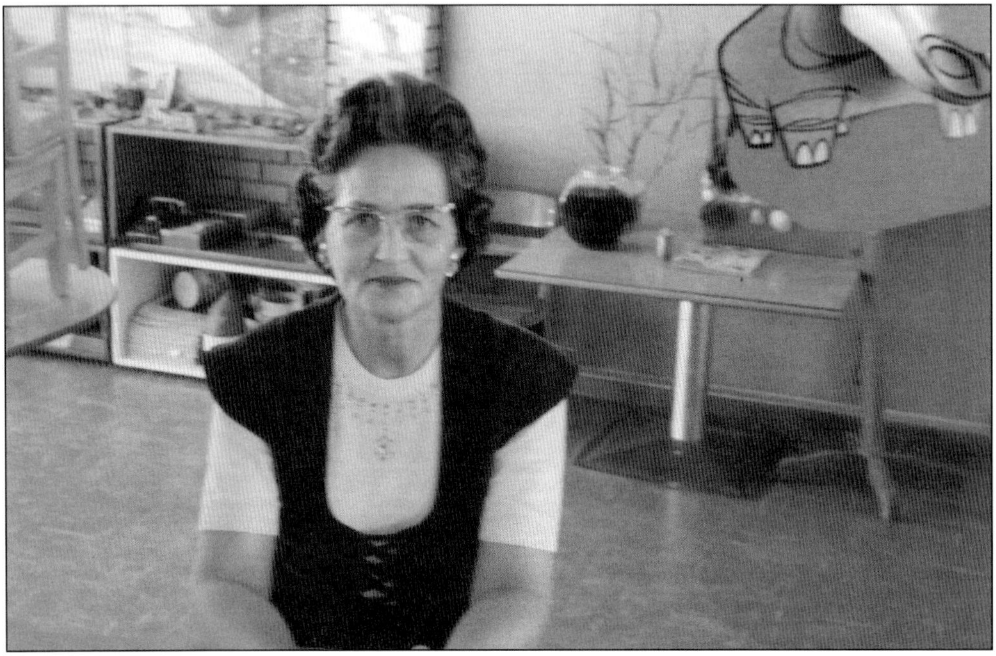

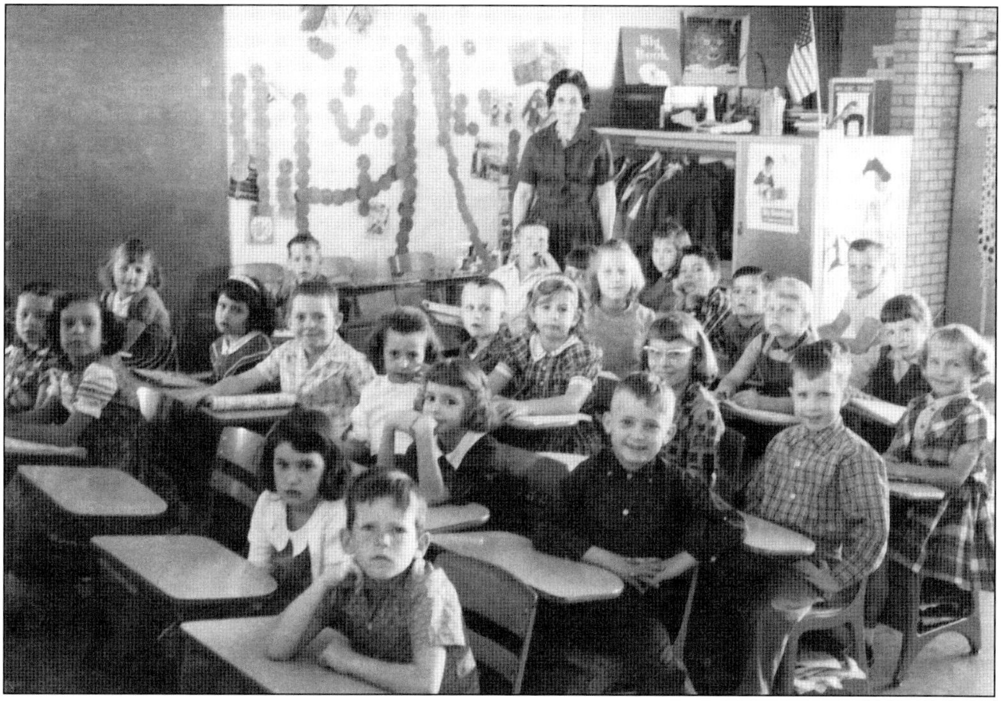

Teacher Virginia Armstrong's 1960–1961 first-grade class numbered around 30 students and produced record numbers of readers using phonics, a system of teaching students how to read. The circles on the back whiteboard were named "bookworms" and represent individual books read by each of Armstrong's first-grade students. Students in Armstrong's class depicted here include several who remained in Mesquite public schools through high school: Patti Allison, the author, Phyllis Rigsby, Toni Watson, Debra Ponder, and Cindy Dean.

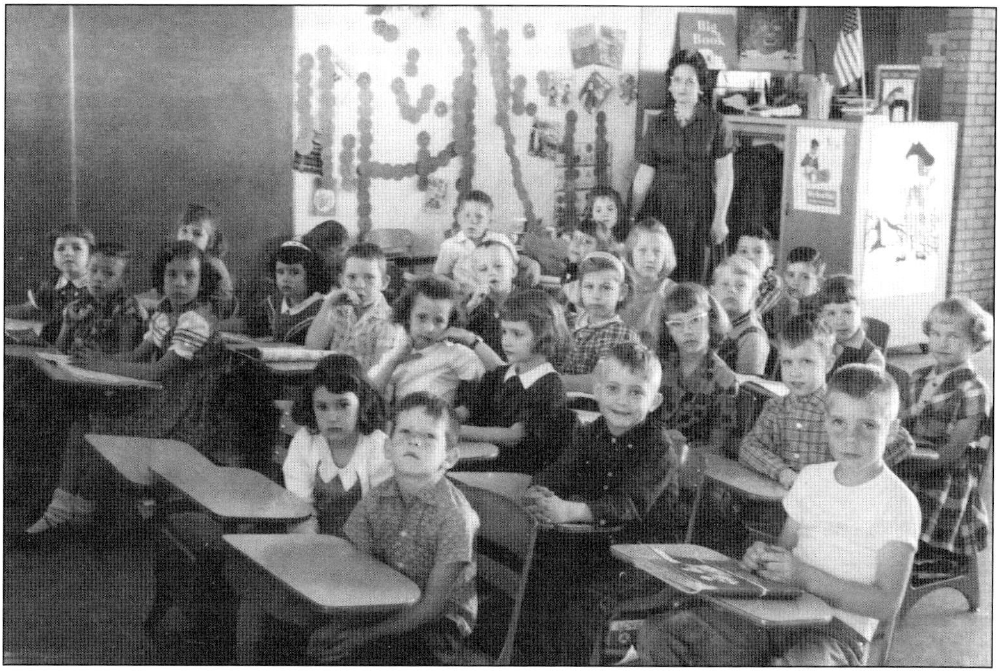

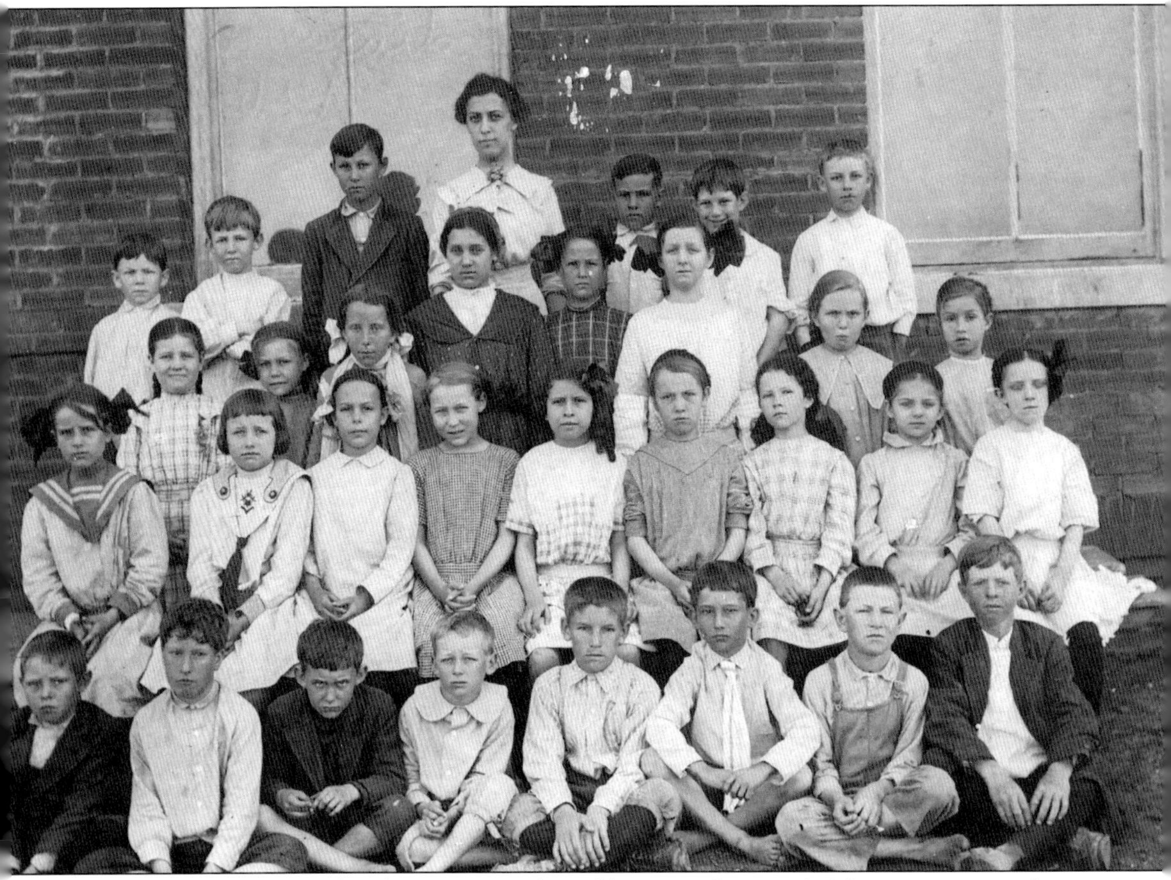

Teacher Edna May Shands Bassett, mother of longtime Sunnyvale-Mesquite piano and organ teacher Beth Bassett, poses with her class at Mesquite School around 1910.

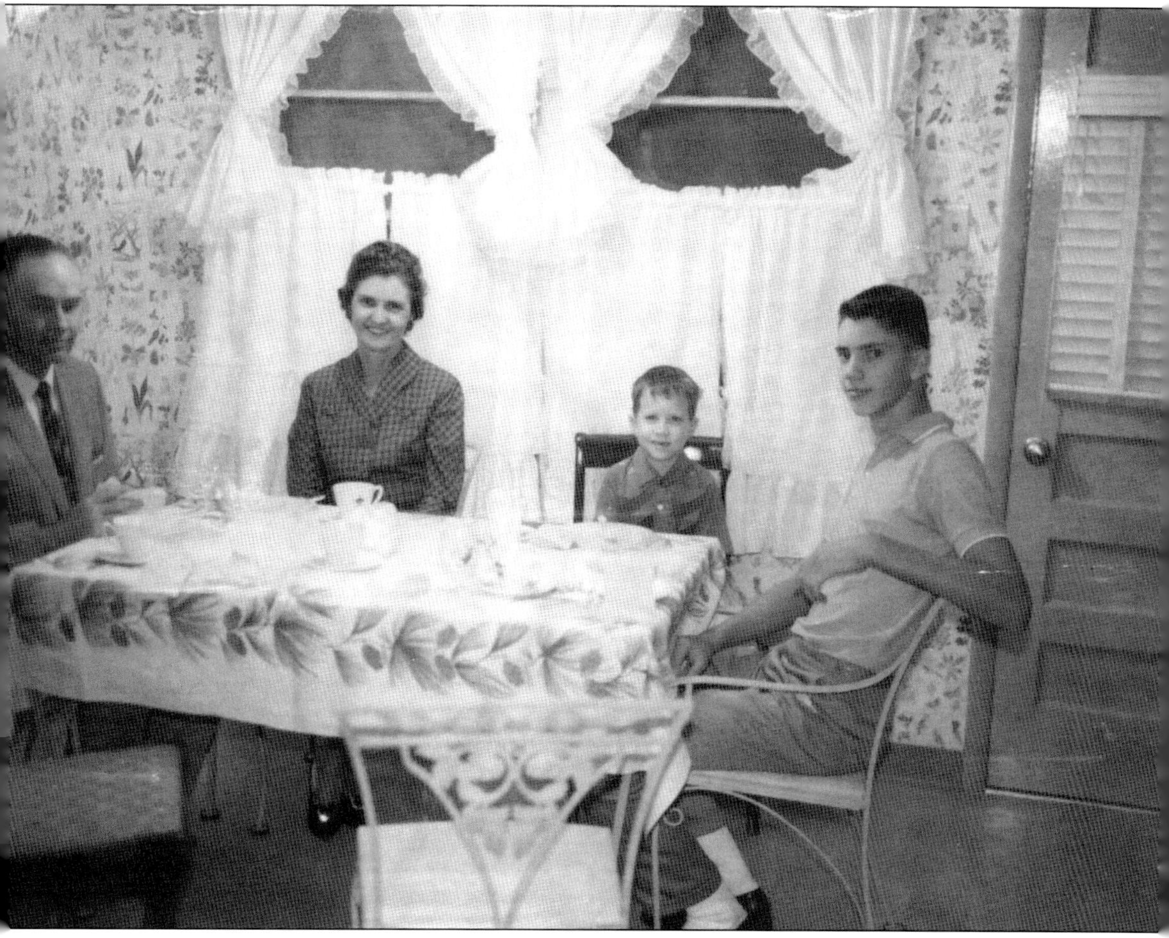

When Mesquite was a Boomtown USA in the 1950s through early 1960s, there was a close sense of community and shared culture between principals and the public they served. Principal Mary Moss and husband, Foy, are pictured dining at the Greenhaw home in the Florence Black Elementary School neighborhood. Principal Moss worked as a teacher in the Mesquite Public Schools and ultimately principal at Florence Black Elementary School. Moss Elementary School is named for Mary Moss.

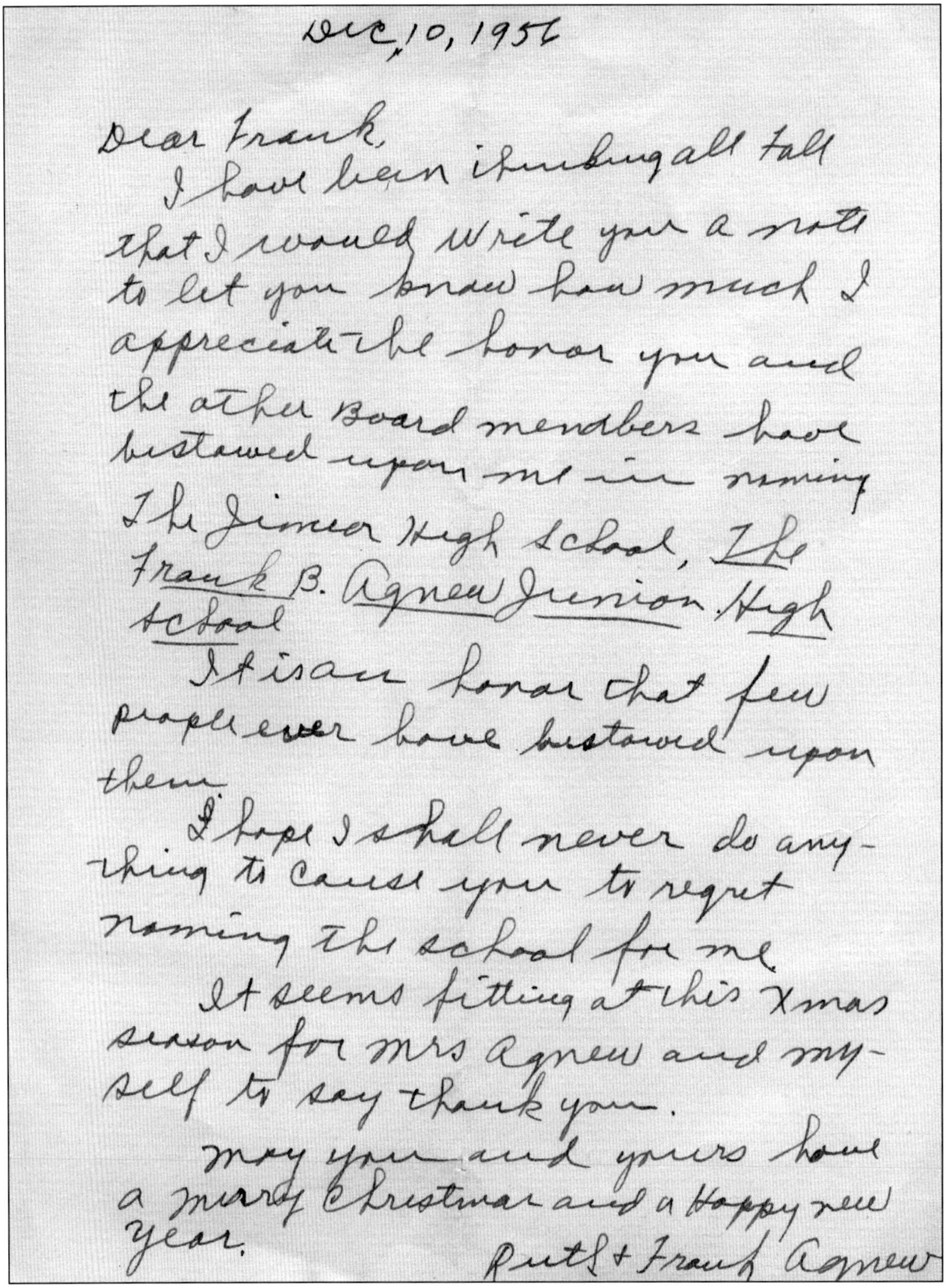

Dec, 10, 1956

Dear Frank,

I have been thinking all fall that I would write you a note to let you know how much I appreciate the honor you and the other Board members have bestowed upon me in naming The Junior High School, The Frank B. Agnew Junior High School

It is an honor that few people ever have bestowed upon them

I hope I shall never do anything to cause you to regret naming the school for me

It seems fitting at this Xmas season for Mrs Agnew and myself to say thank you.

May you and yours have a merry Christmas and a Happy new year.

Ruth & Frank Agnew

Frank B. Agnew was a Mesquite High School mathematics teacher for whom Agnew Middle School was named in 1956. The personal letter from Agnew shown here thanks the board of trustees for the honor and includes his sentiment "I hope I shall never do anything to cause you to regret naming the school for me." Agnew Middle School is located on Wilkinson Street in Mesquite.

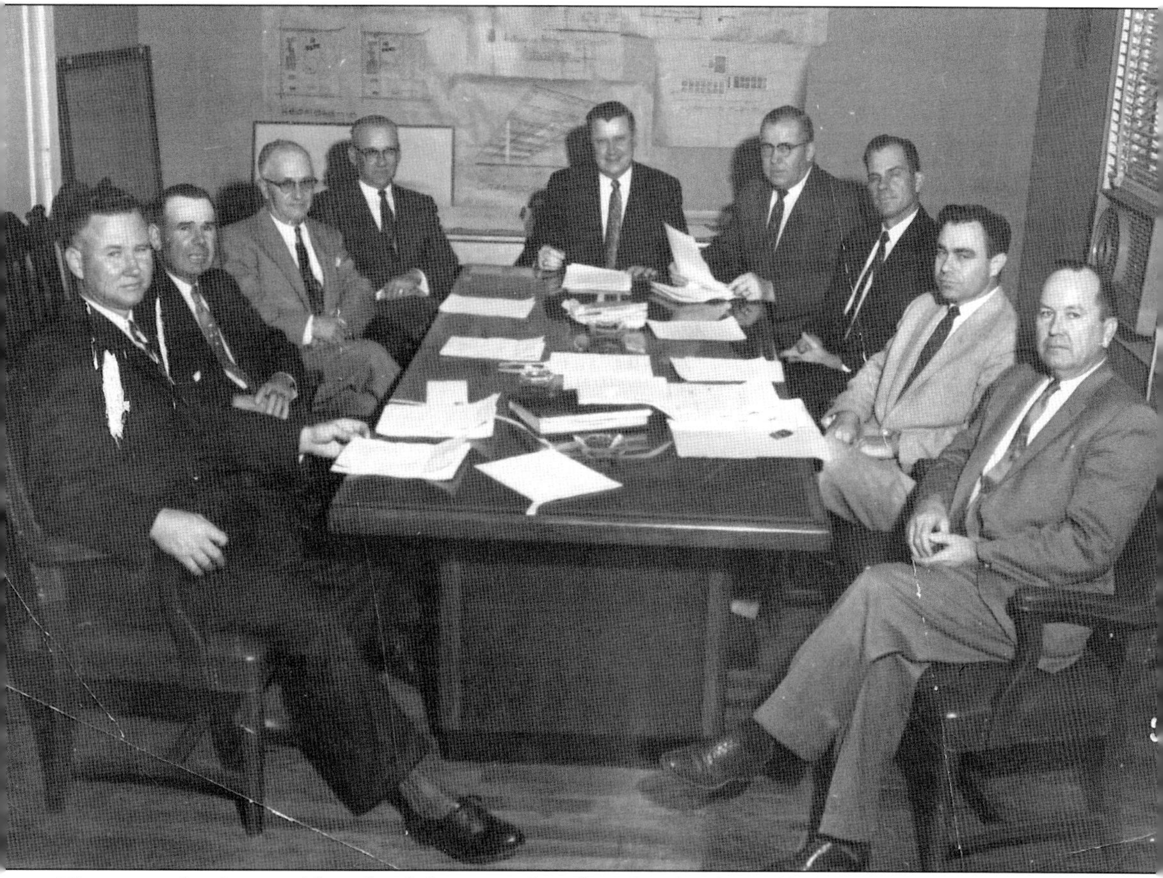

The strength of any public school district is found in the checks and balances provided by the citizen-elected school board which sets policies and the school district administration and employees who carry out those policies. This system of checks and balances ceases to function effectively when the electorate turns out in the tiny numbers that Mesquite and other communities have experienced in recent years. During Mesquite's boomtown years of the 1950s, voters turned out in dramatically higher numbers percentagewise than voters of today to cast their votes in city council and school board elections. The Mesquite Schools Board of Trustees is shown in a photograph taken during a meeting in the mid-1950s.

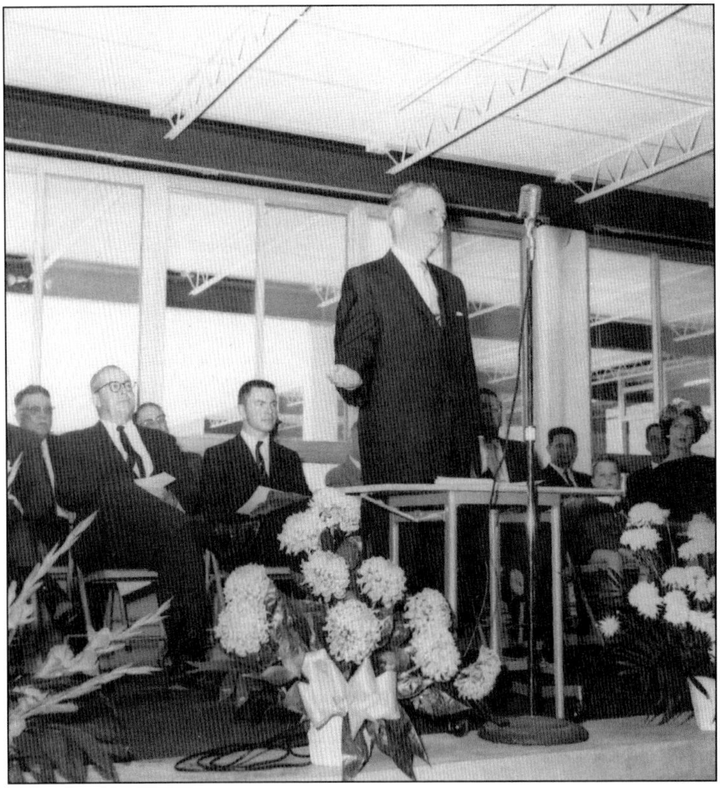

It is a rare happening across the state of Texas when a sitting Texas governor attends and officially dedicates and opens a public school. But this is exactly what happened when Gov. Price Daniel delivered the main address for the opening and dedication of McWhorter Elementary School in 1959. Joining Governor Daniel beside the speaker's podium is a representation of Mesquite citizens, school officials, and religious leaders.

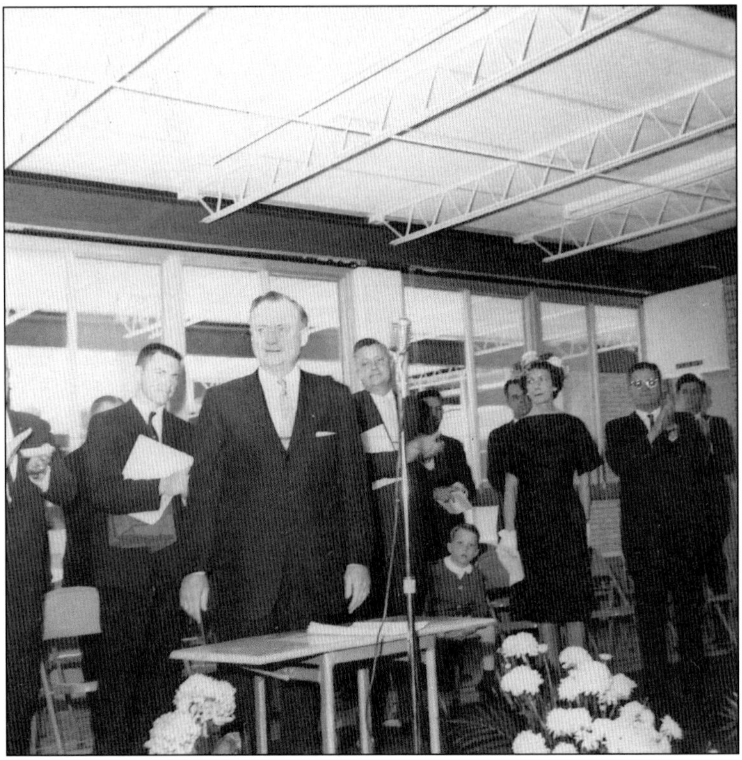

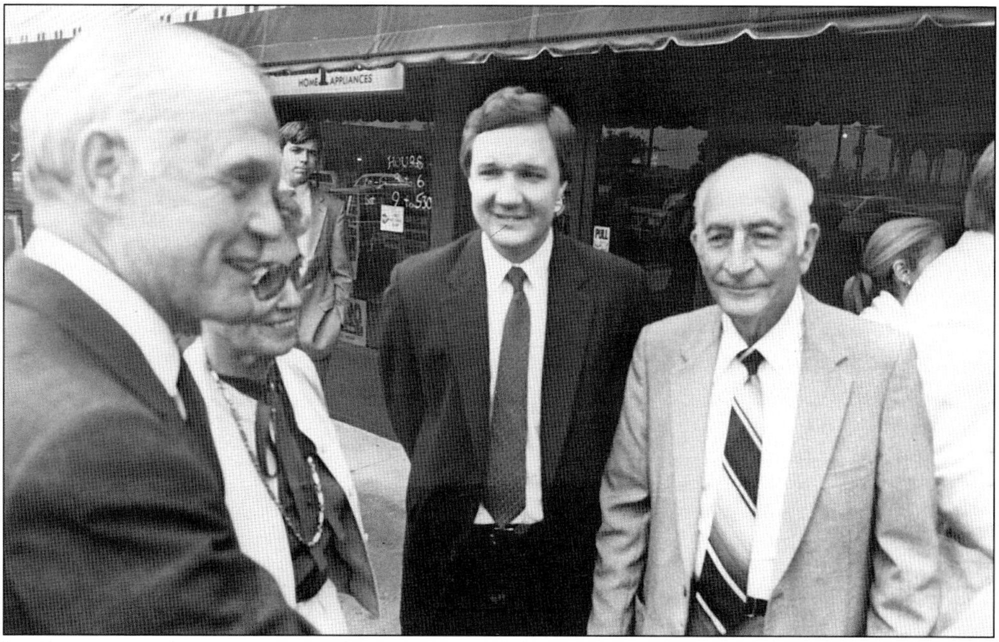

In the not-too-distant past, in the Mesquite of the 1980s, there was consistency in local law enforcement and judicial leadership. A Mesquite citizen and resident could rest assured that his local constable or his local justice of the peace would be a neighbor and a person with deep roots in the town and in the region. His elected representatives would almost always have a clear understanding of which values and people built Mesquite. In these images taken in front of the McWhorter-Greenhaw Building in Mesquite's downtown square when Ohio senator and former astronaut John Glenn (left, both images) brought his US presidential campaign to Mesquite, Constable Homer DeMoss (below, right) and Judge Frank Berry (above, right and second from right, below) are on hand to greet him.

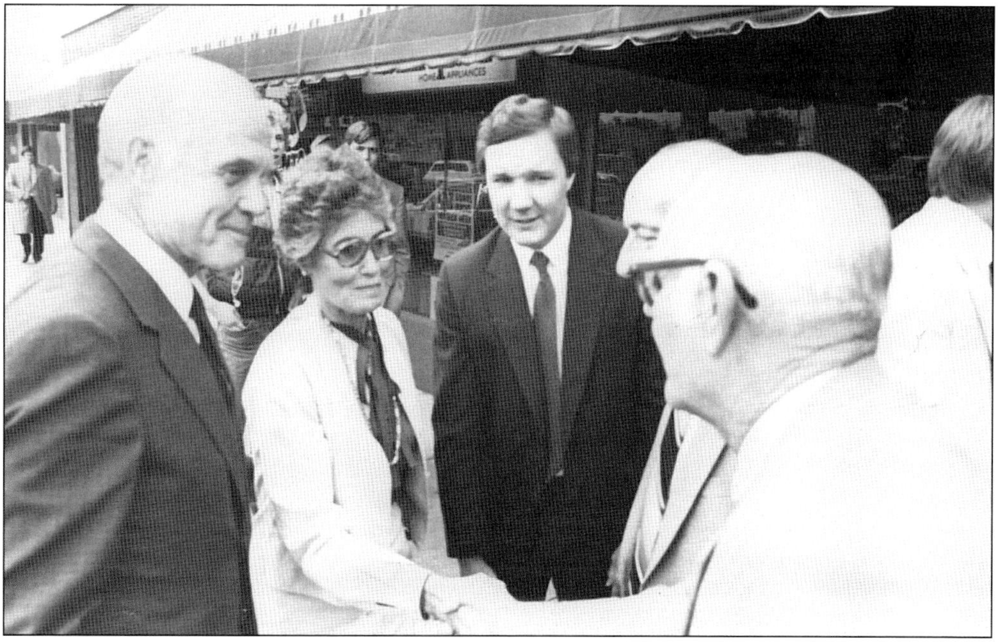

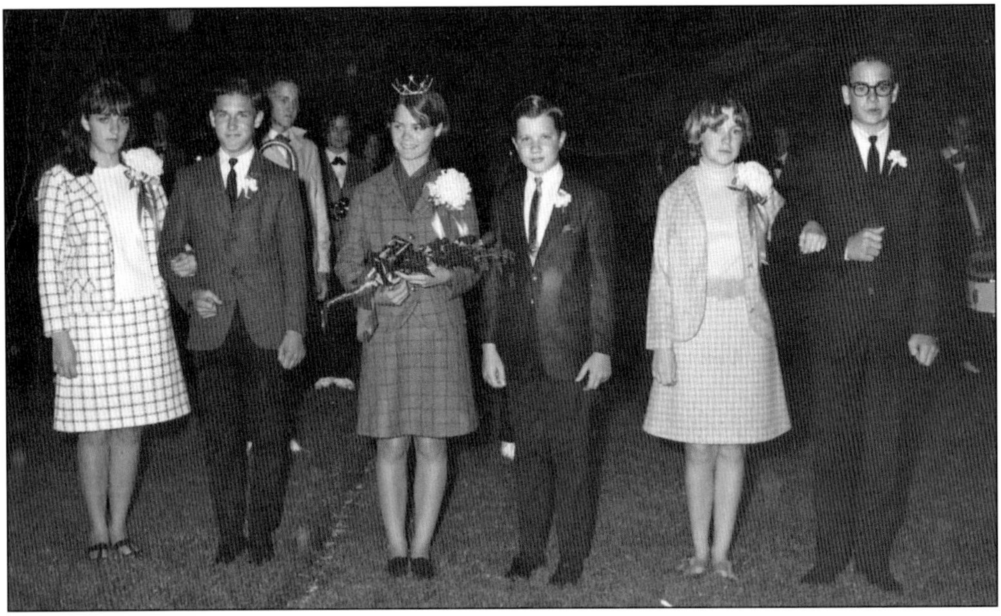

During the boomtown years of the 1950s and 1960s, Mesquite schools encouraged individual achievement, initiative, and academic accomplishment. In the junior high school, there were annual Principal's Awards and annual Hi-Liter Awards chosen by teachers, along with student popularity contests such as favorites and sweethearts. Each spring, the faculty at Agnew Junior High would transport the award recipients to a selected picturesque location off campus. On this special day away from class, a professional photographer would snap pictures of favorites for the school yearbook. One year, it was a photograph shoot in historic downtown Dallas. Another year, it was the opening of the Dallas Quadrangle, a cluster of upscale boutiques with its mod Carnaby Street fashions and unusual architecture. There were also the more traditional school on-site photograph shoots like these, which include sweethearts on a football field and National Junior Honor Society officers at the campus bike rack.

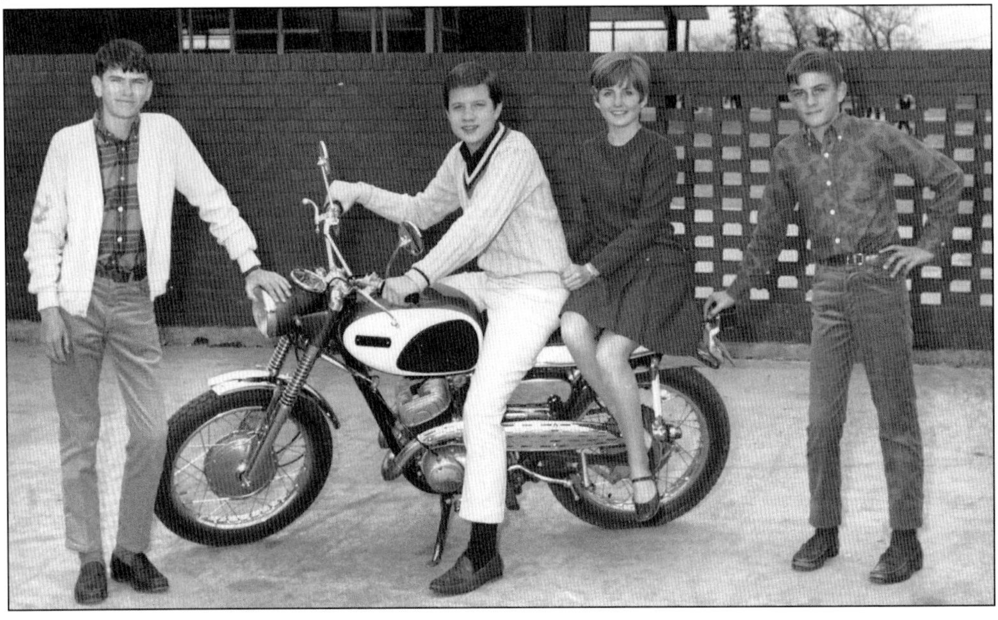

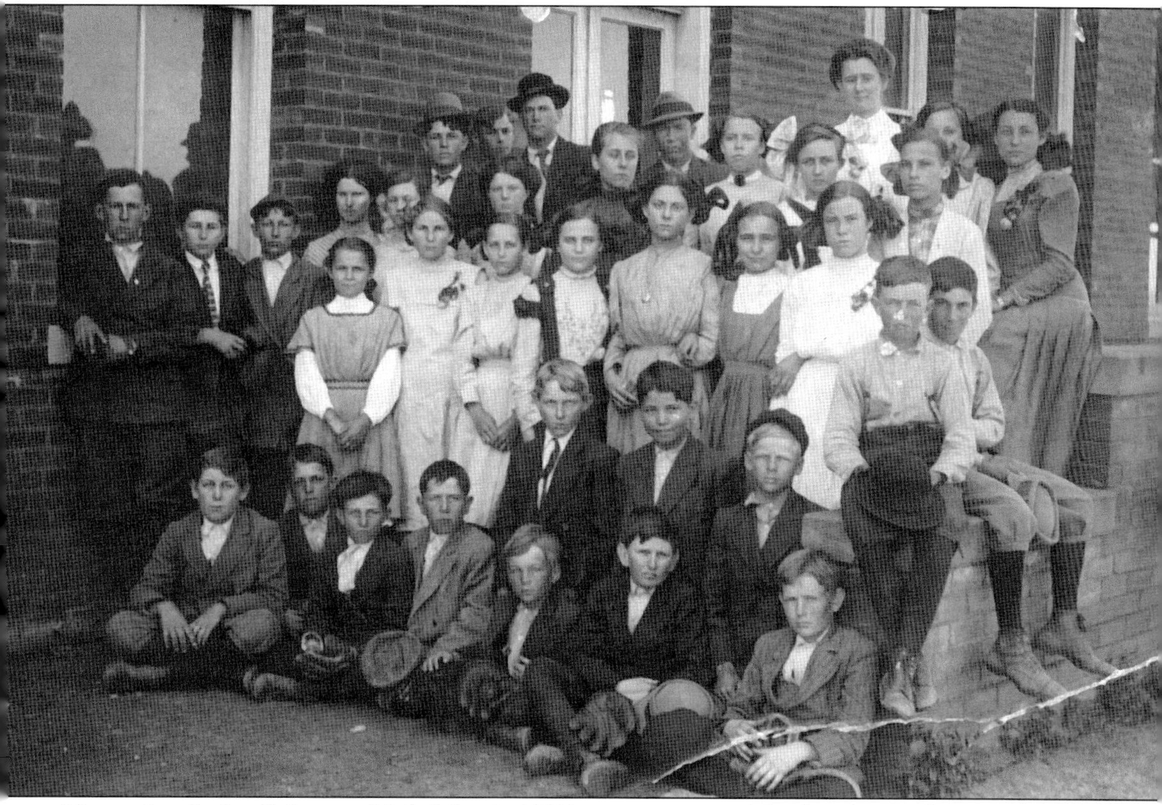

The student body of Mesquite High School of 1910 poses in attire of the day along with Mesquite's sixth and seventh grades. Note the ball gloves and balls with the boys seated in the front row.

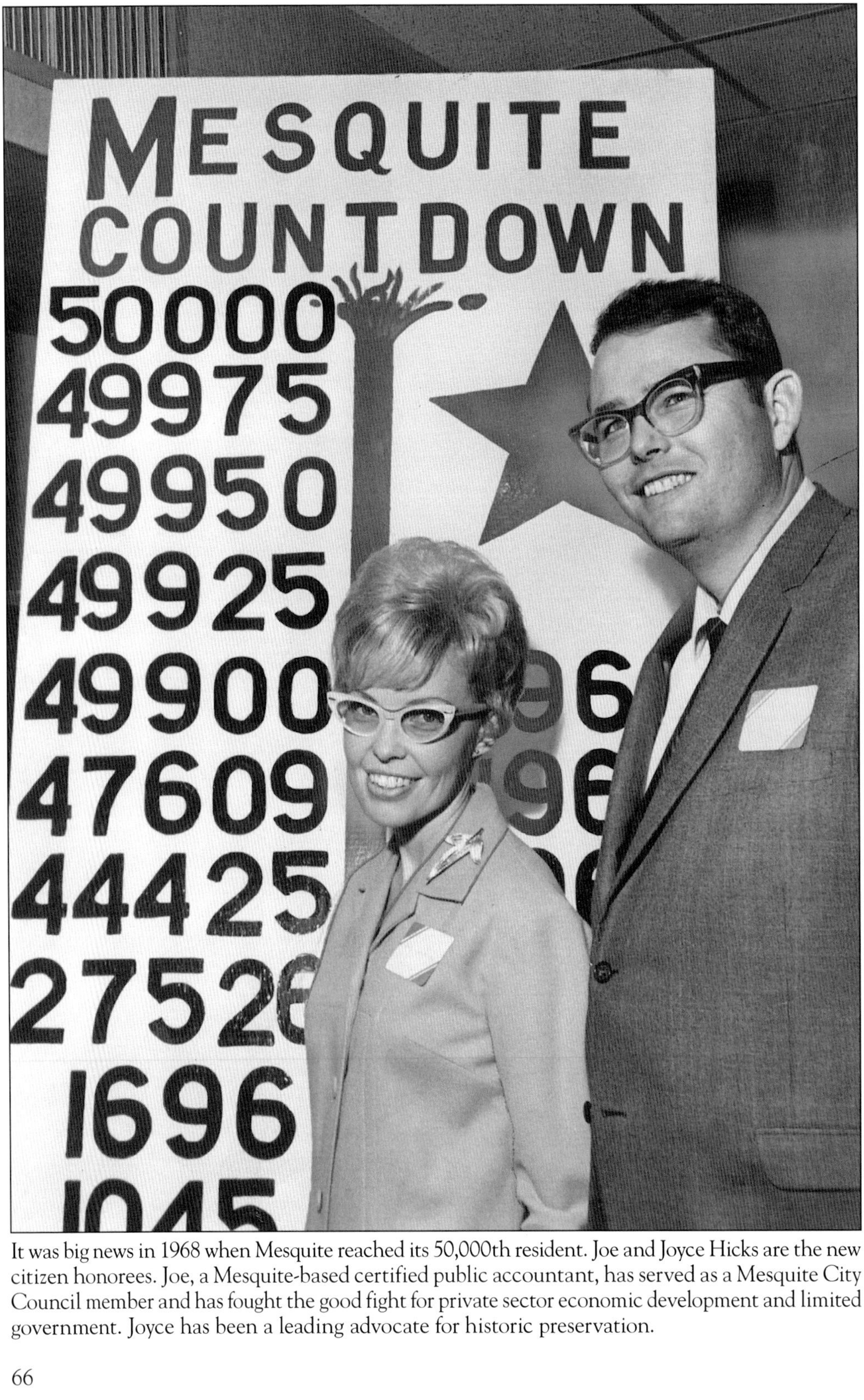

It was big news in 1968 when Mesquite reached its 50,000th resident. Joe and Joyce Hicks are the new citizen honorees. Joe, a Mesquite-based certified public accountant, has served as a Mesquite City Council member and has fought the good fight for private sector economic development and limited government. Joyce has been a leading advocate for historic preservation.

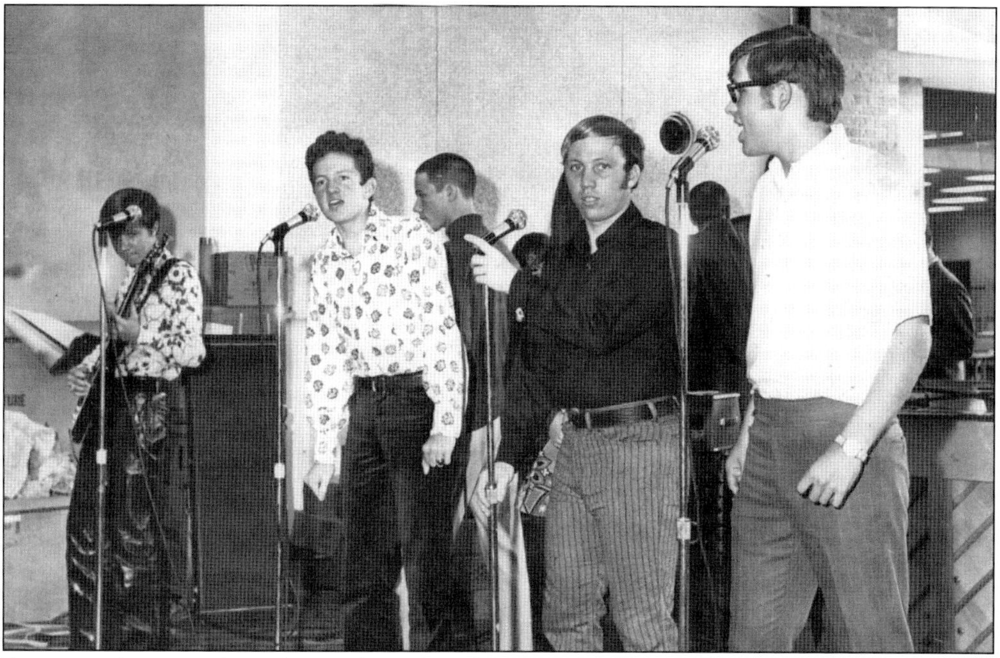

Every so often, just the right combination of fine arts students and teachers come together to create trendsetting concepts in education. From 1970 to 1972, Mesquite High School boasted its very own pop vocal and instrumental band named Contempo '70. Jack Williams and Rosemary Heffley were innovative and supportive choral teachers whose ensembles are shown in these two photographs. The Jack Williams group is shown above, and the Rosemary Heffley group is shown below. The 33 1/3 vinyl albums recorded by the 1972 configuration of Contempo '70 at famous Sellers Sound Studio in Dallas are still in circulation today.

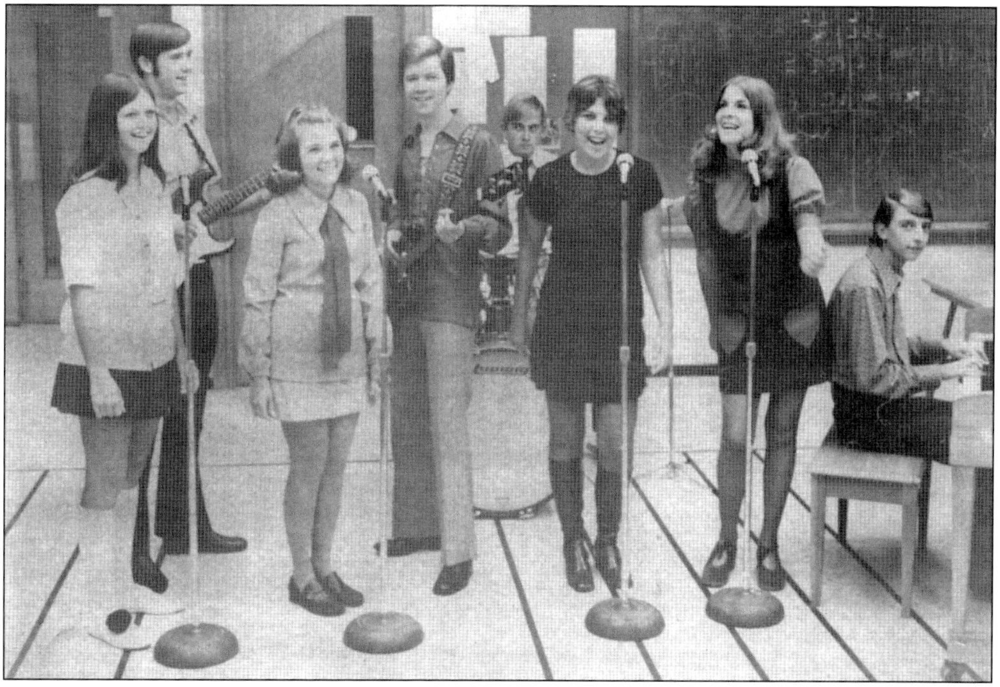

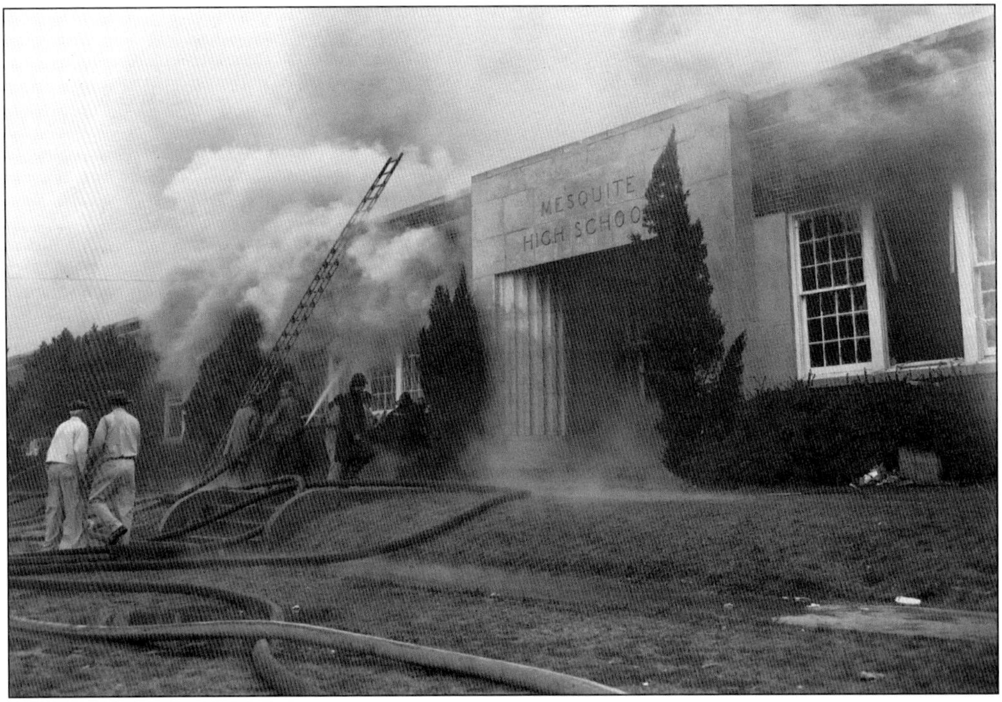

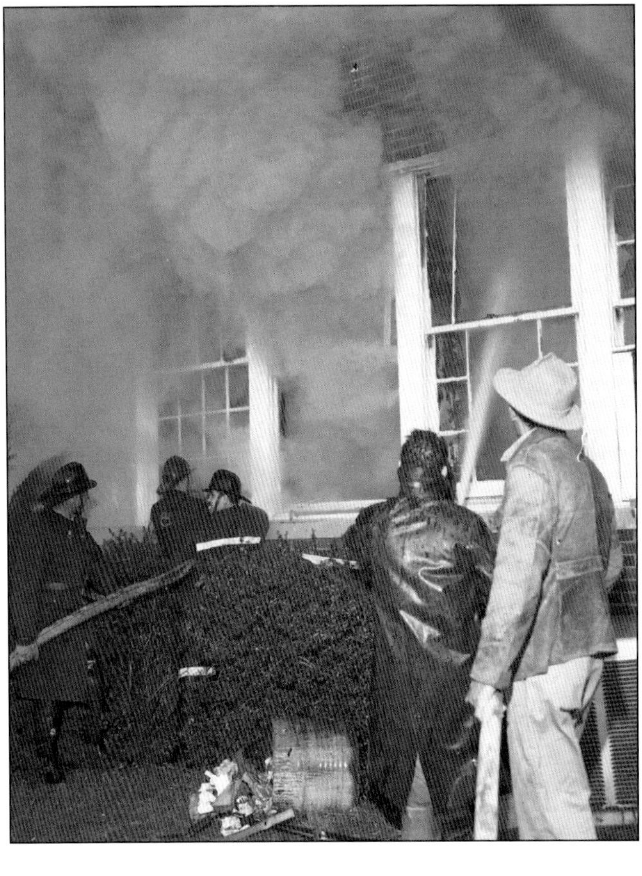

A major fire struck Mesquite High School on March 12, 1952, possibly erupting from an electrical circuit problem near the classroom of social science teacher Florence Black.

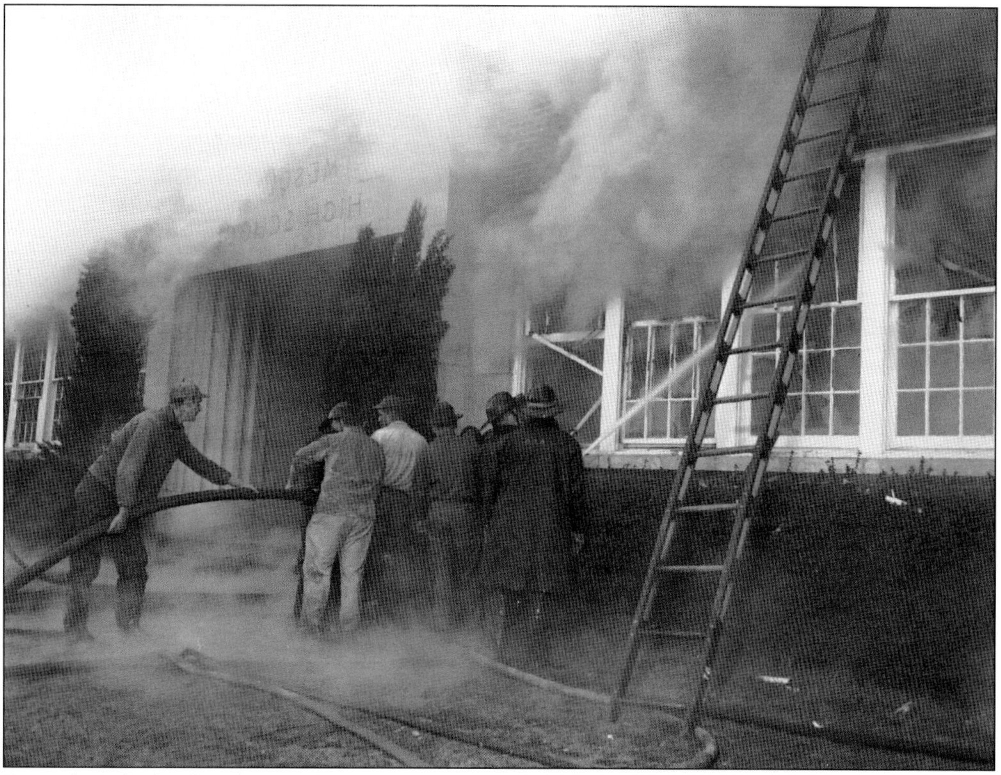

Even though the fire departments of Mesquite, Seagoville, and Dallas fought the blaze, several rooms were destroyed, and the school set up temporary classrooms in local churches and other locations.

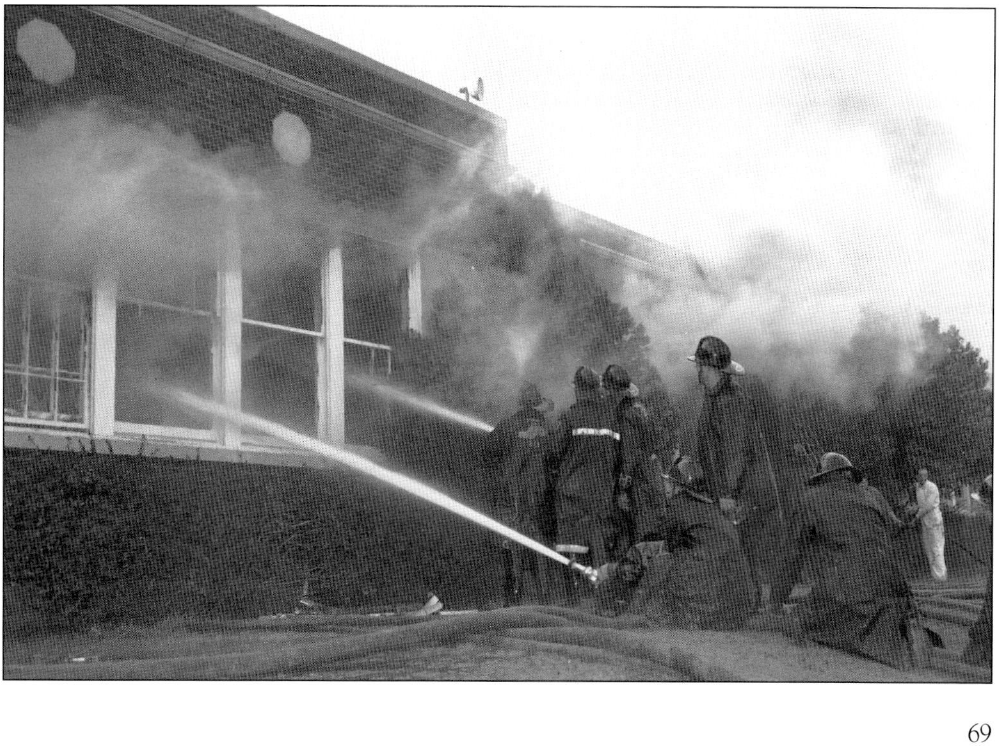

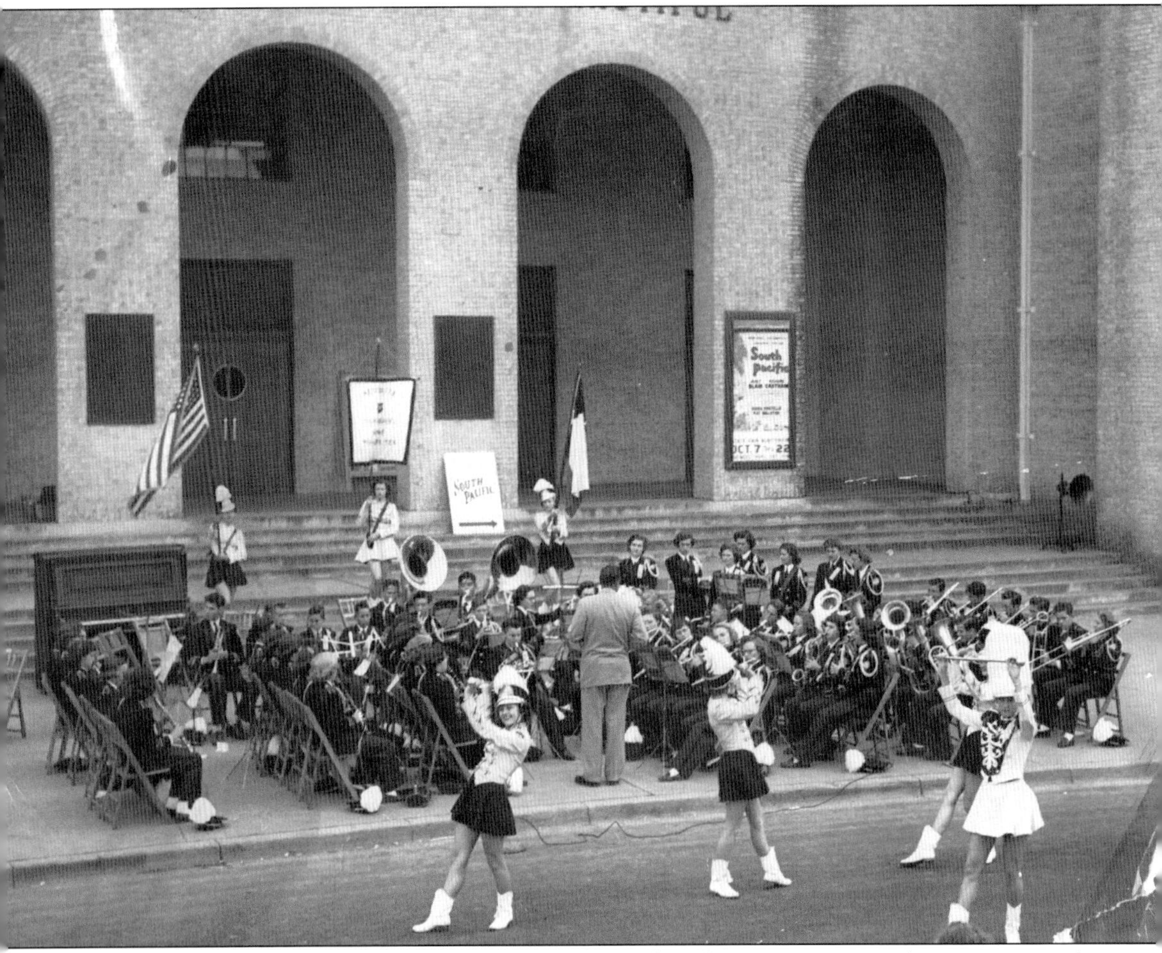

Around 1949–1951, the Mesquite High School Band performs a concert at the entrance to the Dallas Fair Park Music Hall, where the musical *South Pacific* was being staged inside. Frank W. Greenhaw is the band director.

In Mesquite Boomtown USA, its successful and productive chief of police was Leonard Limmer, appointed to the office at the age of 27 in 1963, when Mesquite employed 40 officers. Limmer went on to a later career leading and managing the entire security force of the Dallas–Fort Worth International Airport.

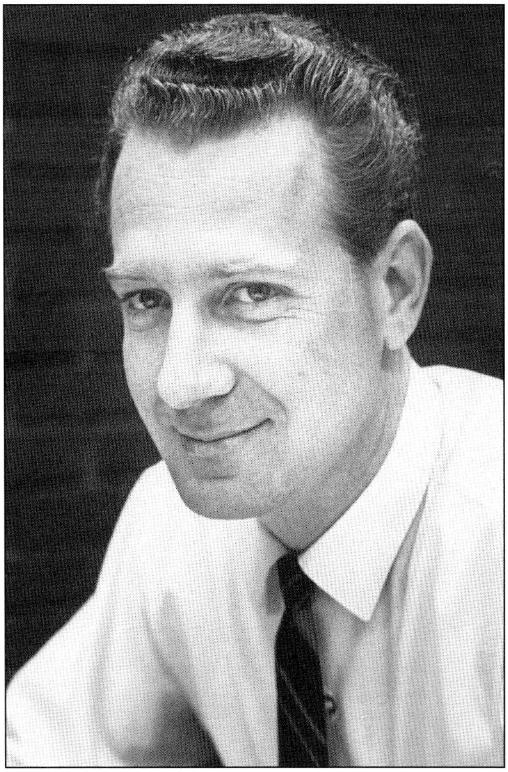

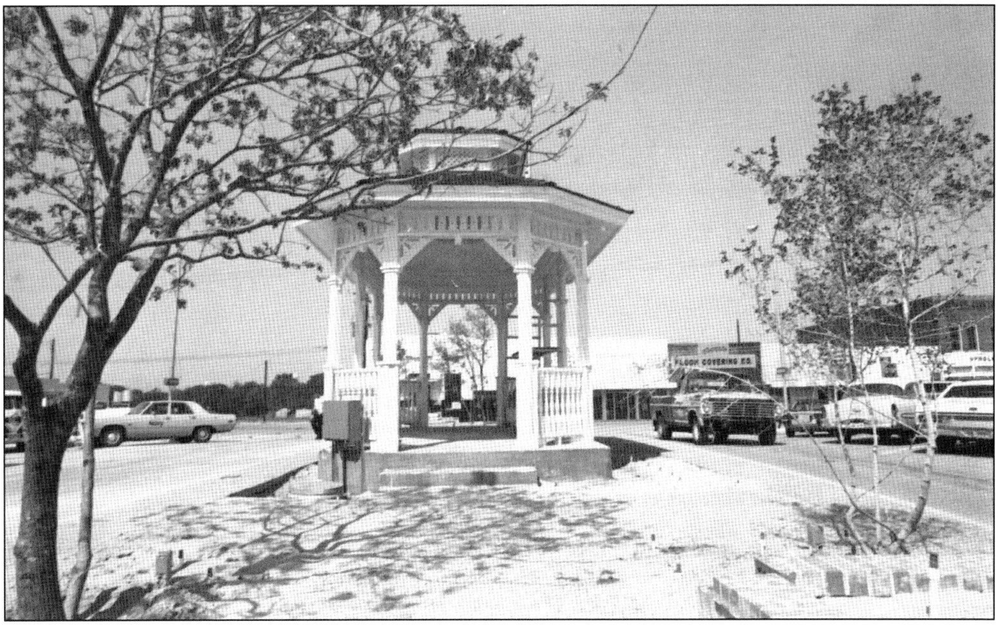

When Mesquite has seen its "best of times," talented citizens and residents have stepped up to the plate and have given of their time, talents, gifts, and services for civic beauty. Architect Joe Crook designed this stately gazebo for the Mesquite Heritage Square during the mid-1970s, and hundreds of people gave monies to landscape the center of the square, bringing back, for a period of time, the square's beautified glory days of the 1930s and 1940s.

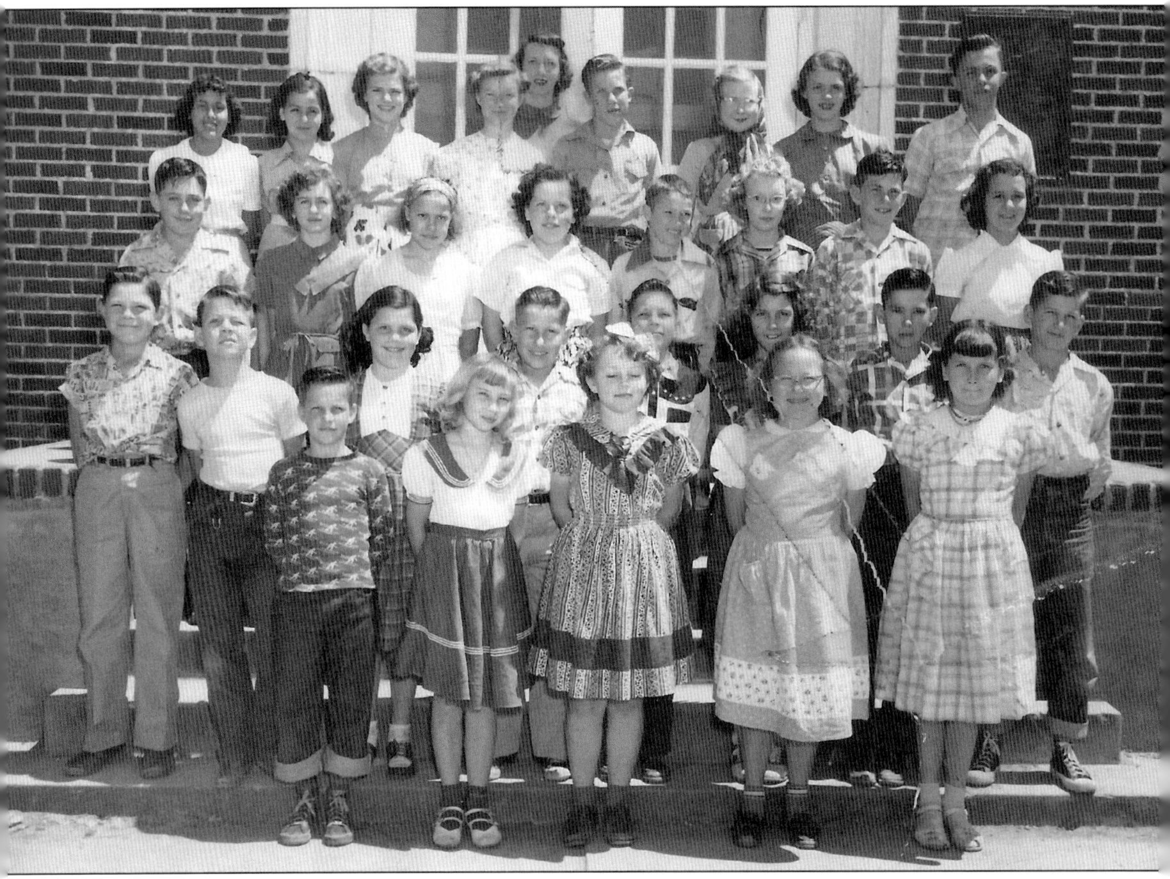

Mesquite Elementary teacher Patricia Ann McWhorter (top row center) is shown with her fifth-grade class in the late 1940s.

In the "worst of Mesquite times," public school officials turned male students' hair length into a holy crusade, concocting, in the words of the *Dallas Morning News*, a hair code "that's as detailed and complex as a set of federal guidelines." Regional and national editorials scoffed at 1980s Mesquite public school officials with opinions such as "dived the full depth of absurdity," "ultimate frontier of asininity," and "hair has become an issue only because the school administrator is acting to enforce a standard that has no intrinsic educational value." The photograph at right depicts Mesquite student Jimmy Ray Lewis in 1980 and his "disruptive influence" hair. *Dallas Times Herald* writer Jim Henderson sarcastically stated, "If I were principal (at North Mesquite High School), I'd line up all the male students every day and look in their noses. Unchecked nose hair obviously is responsible for all the nuttiness that is loose in the land." Among the many whose hairstyle would have precluded him from a Mesquite schools' public education in the Mesquite worst of times was former US president Lyndon B. Johnson, pictured below in 1972. (Below, courtesy of the Lyndon B. Johnson Presidential Library.)

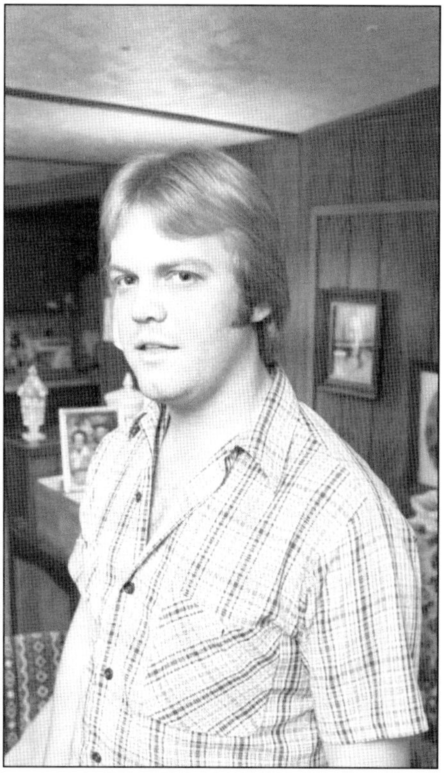

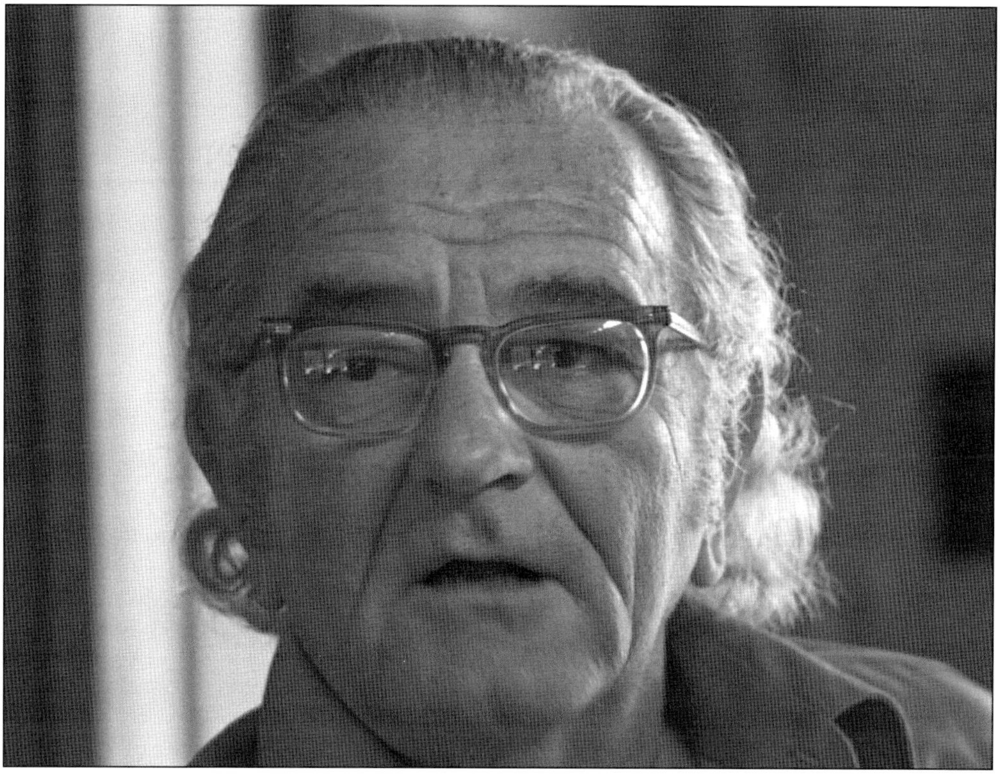

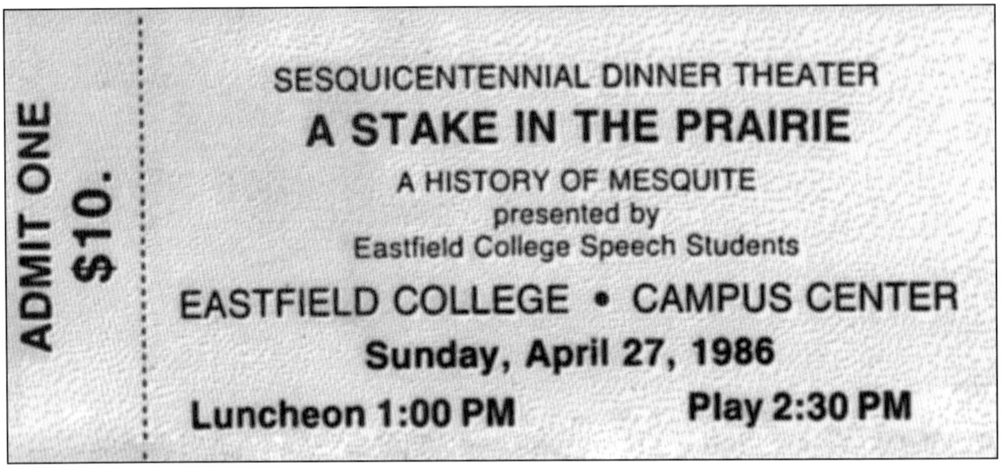

Eastfield College speech and theater teacher Mary Forrest directed this 1986 musical stage play based upon the content of the definitive history of Mesquite, *A Stake in the Prairie*. The cast was comprised of approximately 25 Eastfield College students.

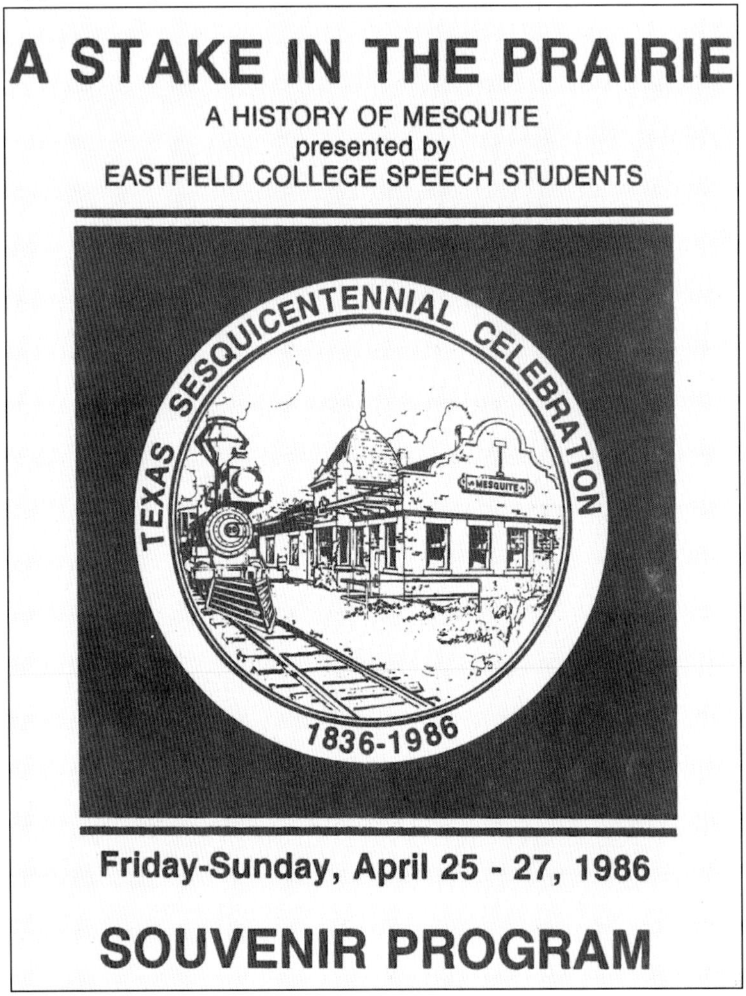

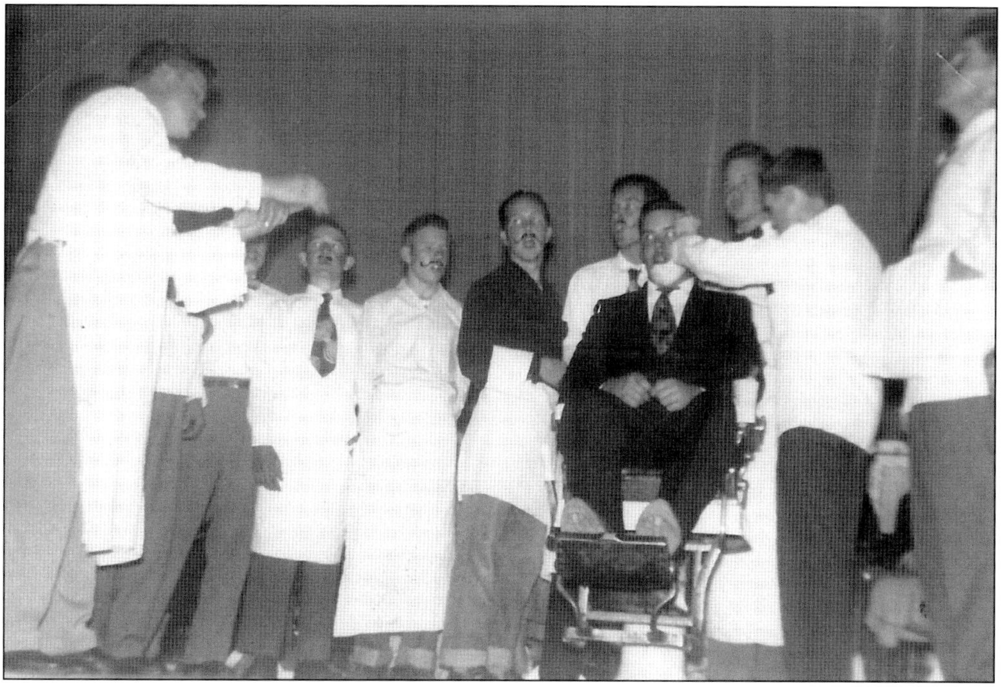

As part of the Outburst program, Frank W. Greenhaw directs Mesquite schools' Barbershop Quartet in the 1949–1950 school year. Outburst was an annual musical extravaganza conceived by Greenhaw and held at Mesquite High School.

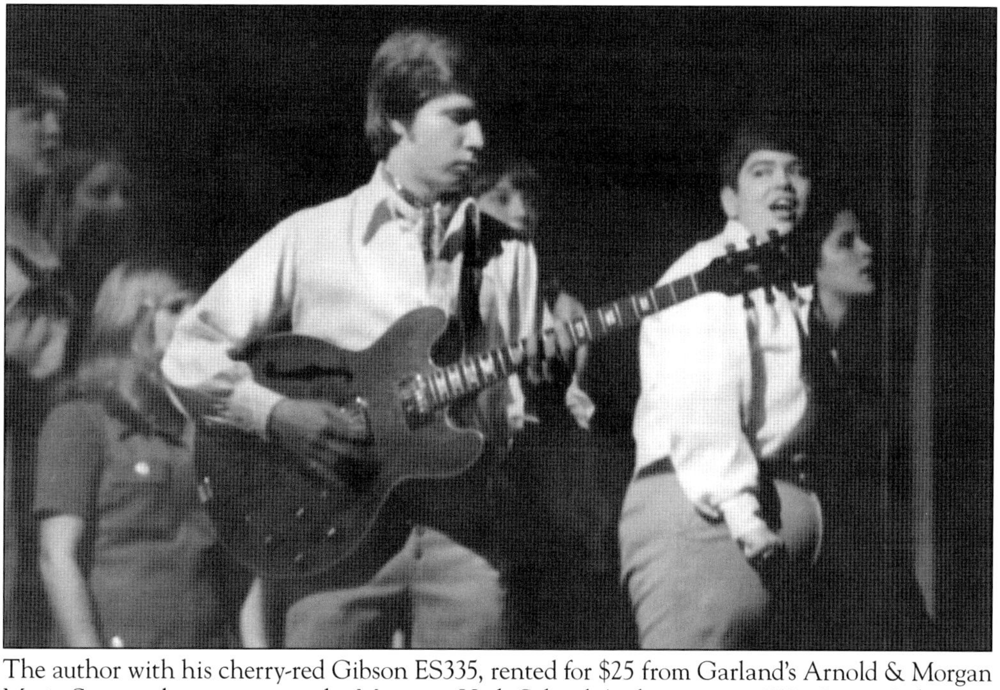

The author with his cherry-red Gibson ES335, rented for $25 from Garland's Arnold & Morgan Music Store, solos on stage at the Mesquite High School Auditorium in 1971. Curtis Cole, seen here at right, contributed much to First Christian Church of Mesquite as minister of music in his adult years.

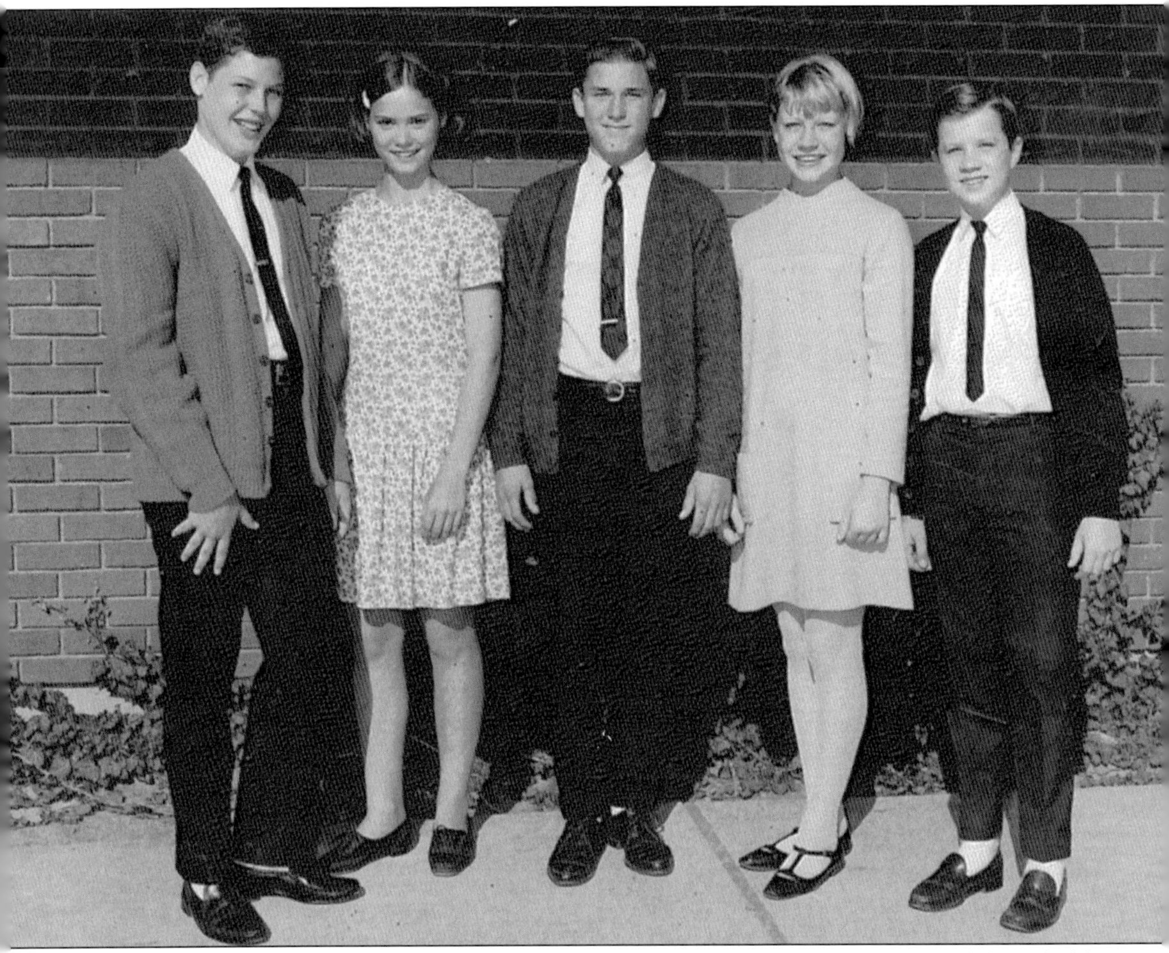

The Agnew Middle School 1967–1968 annual, in which this photograph appears, is titled *Psychedelic Edition*. The Age of Aquarius might have been dawning in parts of the USA with its paisleys, scarves, and ruffles, but these Agnew band officers are still "Ivy League" in their sweaters and ties in Mesquite, Texas. Pictured are, from left to right, Charles Austin, Susan Smith, Johnny Hooper, Jan Wilcox, and the author.

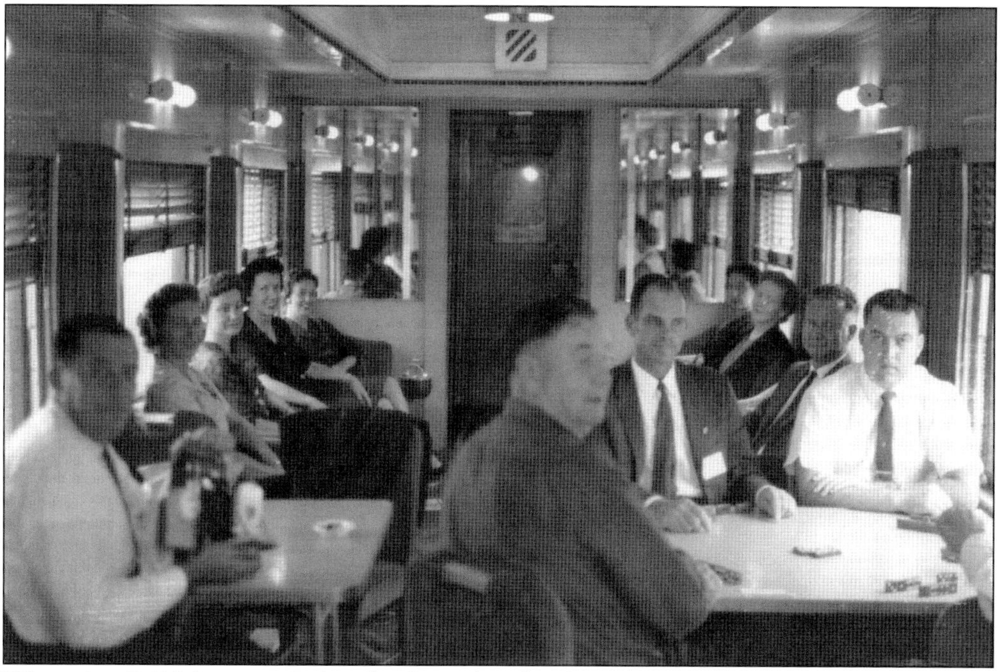

When the 1961 Mesquite High School Band under the direction of William Hooper traveled to Pasadena, California, to participate in the Tournament of Roses Parade, the Texas & Pacific Railway provided the band with its own private cars, including the two cars in the photographs, which housed the city's leading business and community leaders who made the trip. The 1961 Mesquite High School Band was one of only four bands outside California to be invited to perform in the parade that year.

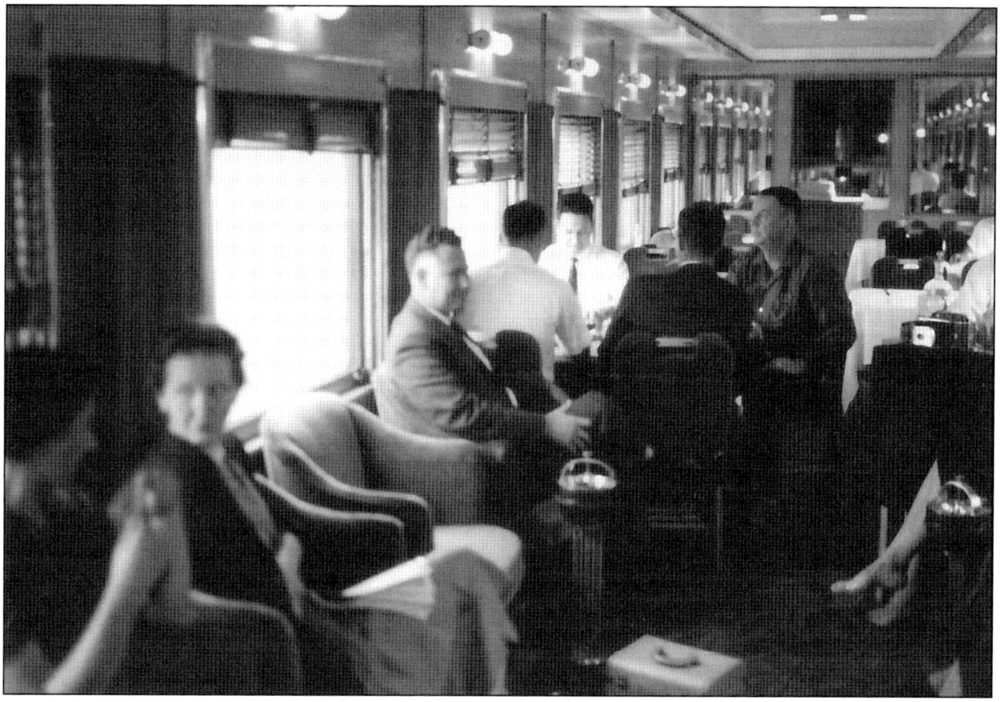

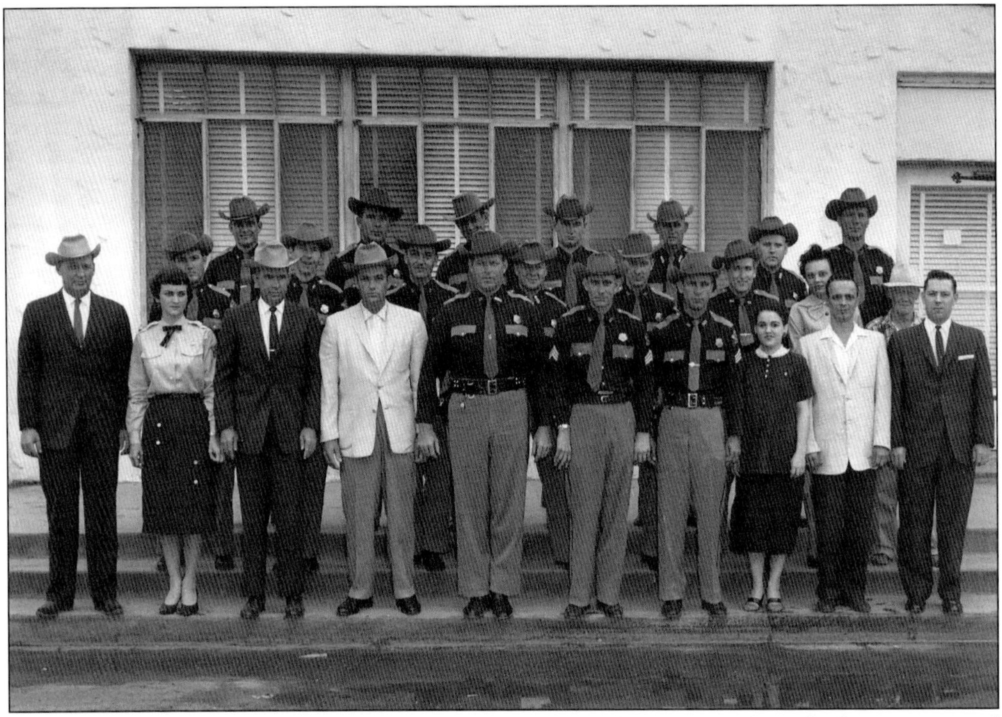

A golden age of Mesquite city government was about to begin in 1959 with the city council appointment of George Schrader as city manager in the council-manager form of government. Schrader (first row, far right) is pictured above with the 1959 Mesquite Police Force in front of Mesquite City Hall. The photograph below depicts an aerial view of a new modernistic Mesquite City Hall constructed during Schrader's tenure.

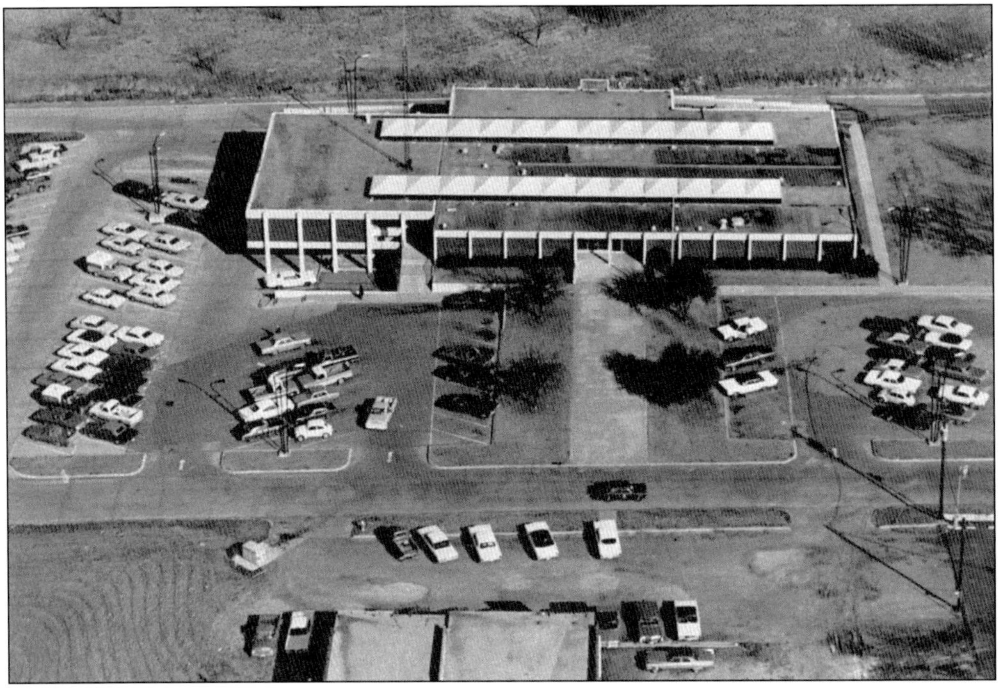

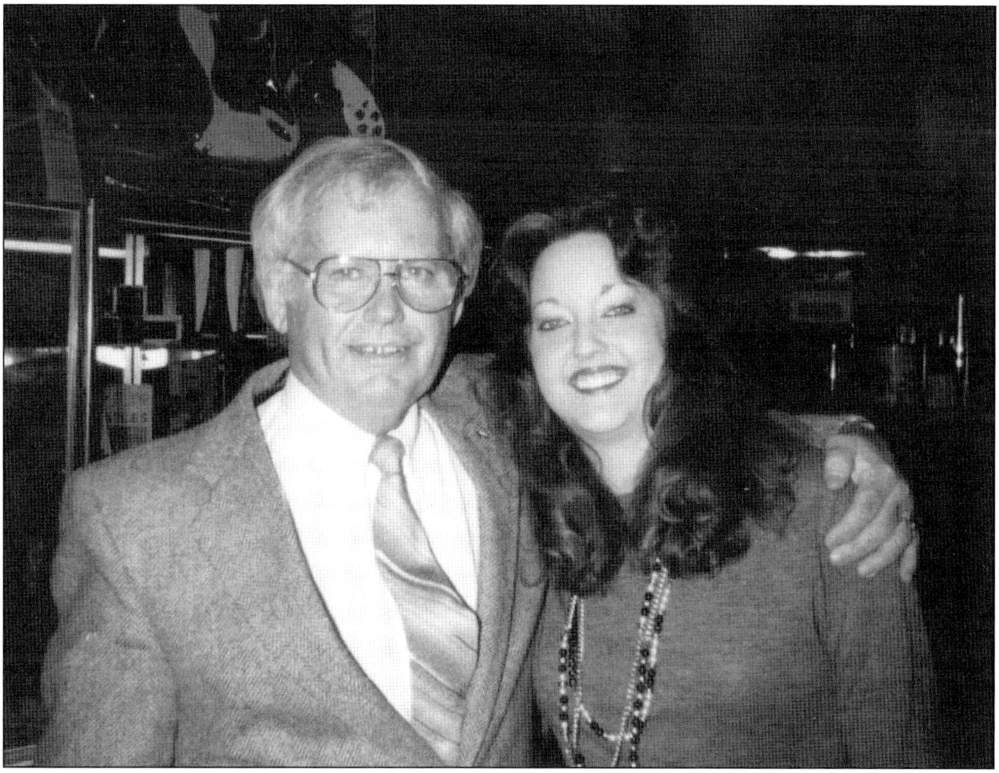

Bill Blackwood, a security installation company owner and Mesquite City Council member, was elected Texas state representative to the seat locals referred to as the "T.H. McDonald seat," so named for the successful and beloved school superintendent turned legislator. Blackwood is pictured above with Jamie Shipman, a famous Mesquite Opry vocalist. The photograph at right shows Mr. and Mrs. T.H. McDonald (front and center) during "Mr. Mac's" tenure as a Texas state representative.

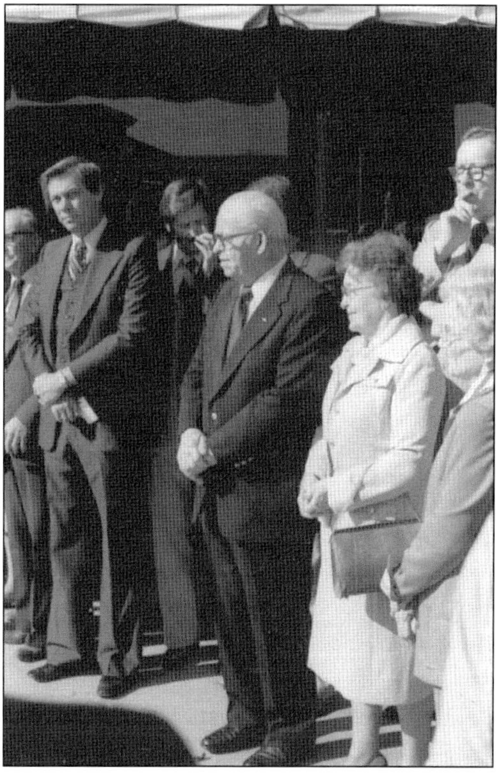

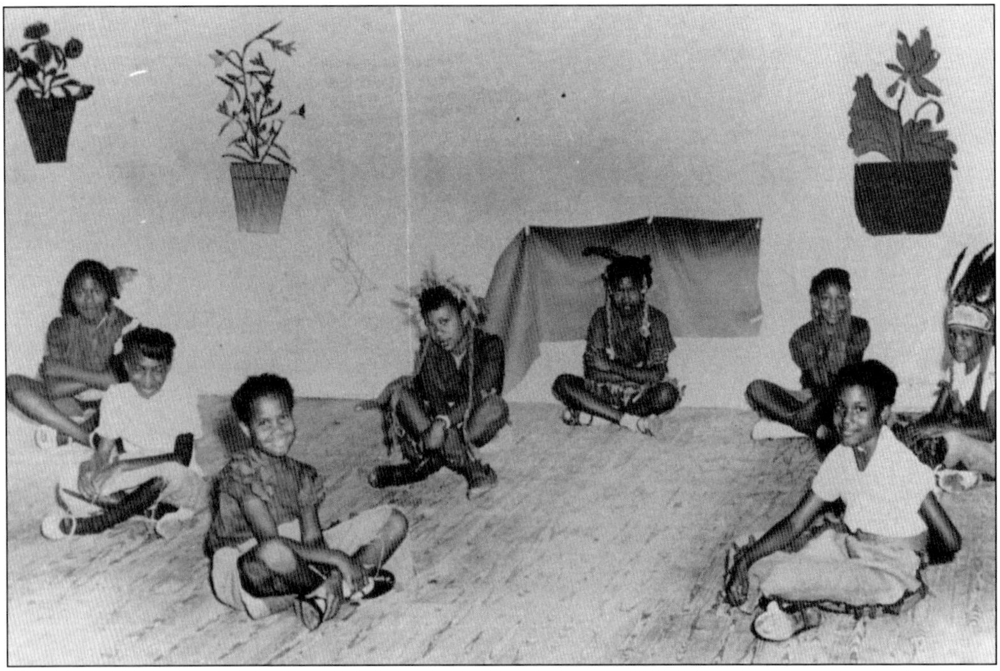

Prior to full integration, these photographs show costume-filled historical plays performed by students at Carver School. In 1965, Mesquite was the first of the Dallas County public schools to become fully integrated.

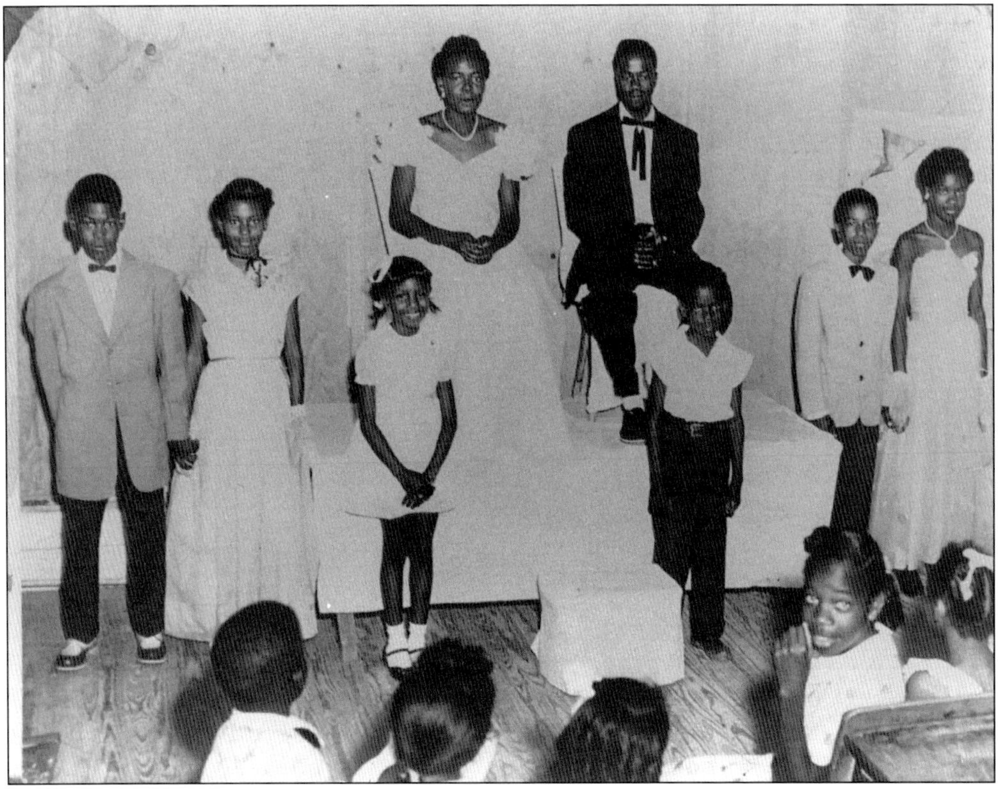

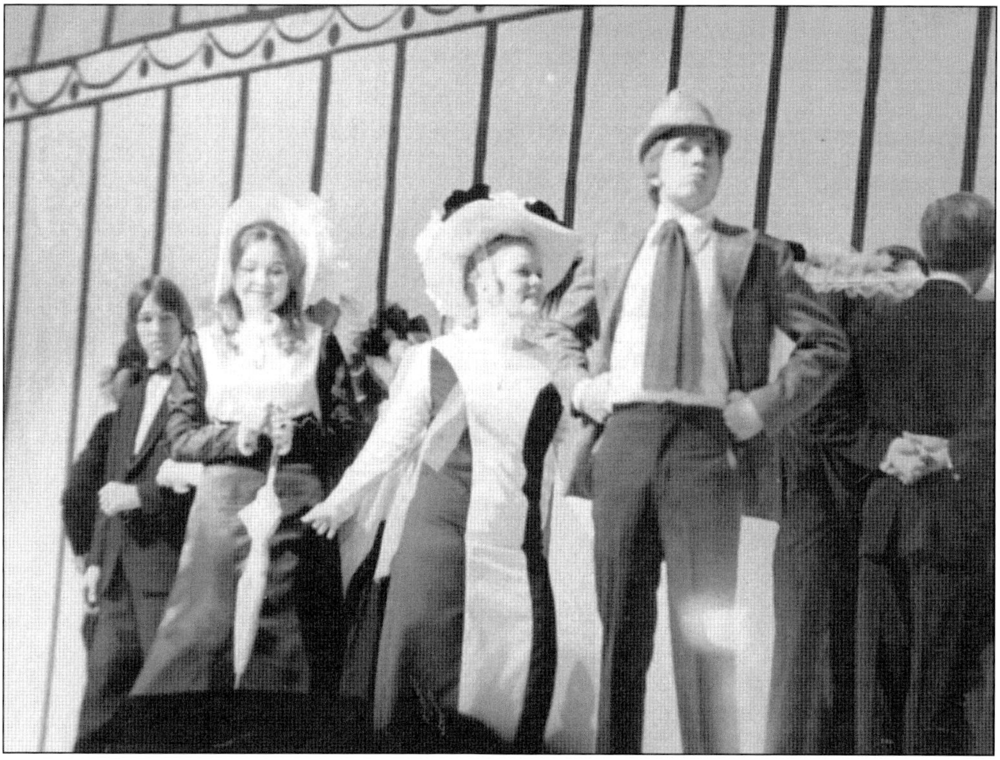

One of the most ambitious of the Sue Braden–directed Mesquite High School musicals was the 1972 production of *My Fair Lady*, in which the student actors/singers spoke and sang with British accents.

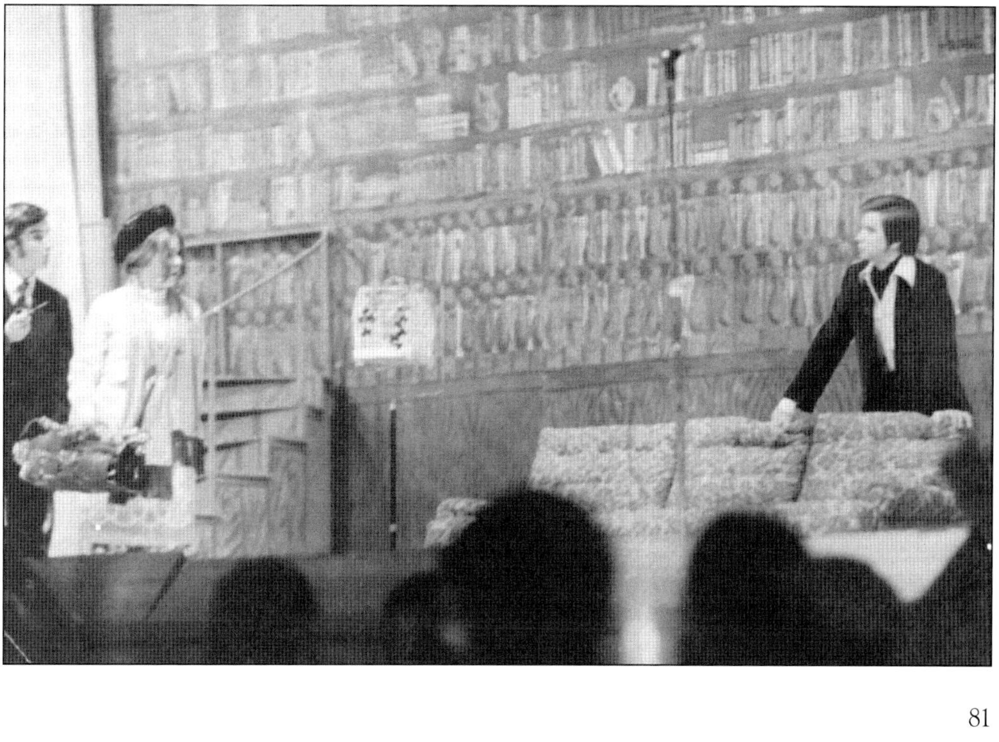

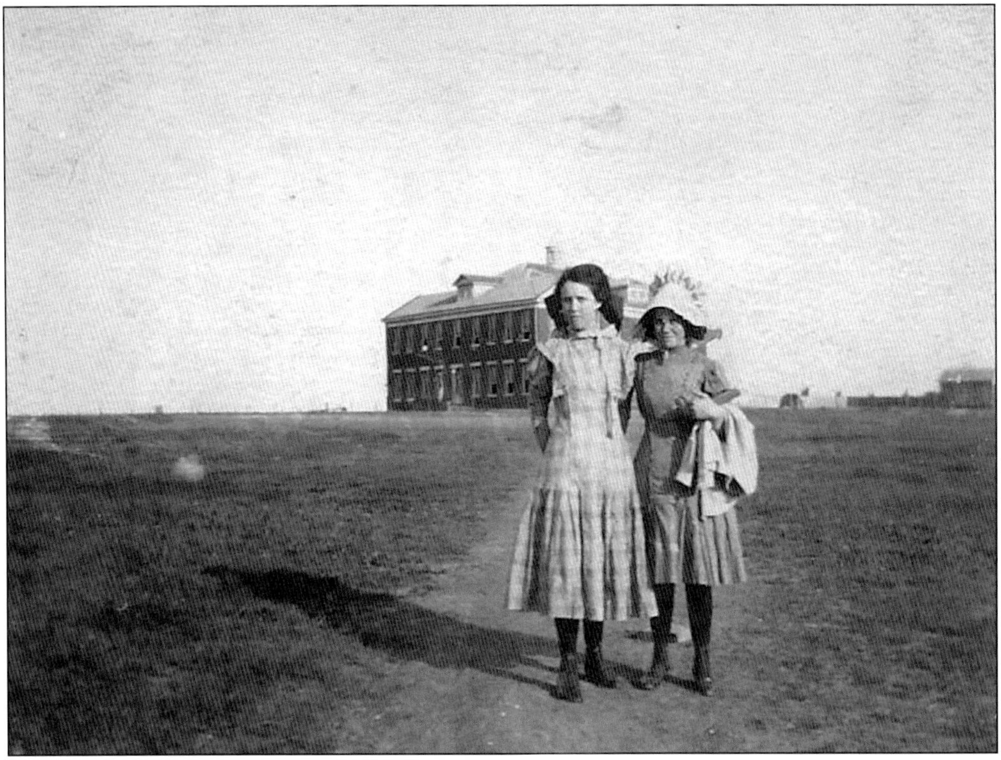

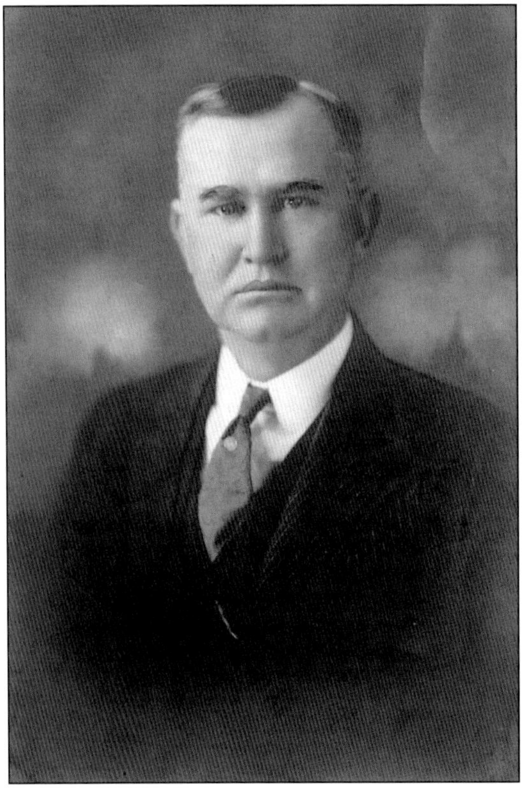

Two Mesquite girls stand in an open field in front of what appears to be the first Mesquite public school building, which would place this photograph around the year 1901. The other structures in the background are not close enough to be identified. (Courtesy of Historic Mesquite, Inc.)

This studio portrait depicts John S. Lawrence, who was the son of Stephen Decatur Lawrence and his first wife, Louisa Porter Lawrence. John was involved in several early business ventures in Mesquite and was Mesquite mayor in 1917–1923, 1925–1928, and 1949–1953. He holds the distinction of being the only person in history to have been reelected mayor of Mesquite after having served time in prison and been pardoned by Texas governor Miriam "Ma" Ferguson. The pardon completely restored his civil rights. (Courtesy of Historic Mesquite, Inc.)

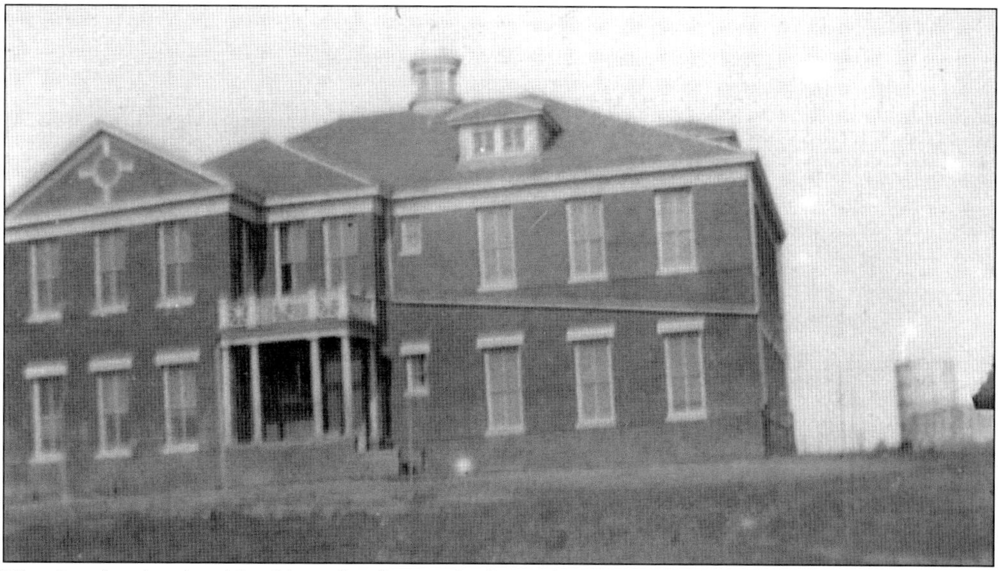

The first brick school building for the newly formed Mesquite Independent School District is shown in 1901. The two-story structure was in use for many years before the expansion of the school district facilities in neighborhoods. A cistern is visible to the right of the building. (Courtesy of Historic Mesquite, Inc.)

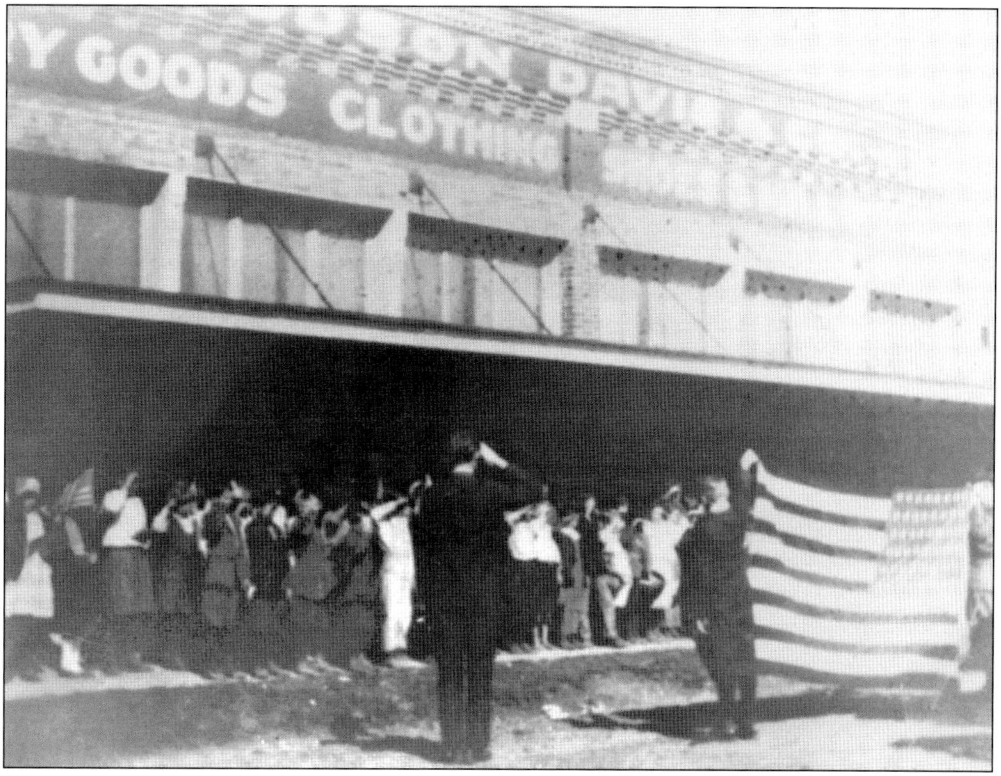

These Mesquite schoolchildren are saluting the American flag to celebrate the end of World War I on Armistice Day in 1919, as they gather on the town square in front of the Hudson Davis & Co. store.

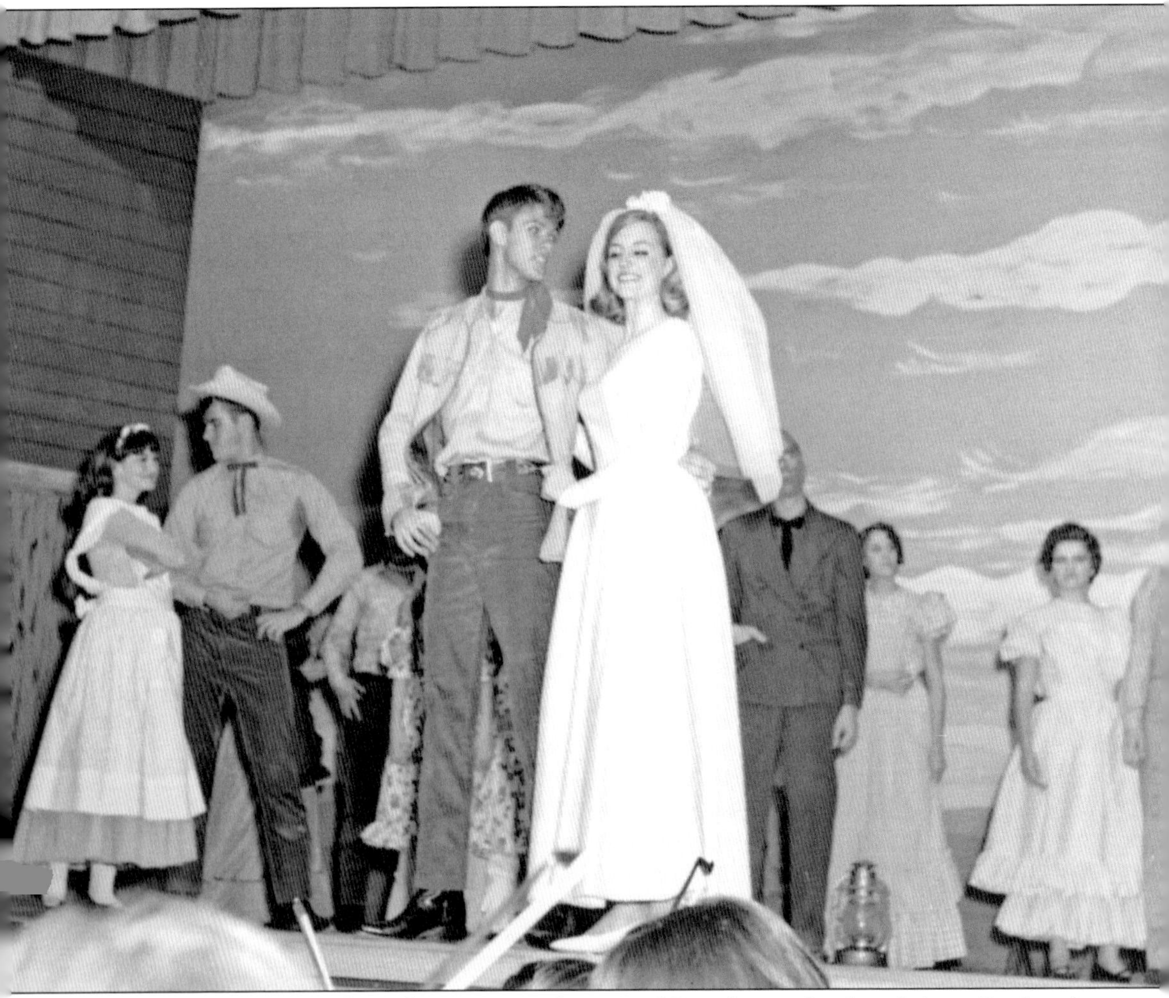

Mesquite can boast of a truly great star of stage and Broadway—Stephen Lehew. Stephen has had an illustrious, long career in musical theater and was chosen for the revue *Rodgers and Hart* by Richard Rodgers himself. Stephen was featured vocalist for touring stage shows with composer Marvin Hamlisch. He has even starred in the title role in *Jesus Christ Superstar*. In this photograph, Stephen (as cast lead character Curly) sings front and center stage to Patricia West (another of the greatest vocalists Mesquite has produced) in the 1966–1967 school year Mesquite High School production of *Oklahoma!*, which officially opened the new high school auditorium. Behind center stage, to the left, are costars Diana Barber and Randy Root. Teacher Sue Braden directed the production in her first year at Mesquite High School. (Courtesy of Stephen Lehew.)

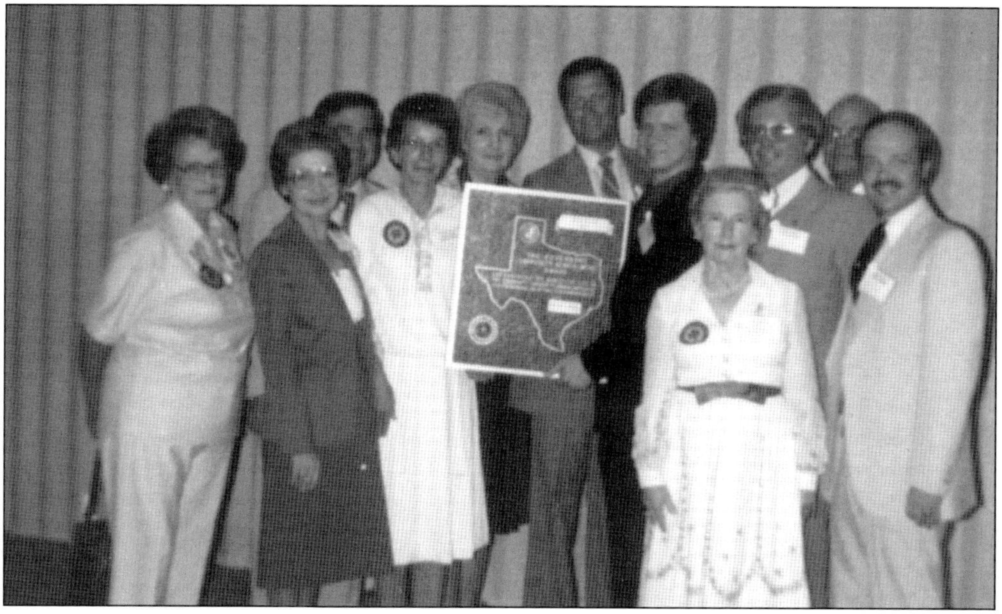

Mesquite in 1981 edged out Dallas, Houston, San Antonio, and all other 60,000-plus-population Texas cities to win the 1981 Governor's Achievement Award for exemplary beautification efforts. In this photograph, members of the Mesquite City Council and the appointed Mesquite Environmental and Beautification Commission pose with the official plaque and Mayor Len Gibbens (sixth from left) and city council members John Childs (third from left) and Bill Blackwood (third from right).

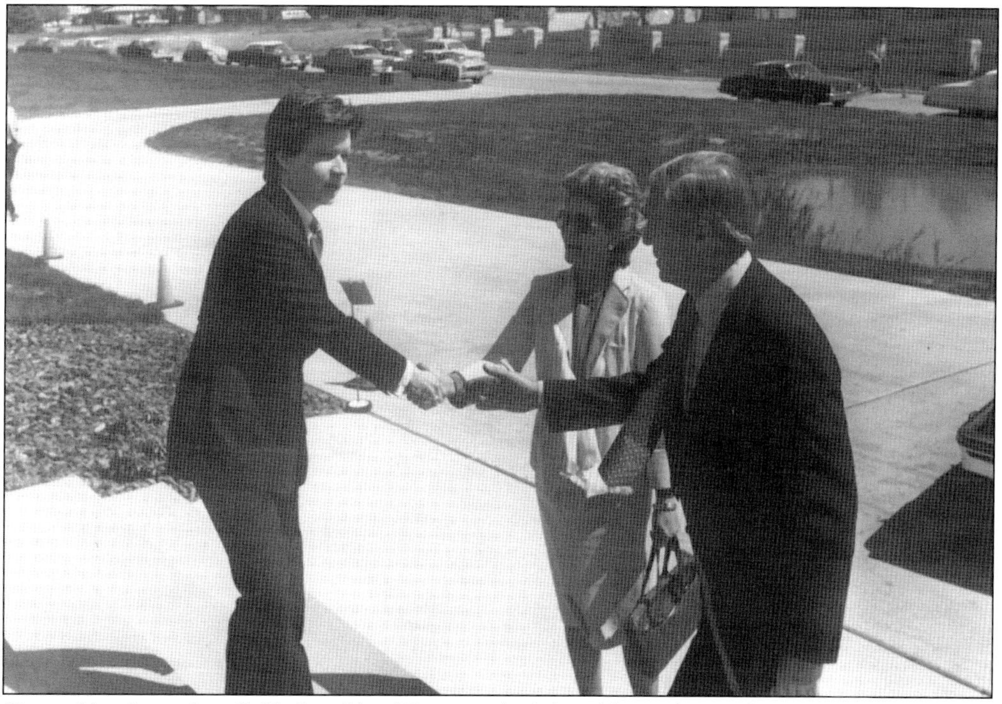

Greeted by the author (left), Sen. Lloyd Bentsen (right) and his wife, Beryl Ann Longino Bentsen, arrive in the company of a Mesquite Police escort to a reception for civic and business leaders in the newly developed Mesquite subdivision, Woodstream Estates.

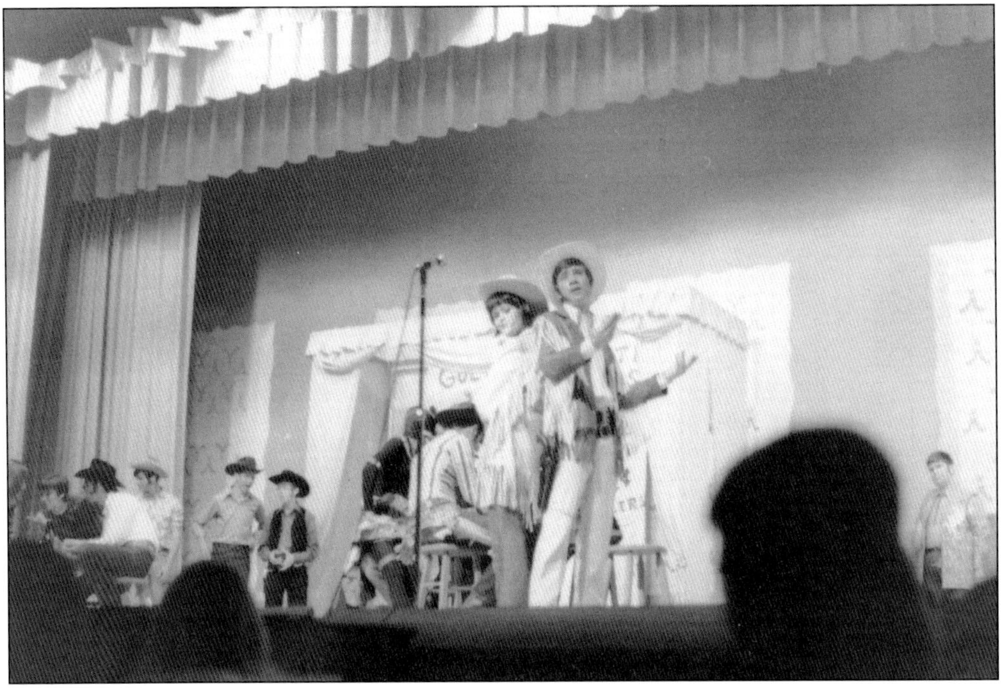

In contrast to the British accents of *My Fair Lady*, Mesquite High School's 1971 theater production of *Calamity Jane*, directed by Sue Braden, reverted to cowboys, Indians, and the Old West. Students nicknamed the production "Calamity Janet" after the leading lady, Janet Page. The author played Wild Bill Hickok and wishes to thank future rodeo champion and fellow classmate Monty Henson for the loan of the fringed leather jacket worn in the musical.

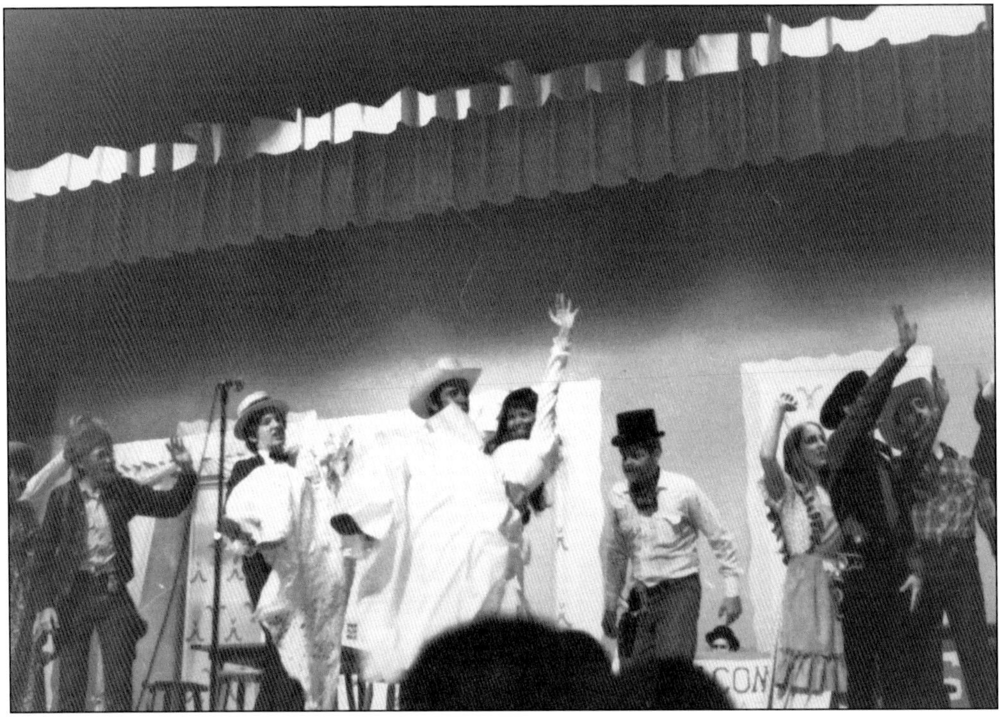

Vanston principal George Childress asked musician Frank W. Greenhaw to compose a song that could be easily learned and effectively sung by seventh, eighth, and ninth graders. The "Our Vanston Junior High" original 1965 manuscript, hand-penned by composer Frank W. Greenhaw, is shown here. At one time in Mesquite, students and their families could even sing their official school songs. "Singing Glory to the Maroon and White" is a melodic, uplifting, school song for Mesquite High School, as is this school song for Vanston Junior High.

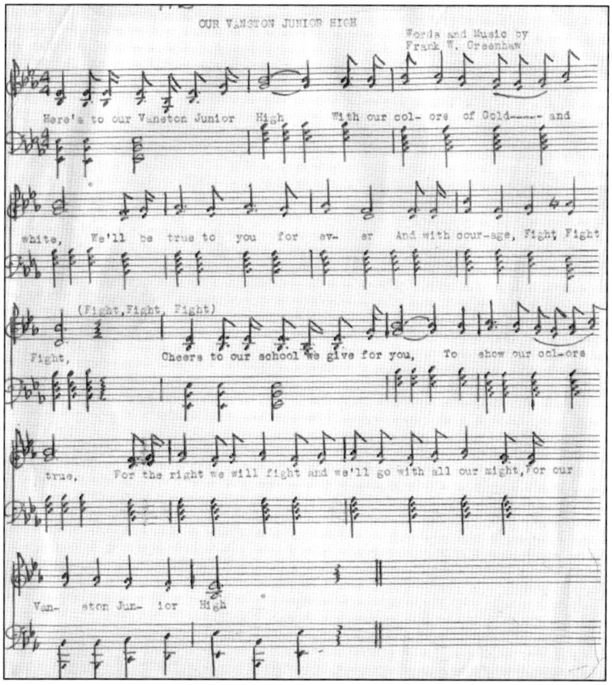

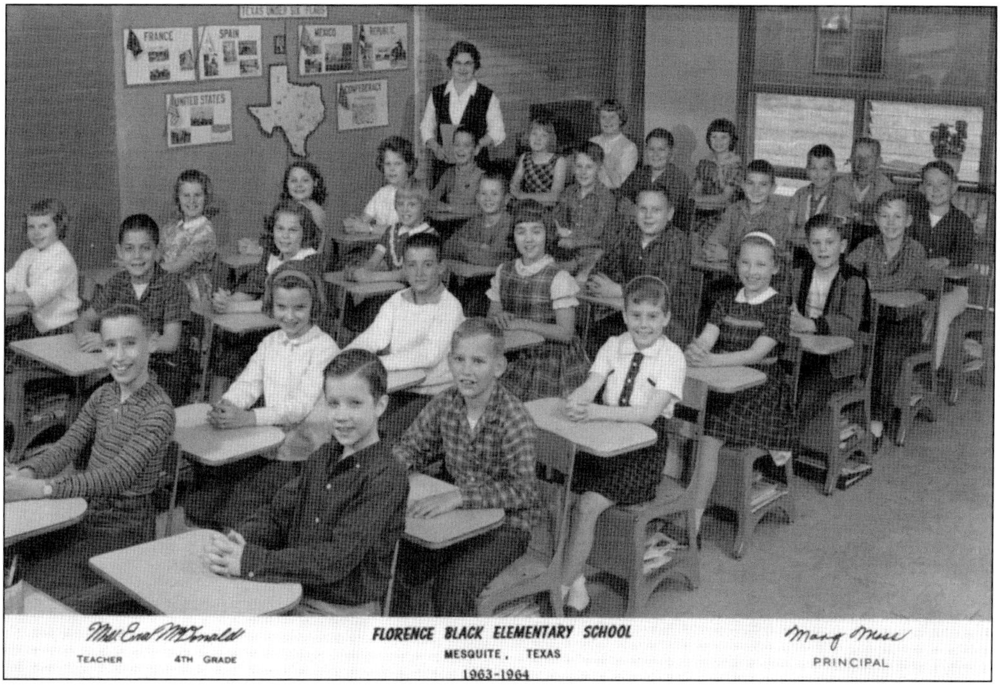

Exemplary fourth-grade teacher Era (Mrs. T.H.) McDonald was an inspiring mentor. Her classroom at Florence Black Elementary School was not air-conditioned, and television sets were not part of the district's equipment. McWhorter-Greenhaw Hardware delivered an RCA television set for the students to watch Pres. John F. Kennedy's historic visit to Dallas, Texas. The president was accompanied by First Lady Jacqueline Kennedy, Vice Pres. Lyndon B. Johnson, and Texas governor John Connally.

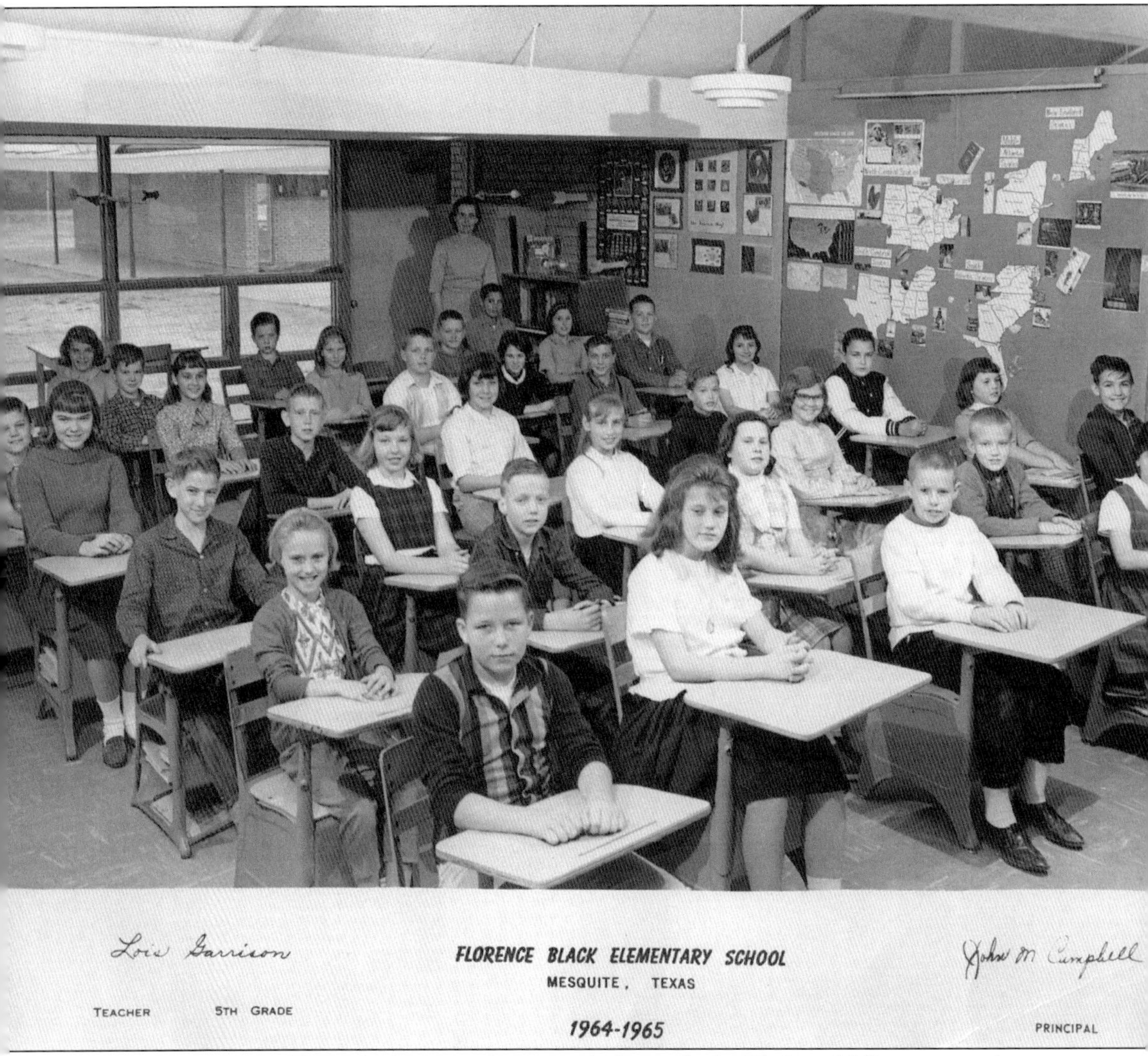

Lois Garrison's fifth-grade classroom began each day with the Pledge of Allegiance and a prayer. The 1964–1965 class was in full-academic mode when the Beatles played at Memorial Auditorium in Dallas, Texas, on September 18, 1964. Frank and Pat Greenhaw chaperoned their son, Art, and his friends Deborah and Honor Franklin to the "concert of the century." After the Beatles' American debut, music performances at Florence Black Elementary School were forever changed when students demanded the inclusion of such great hits as "Twist and Shout," "I Saw Her Standing There," and "This Boy."

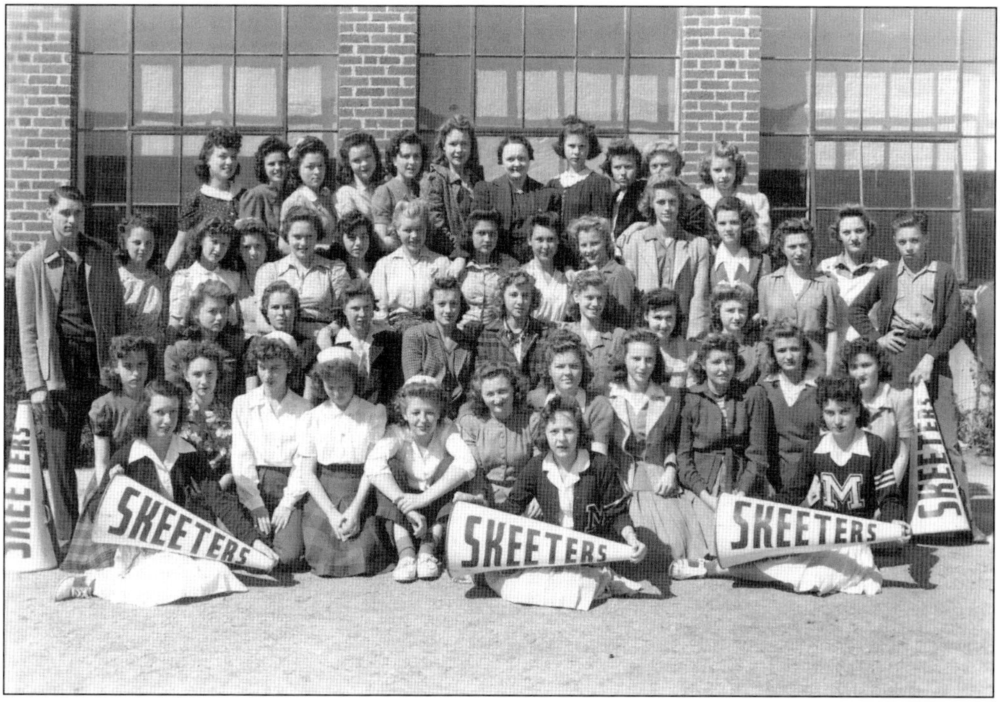

Cheerleaders and the pep squad are shown in front of Mesquite High School in this 1941–1942 school year photograph.

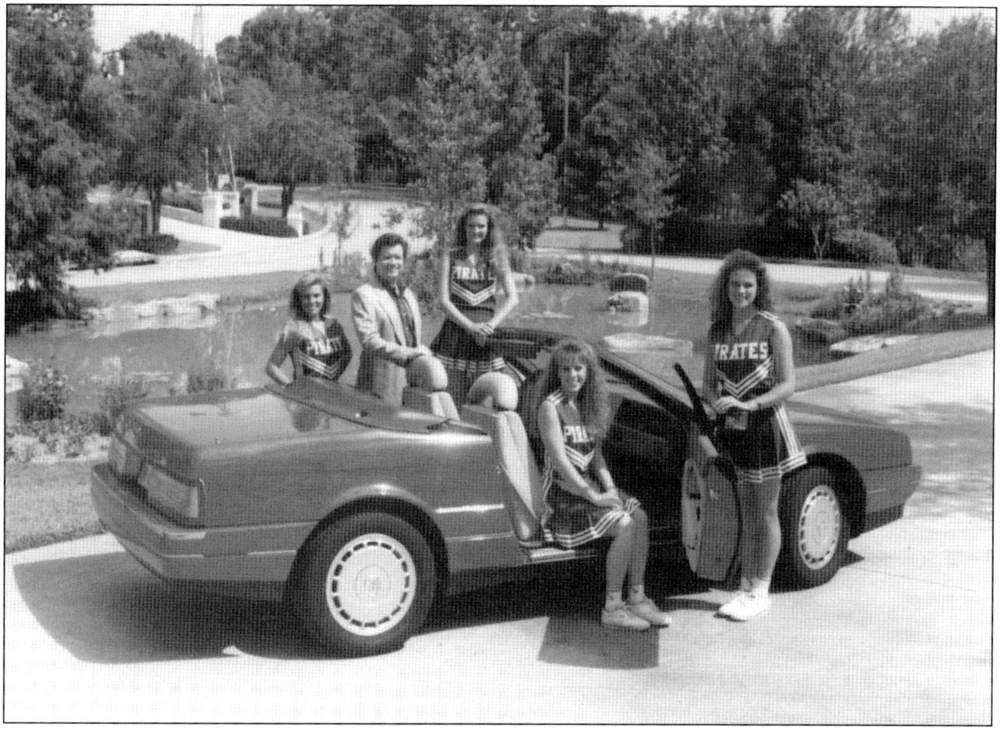

Approximately 50 years later in 1991, cheerleaders from Mesquite's Poteet High School pose in a south Mesquite residential subdivision with author.

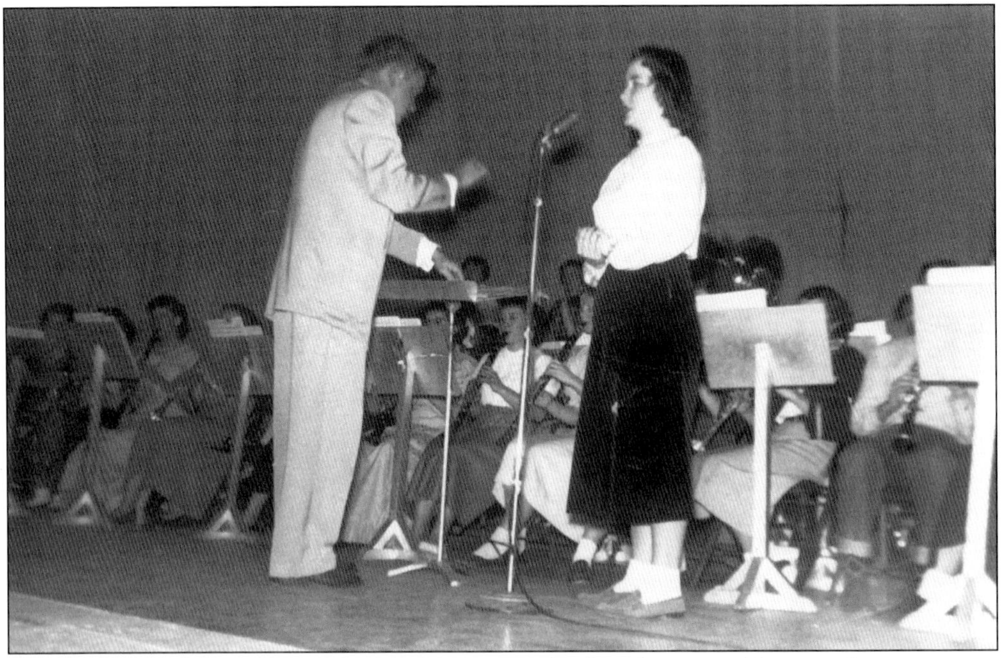

In the best of community times of Mesquite, Texas, school graduates would stay in the community in which they were raised and continue to build for future generations. A shining example is Eunice Wheat Futrell, shown here singing with the MHS band under the direction of Frank W. Greenhaw. As of 2015, Eunice continues to build and work for her hometown of Mesquite.

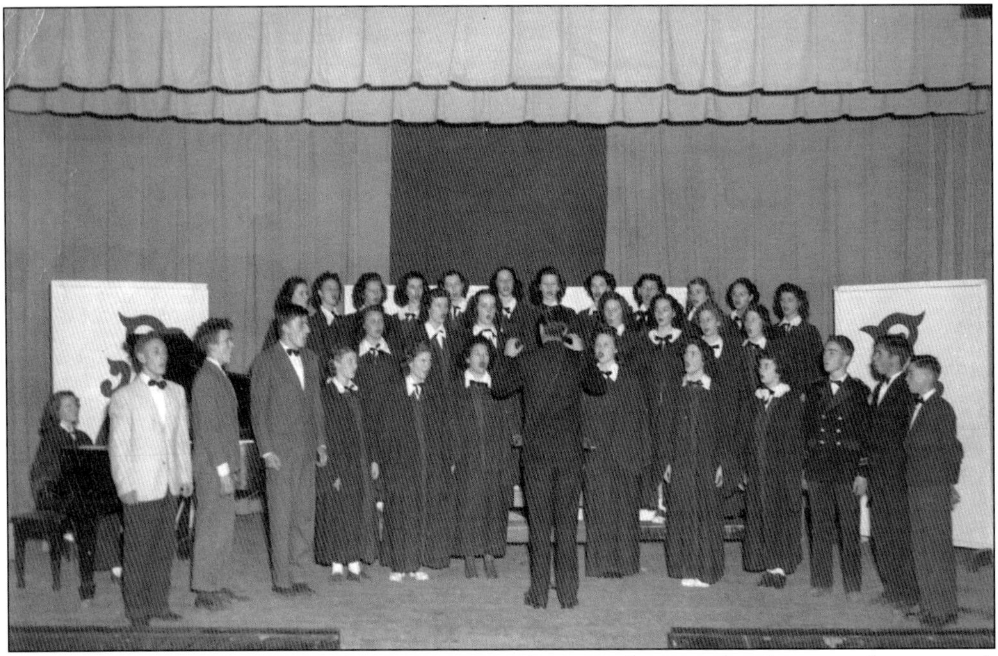

Immediately after World War II, there was a strong desire on the part of students to achieve, excel, and be successful in accordance with the American Dream. Because these dedicated students memorized all their music, music stands and handheld sheet music were not necessary. Note the intensity with which they focus on the nuances of their director, Frank W. Greenhaw.

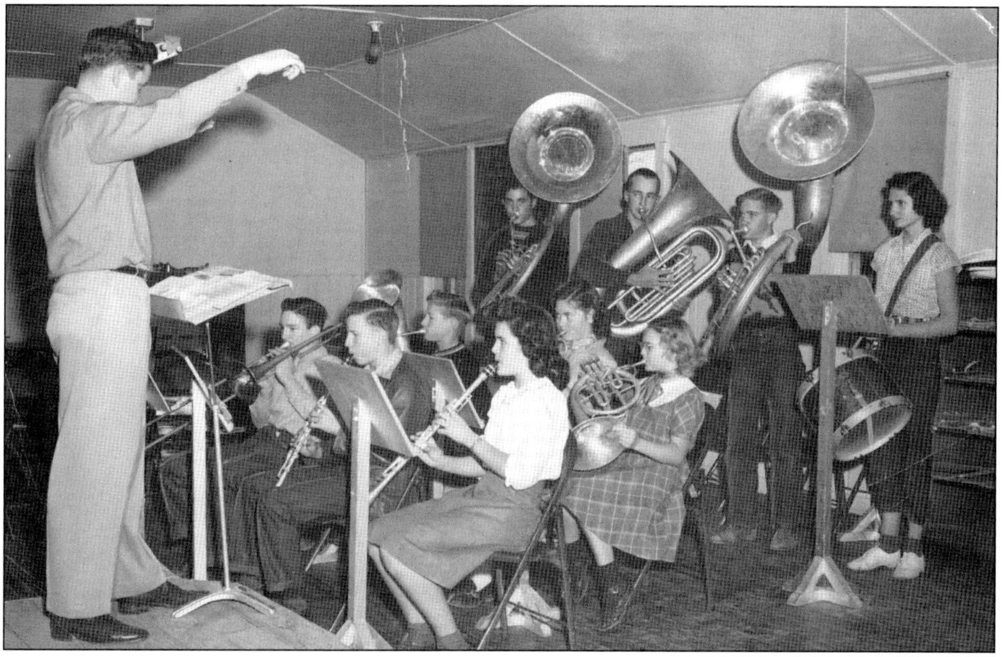

According to Proverbs 22:6, one should "raise up a child in the way he should go, and when he is old, he shall not depart from it." Note the young age of the players performing in this concert band. In the builder generation of Mesquite, the youngest of the young were expected to perform in concert situations with a similar zeal to that of their older brothers and sisters.

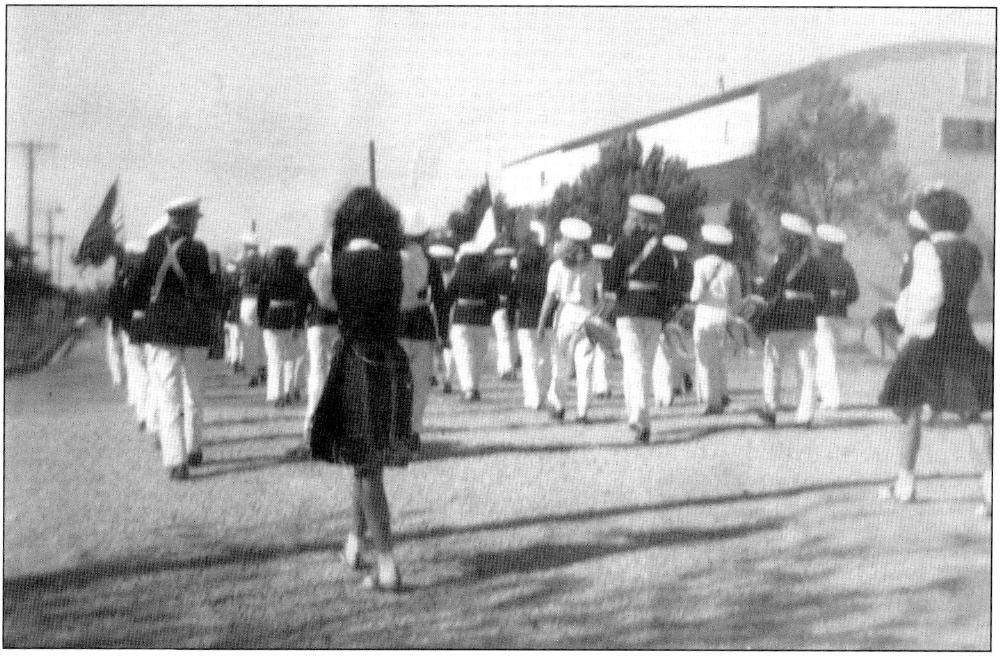

Mesquite boasted a 75-by-125-foot coliseum constructed in 1930 on the southeast corner of Mesquite High School property. It ultimately cost $6,000 and was completely funded by subscription. The Mesquite Chamber of Commerce, the Mesquite School Board, and the Mesquite Fair Association initially sponsored the coliseum, also known as the Mesquite Gymnasium.

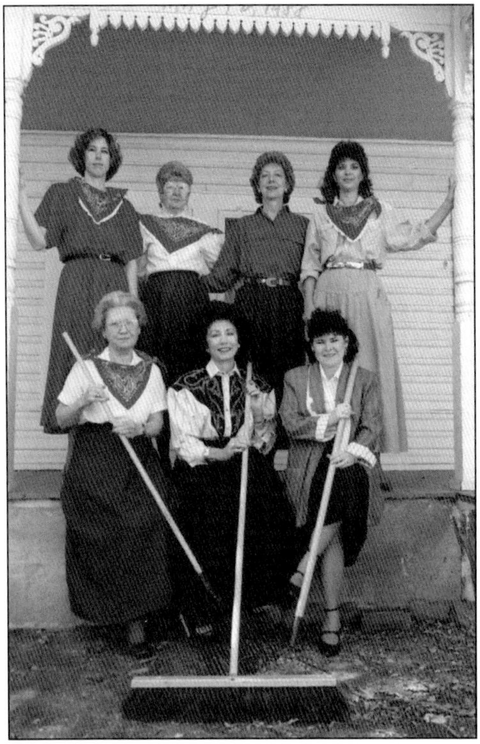

Mesquite women throughout the 1980s and 1990s continued to lead in civic affairs and historic preservation. In 1987, this group of community restorers, with shovels in hand, prepares to break ground for the eventual opening to the public of the Florence Ranch Homestead.

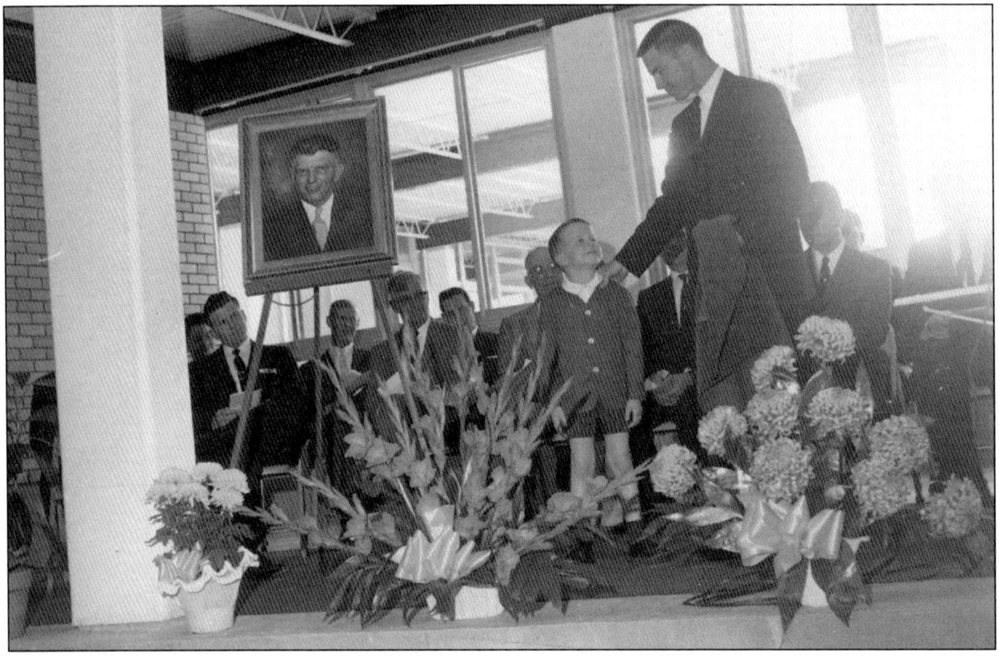

In the best of Mesquite times, principals and teachers watched over their students from earliest elementary school days until high school graduation. Here, the first principal, Jerry Irons, greets the author (and grandson of the school's namesake) at the 1959 official dedication of Ferd McWhorter Elementary School. Civic leaders in the first row include, from left to right, Bob Robinson, Leslie Brown, and N.E. Shands.

Three

Arts and Religion

Culture, Family, Flag, and Faith

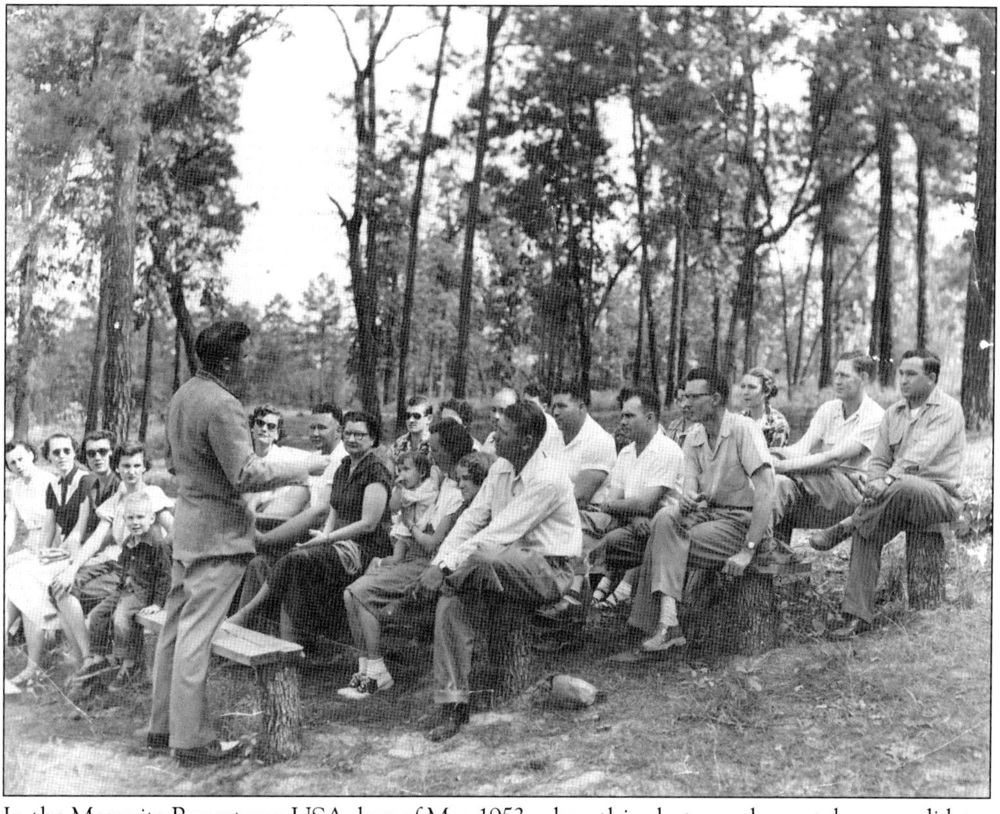

In the Mesquite Boomtown USA days of May 1953, when this photograph was taken, candidates for community public office did not simply decide to run, they were asked to run by their fellow citizens on the basis of leadership, ethics, morals, and sense of duty. Sprinkled throughout this gathering of laymen and laywomen on a Christian retreat are future city councilman and school trustee J.J. McGlothlin, City Councilman Emitt Evans, and school trustees Robert Lawson and Frank W. Greenhaw, teacher of this session.

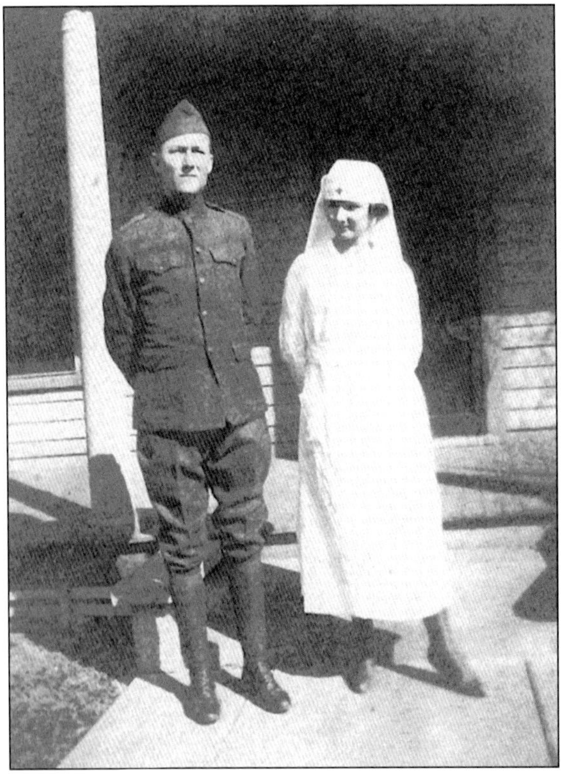

During World War I, all members of age in the Holley family served to defend their country. Soldier Raymond Holley stands next to nurse Elsie Holley prior to Raymond's deployment to France in 1918. Brother Anson Holley practices rifle maneuvers prior to his deployment to war-torn Europe.

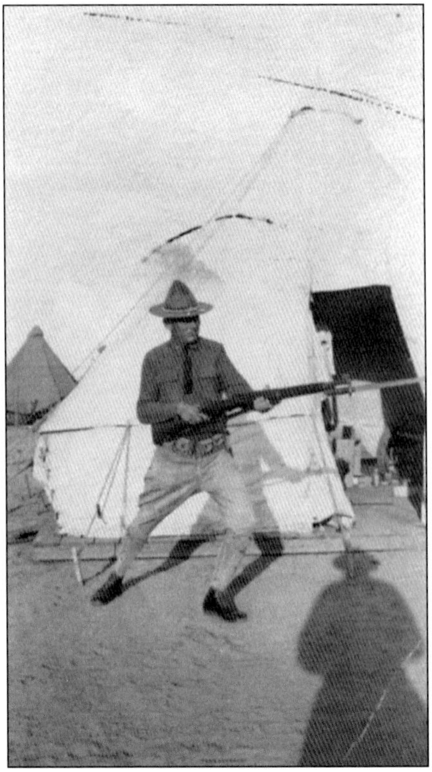

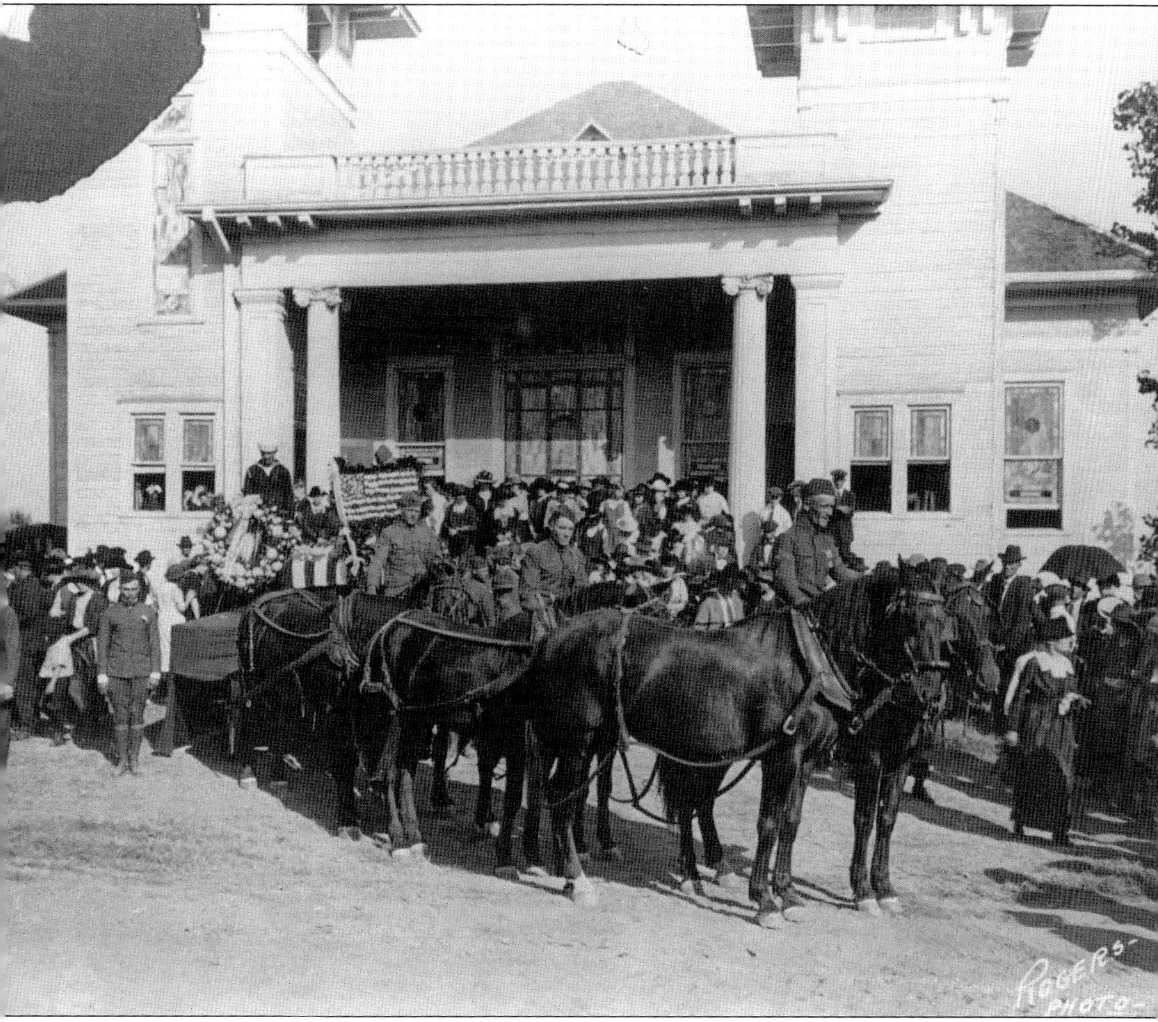

World War I soldier Louis W. Casey of Mesquite was killed in action in 1918, but it was not until 1921 that the body arrived home for burial. A military color guard bears the coffin at services at First Methodist Church of Mesquite on October 18, 1921.

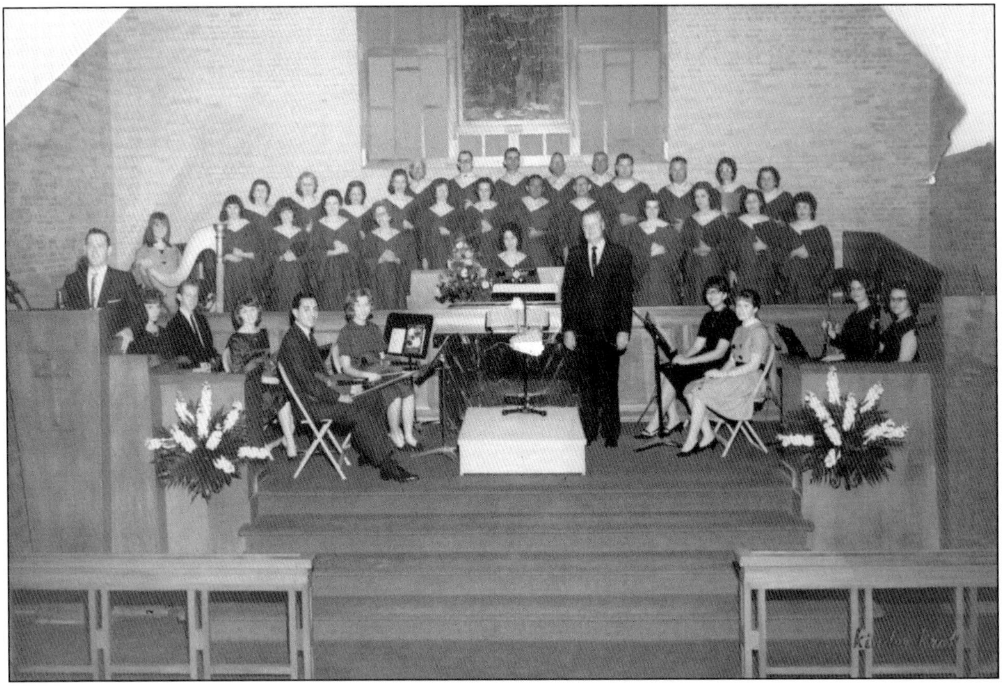

When one of the greatest generations of men who built Mesquite brought its leadership to Mesquite mainline churches in the 1950s and 1960s, church attendance and church influence in the city boomed. Above, Mesquite city manager George Schrader is set to narrate a First Methodist Church of Mesquite choir program in 1964 with Mesquite businessman, musician, and educator Frank W. Greenhaw about to direct the choir and orchestra. The photograph below in this series depicts the musical performance in progress.

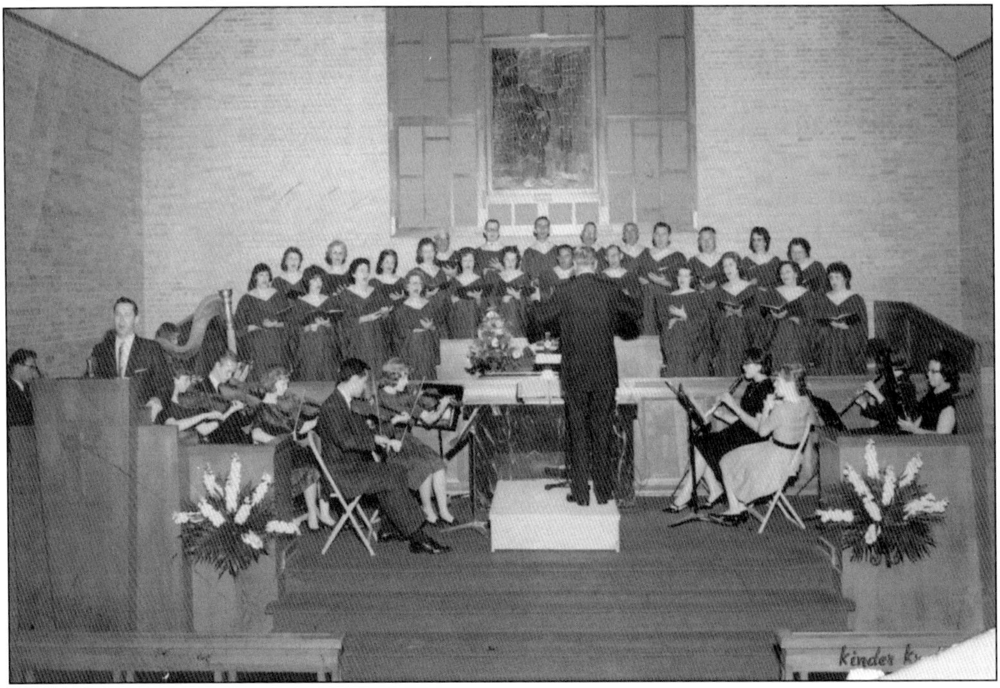

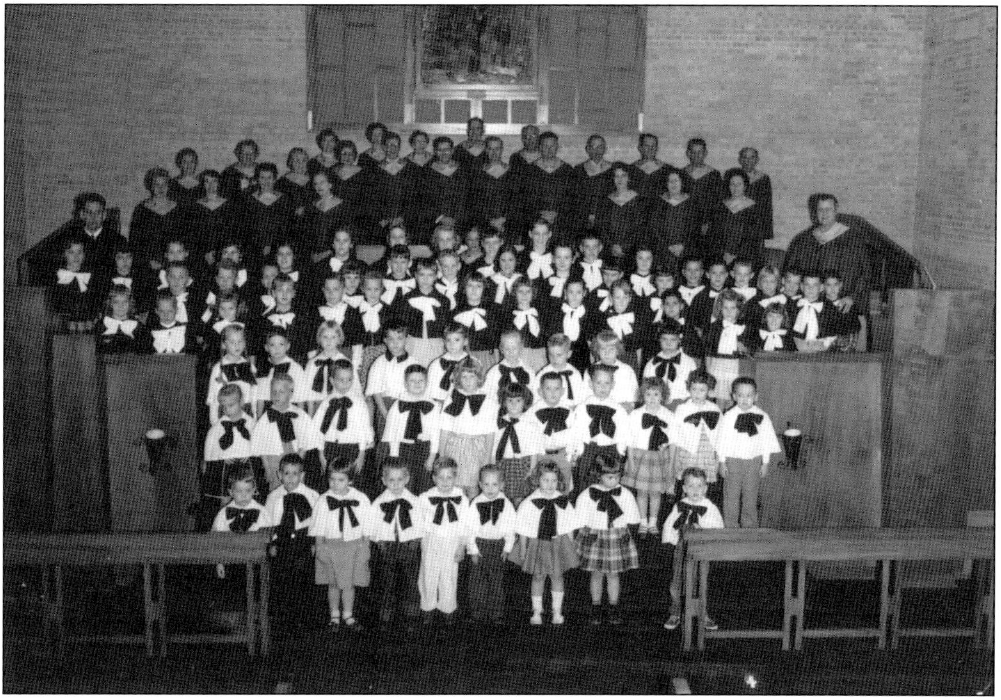

In 1957, First Methodist Church of Mesquite developed a large and vibrant children's choir, as did other Mesquite churches. At the time of these photographs, crime was virtually nonexistent locally, and fathers and men were almost always a major part of home, civic, and church membership. The private sector in Mesquite was flourishing, and single-family homebuilding was booming.

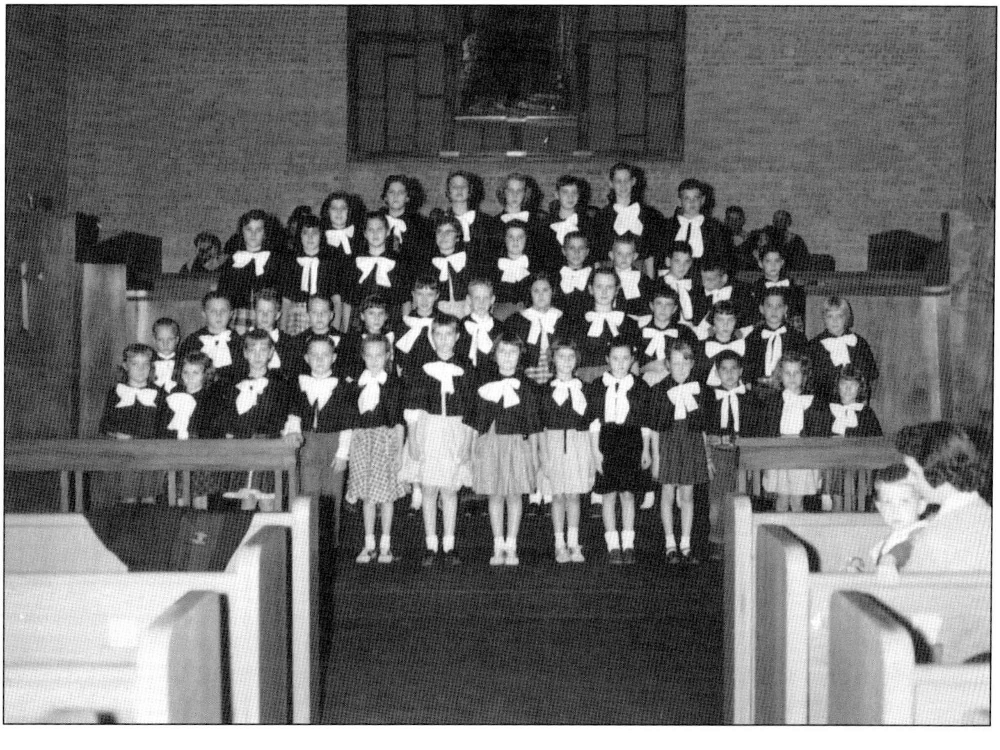

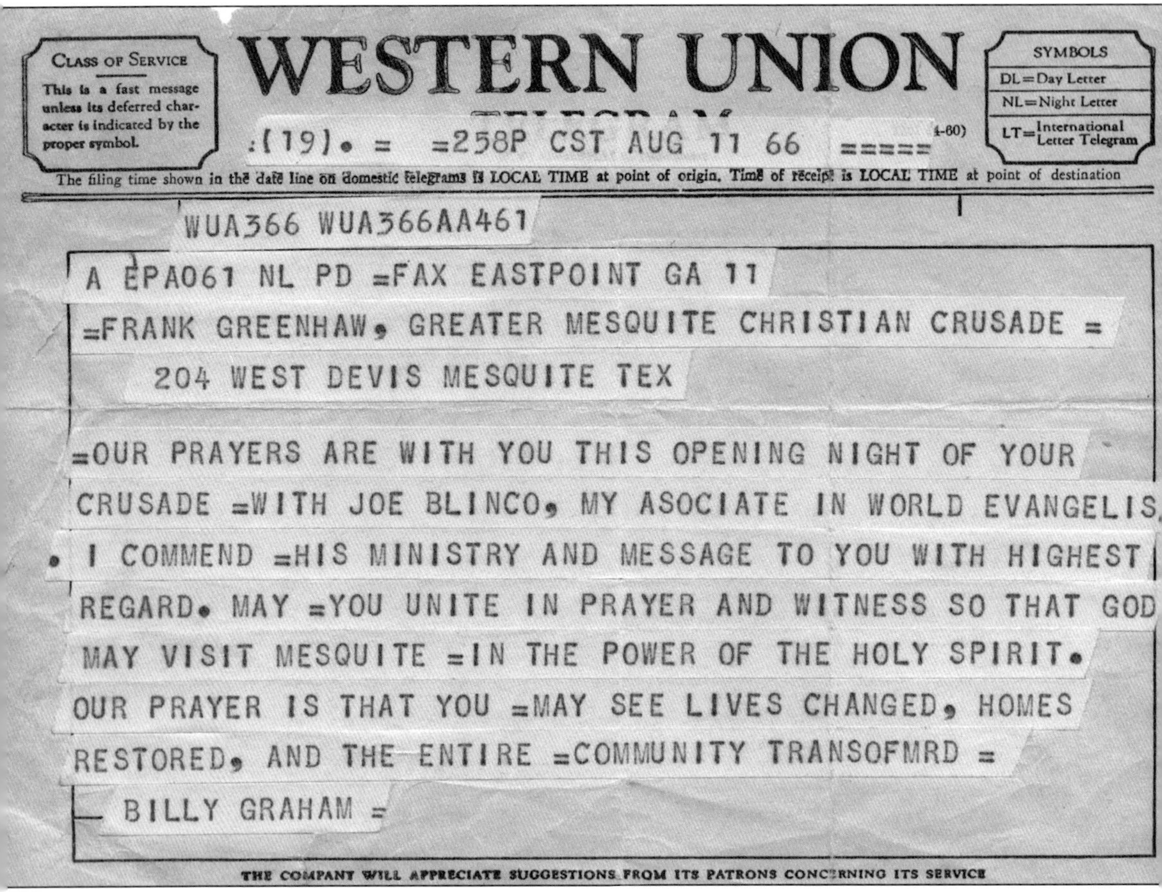
CLASS OF SERVICE
This is a fast message unless its deferred character is indicated by the proper symbol.

WESTERN UNION

SYMBOLS
DL=Day Letter
NL=Night Letter
LT=International Letter Telegram

:(19). = =258P CST AUG 11 66 =====

The filing time shown in the date line on domestic telegrams is LOCAL TIME at point of origin. Time of receipt is LOCAL TIME at point of destination

WUA366 WUA366AA461

A EPA061 NL PD =FAX EASTPOINT GA 11
=FRANK GREENHAW, GREATER MESQUITE CHRISTIAN CRUSADE =
204 WEST DEVIS MESQUITE TEX

=OUR PRAYERS ARE WITH YOU THIS OPENING NIGHT OF YOUR CRUSADE =WITH JOE BLINCO, MY ASOCIATE IN WORLD EVANGELIS. I COMMEND =HIS MINISTRY AND MESSAGE TO YOU WITH HIGHEST REGARD. MAY =YOU UNITE IN PRAYER AND WITNESS SO THAT GOD MAY VISIT MESQUITE =IN THE POWER OF THE HOLY SPIRIT. OUR PRAYER IS THAT YOU =MAY SEE LIVES CHANGED, HOMES RESTORED, AND THE ENTIRE =COMMUNITY TRANSOFMRD =
BILLY GRAHAM =

THE COMPANY WILL APPRECIATE SUGGESTIONS FROM ITS PATRONS CONCERNING ITS SERVICE

The biggest religious event in the history of Mesquite occurred in August 1966 in the form of the Greater Mesquite Christian Crusade, which drew thousands of people to the Mesquite High School Athletic Field (now Hanby Stadium). Over a two-week period, the faithful came from the entire region to hear Billy Graham's associate evangelist Joe Blinco preach the gospel. Soloist and movie star Ethel Waters and a choir of Mesquite singers provided the music for the event. This image depicts the treasured telegram from Billy Graham to crusade chairman Frank W. Greenhaw.

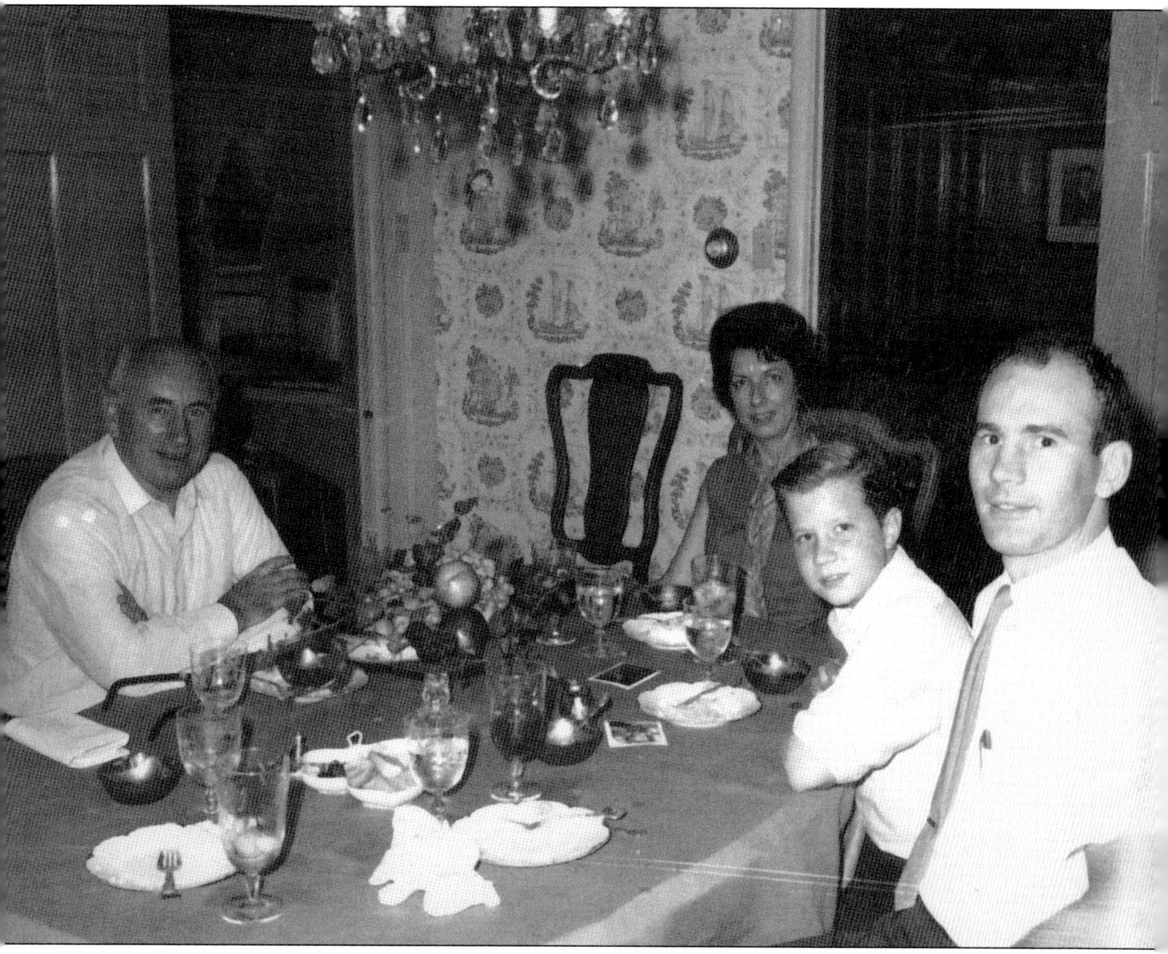

The Billy Graham Evangelistic Association's Greater Mesquite Christian Crusade featured evangelist Joe Blinco (far left), who was accompanied to Mesquite by crusade coordinator Sterling Huston (far right). The gentlemen dined in the home of Patricia McWhorter Greenhaw, seen here with her son Art. The Mesquite crusade was the first major crusade for Graham associate Huston, who went on to become director of all Graham's crusades for the entire North American continent.

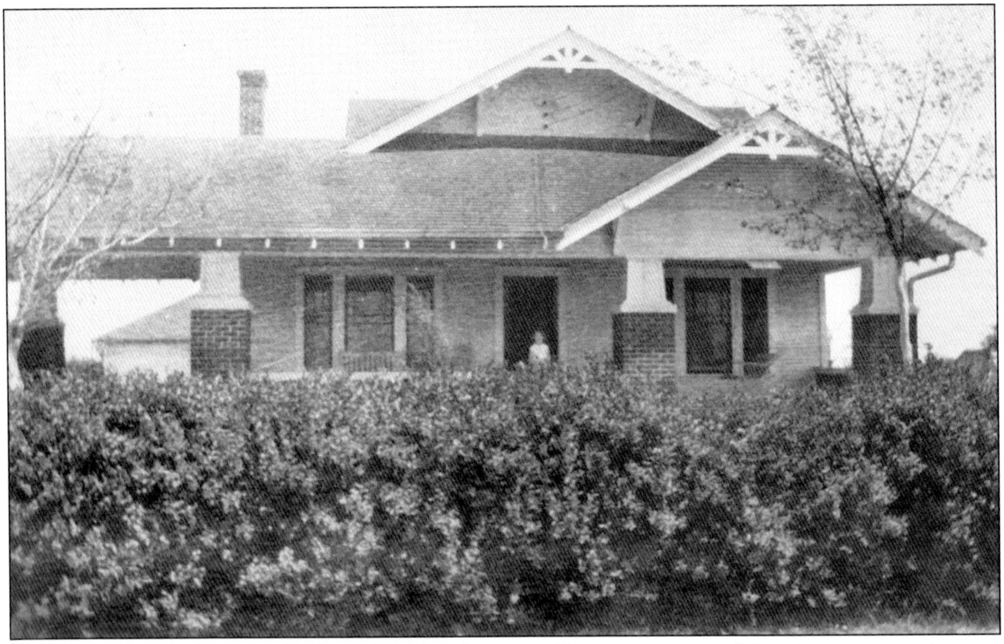

Mesquite natives lament the fact that South Bryan Street, a street of fine homes once known as "Silk Stocking Row," lost almost every significant house when Bryan-Belt Line was widened and the street became mixed-use in the mid-1970s. The home of the Holley-McWhorter families at 504 South Bryan Street in Mesquite stood from 1926 until its demolition in the mid-1970s. "Little Bee," as she was known to her doting family, stands in front of her beloved home place. Patricia Ann McWhorter Greenhaw would grow up to become a civic and philanthropic leader in the region and state through service on many boards and committees, to include the Dallas County Historical Society, the Methodist Children's Home, and the Mesquite Heritage Square Bicentennial Committee.

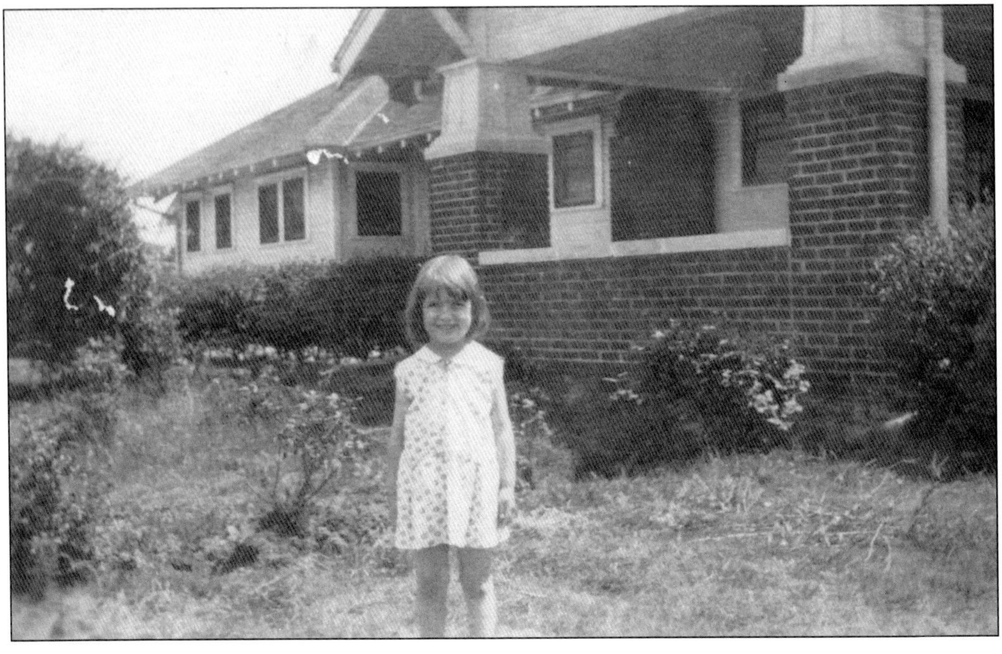

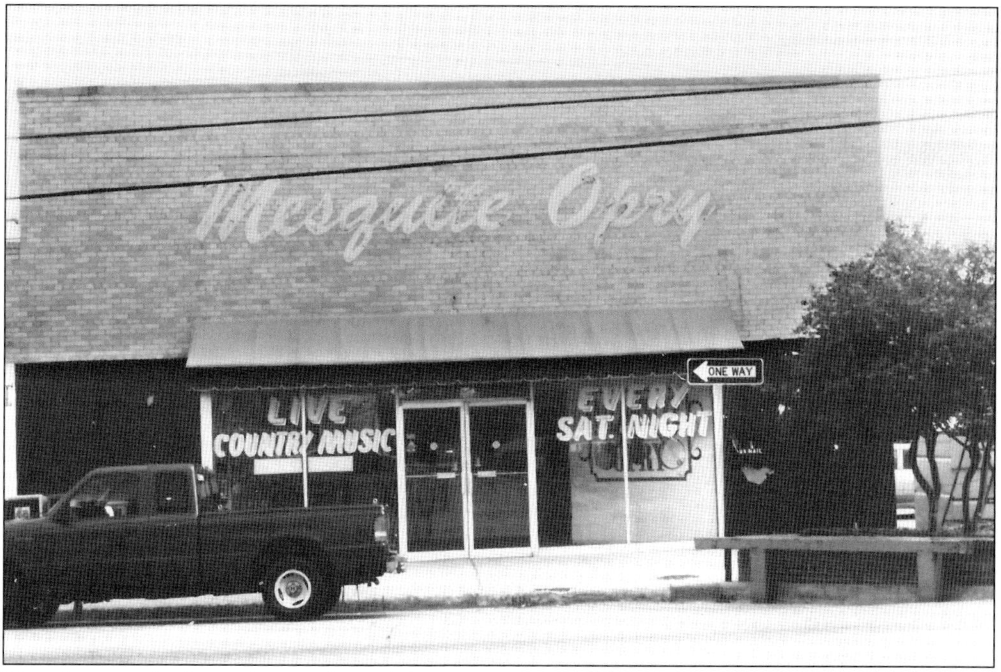

The photograph above depicts the well-known exterior of the Mesquite Opry on the south side of the Mesquite Heritage Square. Even into the 1990s, after the Mesquite Opry changed ownership and became the Rodeo City Music Hall, its country music jamborees played to sold-out houses. In October 1999, all 450 seats were filled, with standing room only for the historic collaboration of the Light Crust Doughboys, gospel legend James Blackwood, and the Singing Wills Family. It was on the occasion of this Friday evening performance when James Blackwood saw the heavy traffic motoring down Davis Street making its way to the concert venue and commented, "You would think that we are in downtown Los Angeles."

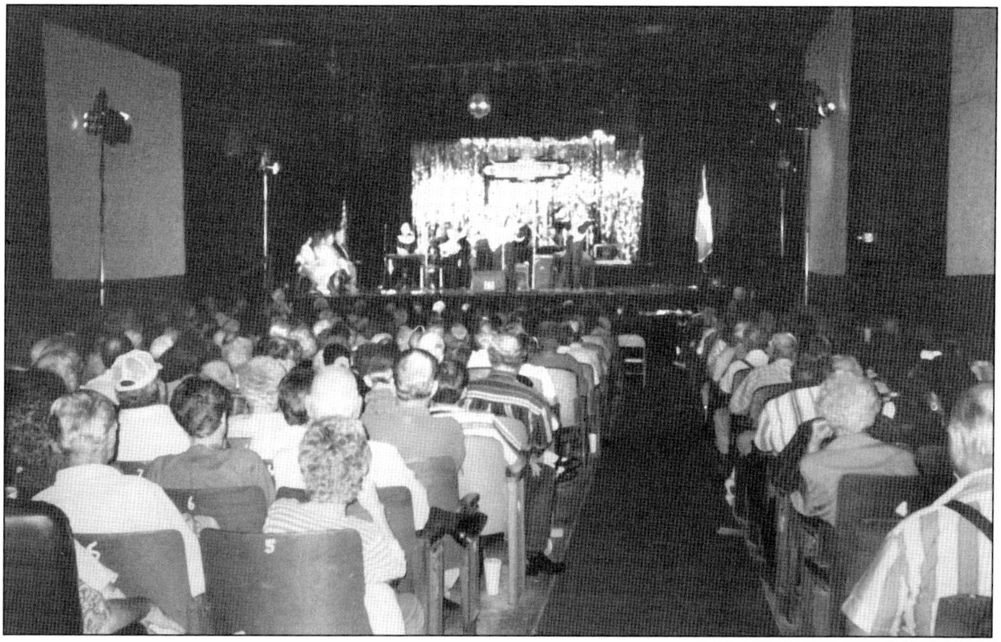

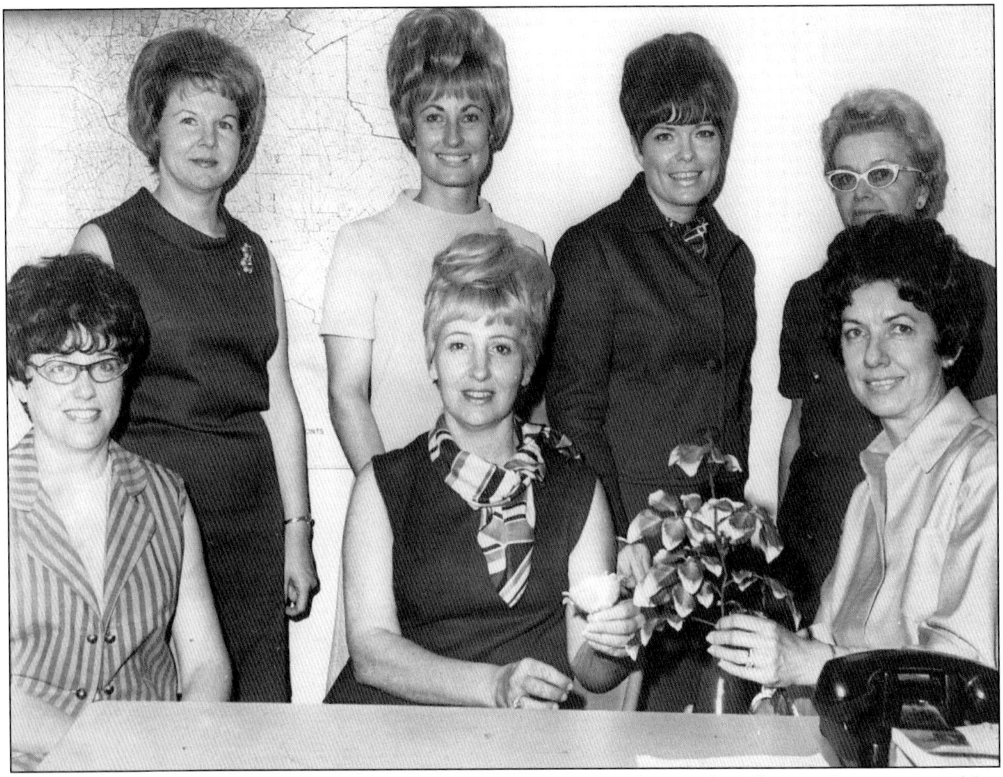

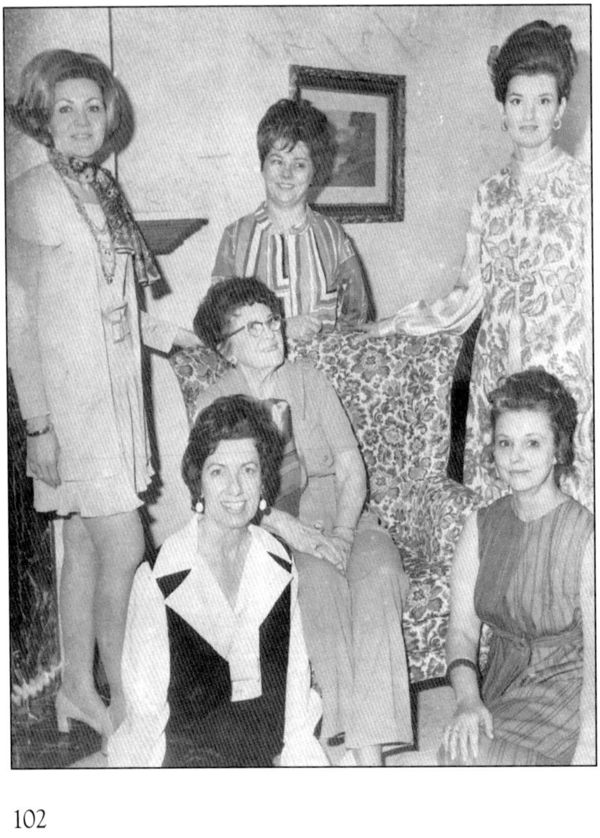

A town's influential women mold its culture. A town's influential women embrace its moral and philanthropic causes. A town's influential women determine its success as a beacon of volunteerism. In the years when Mesquite's private sector and heritage districts were thriving, undergirding all the success were the women who supported the best local candidates for office, the women who volunteered and worked for a town filled with art, culture, and prosperity, a "shining city on a hill." Presidents and representatives from Mesquite's various women's clubs (Mesquite Council of Women's Clubs) are pictured in the above photograph. Mesquite Woman's Club members wearing the day's high fashions from Mesquite store Toby's Ladies Wear are pictured in the photograph at left.

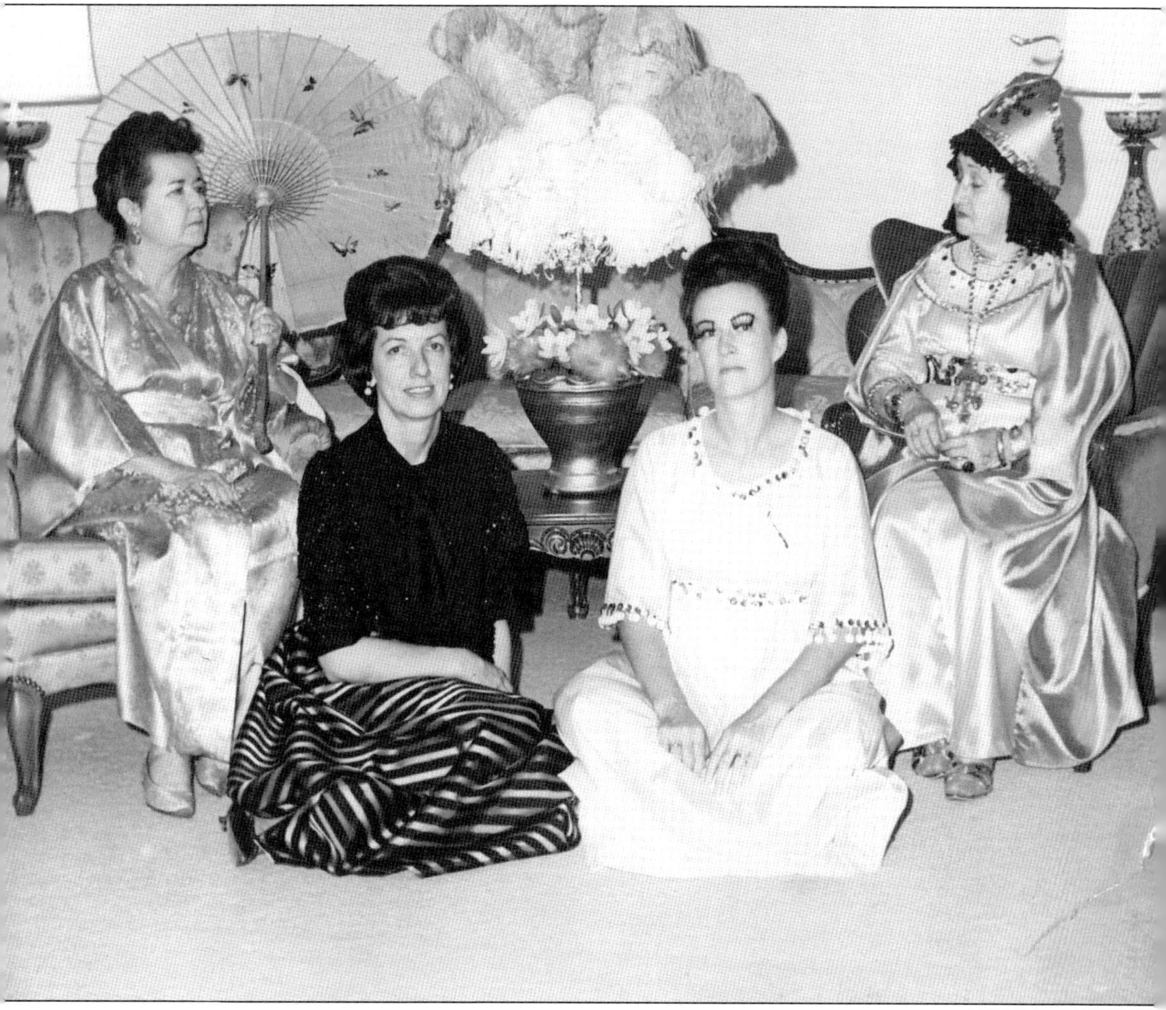

Members of the Mesquite Woman's Club in the 1960s are pictured here in period costumes during the presentation of a program on world history and world fashion. The club, established in 1936 and the oldest woman's organization in the city, was an outgrowth of the Woman's Civic Club. First National Bank of Mesquite hosted in its boardroom the first meeting of the club, where Elsie Holley Shands was elected as its first president.

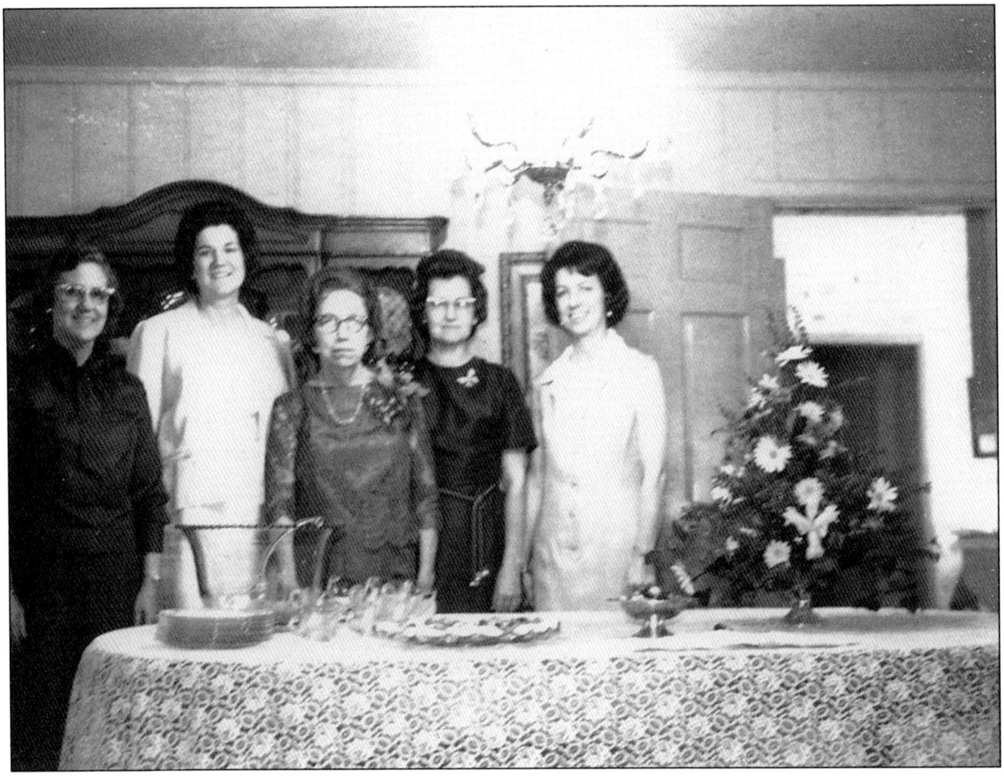

The Mesquite Woman's Club and the local chapter of the American Association of University Women (AAUW) were two of the most influential organizations in Mesquite's boomtown years. The AAUW hosted teas for Mesquite High School senior girls and instructed them in the social and entertaining graces.

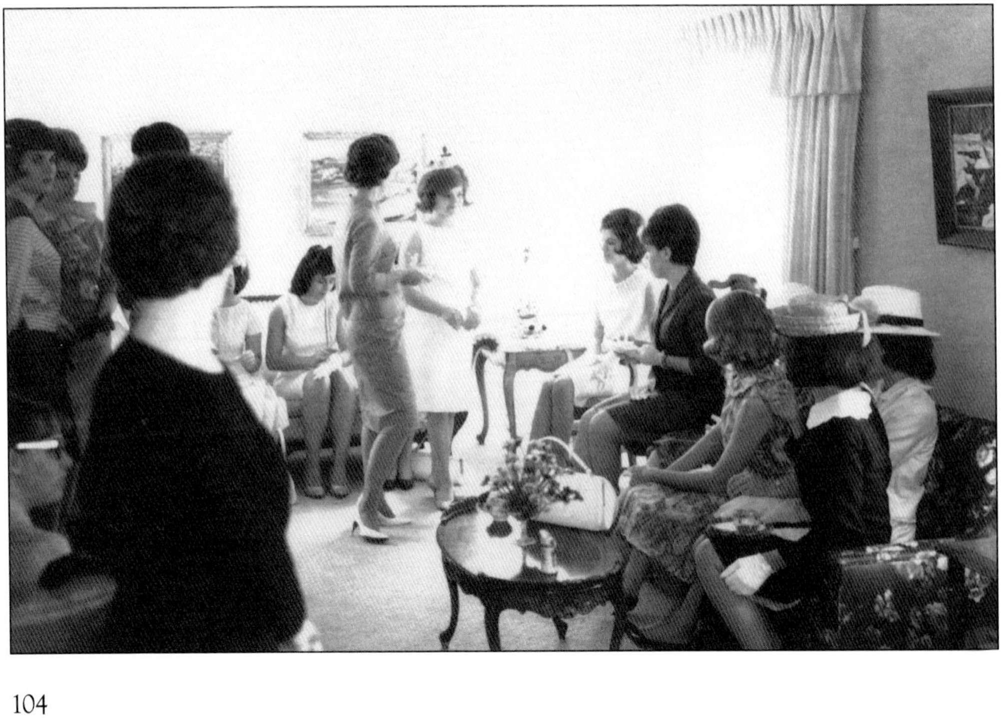

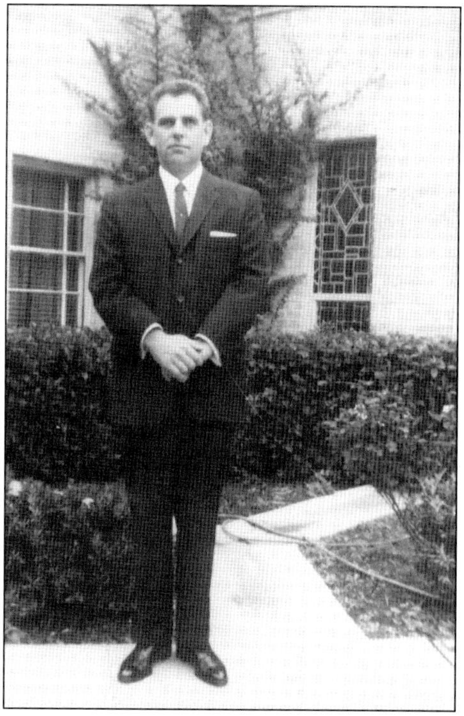

In the builder and the boomtown years of Mesquite in the 1920s through 1980s, there were town pastors and town music directors who, through their personalities and resolve, transcended denominations and dissolved religious and social barriers. They regularly visited church members and nonmembers alike who were hospitalized, they ministered in prisons, they comforted the aged, and they led community religious services. Among the town pastors and town music directors were music men Walter L. Wilkinson, Frank W. Greenhaw, and William Hooper and pastors Earl Kifer, Earl Harvey, Buist Wilson, Hulon Hood, M.V. Pruitt, and Thomas Wilbanks. Kifer is depicted in the photograph at right. Wilson (left) and Greenhaw are depicted in the photograph below.

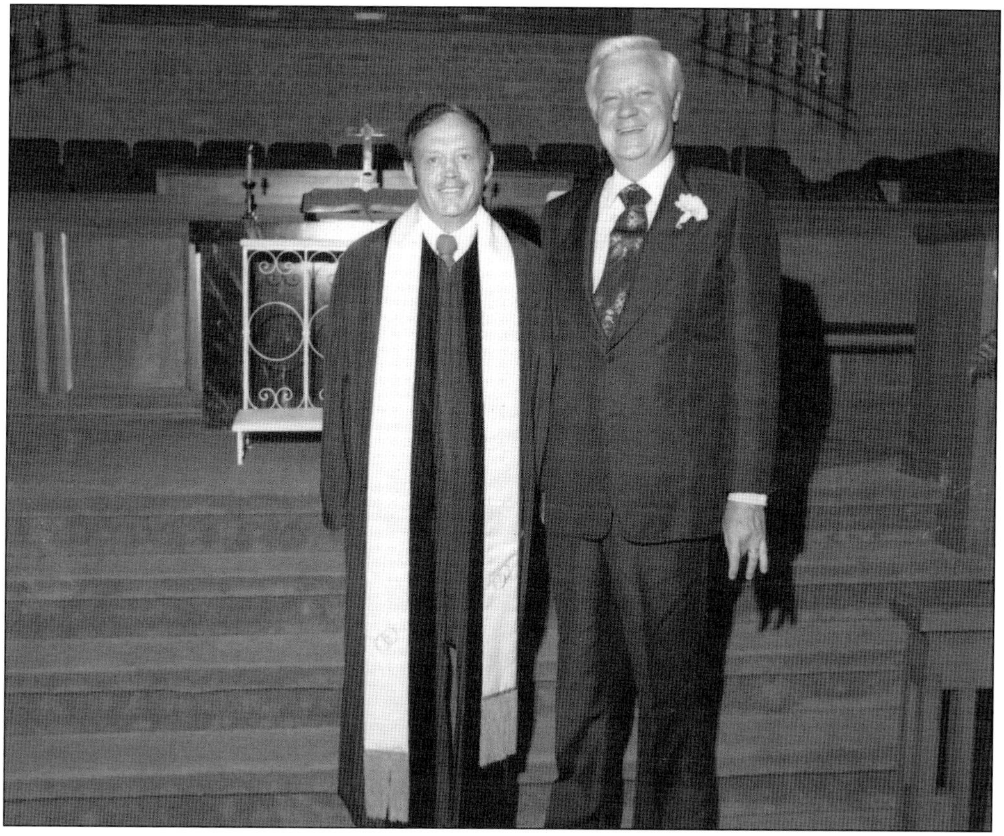

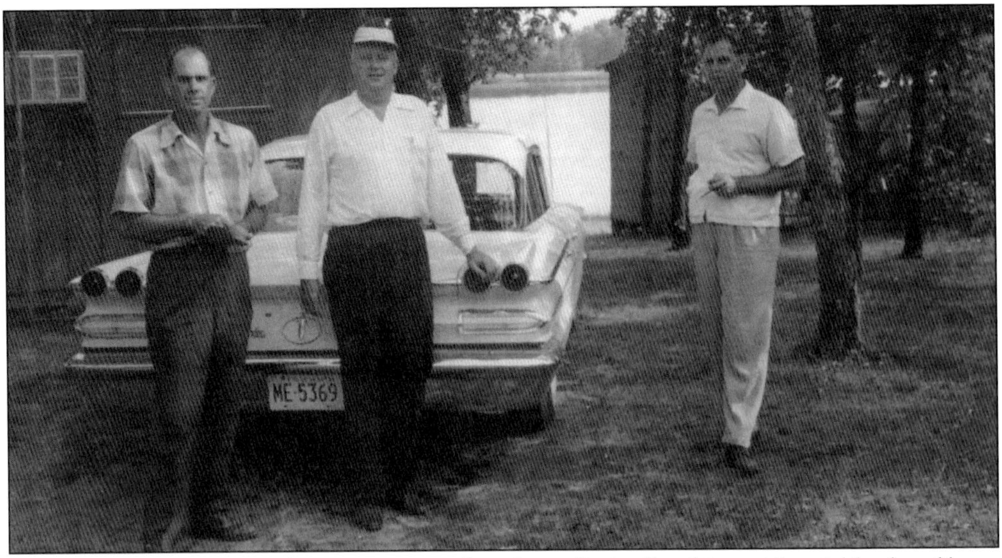

Town pastors in Mesquite's boom years were "men's men" who flew kites with neighborhood boys, who attended Dallas Sportatorium wrestling matches with their congregation's teenagers, who fished and hunted with the adult parish flock, and who provided invocations and blessings at local events. The author is an eyewitness to town pastors who did all of the above as their Mesquite congregations reached record membership numbers. Rev. Earl Kifer is pictured above (right) with M.E. Hamm (left) and Frank W. Greenhaw; Rev. Kifer fishes with church members. Pictured below (top row, far right), Rev. Earl Harvey encourages period 1860s clothing in celebration of the First Methodist Church 100-year anniversary in 1963.

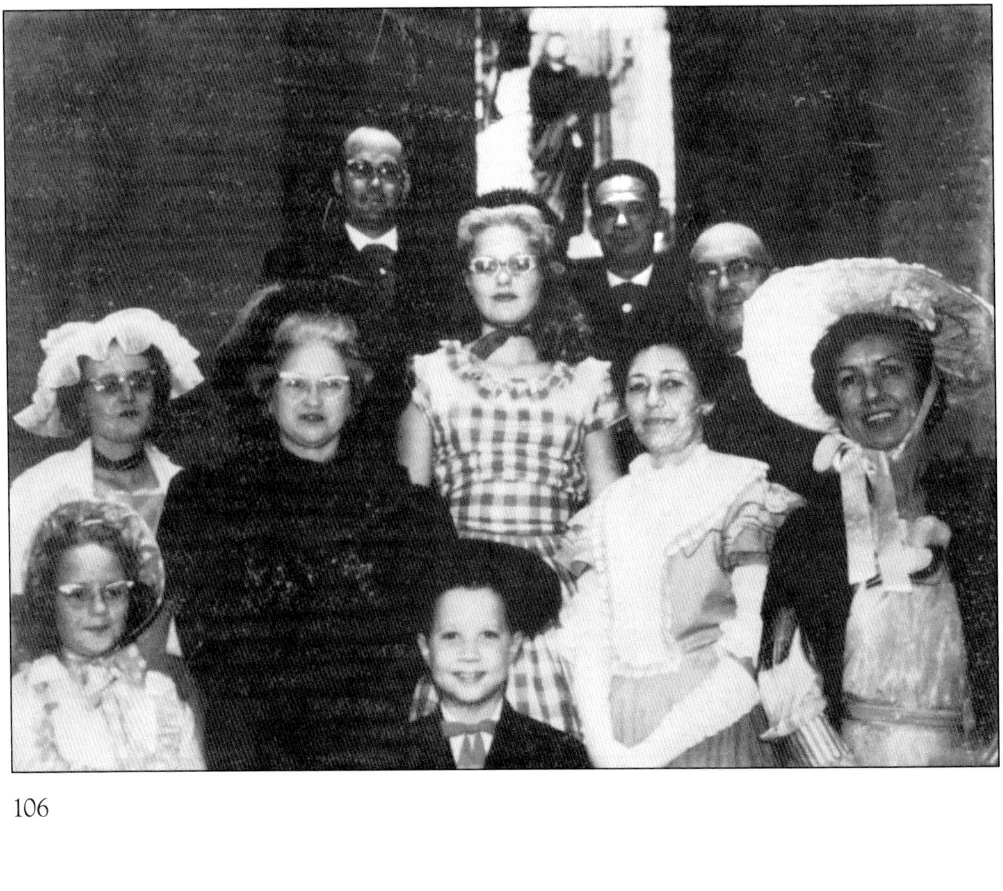

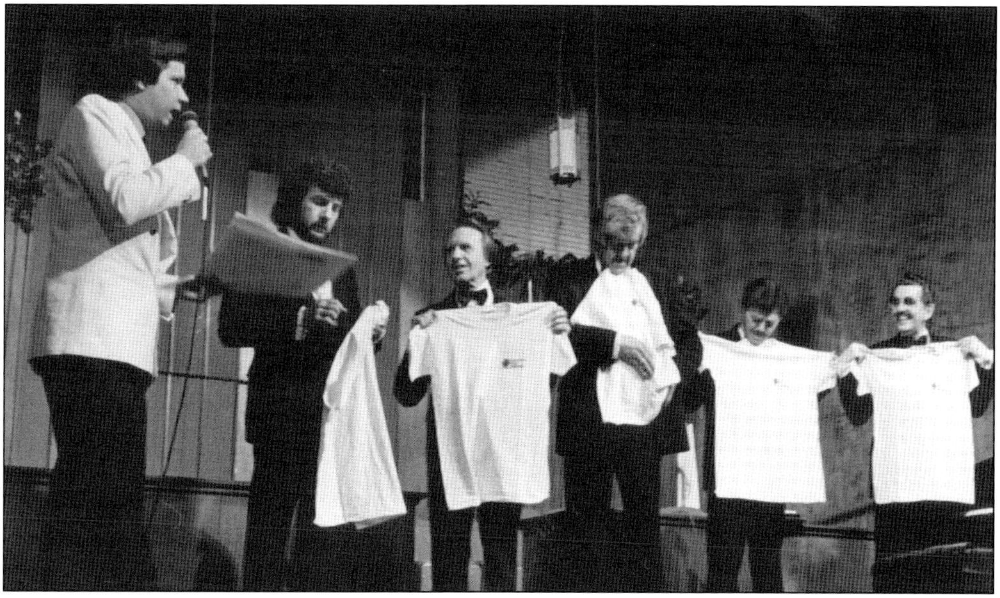

Looking back on it today, it was an almost unbelievable cultural and artistic achievement. During the years 1982–1985 alone, the Mesquite Folk Festival brought to town an incredible array of folk arts performers and musicians the likes of which few suburban towns have experienced in their variety. A partial list of Mesquite Folk Festival iconic musicians concertizing in the city thanks to the vision of early-1980s Eastfield College officials, Mesquite Performing Arts Council, and City of Mesquite officials includes Odetta, the Masters Five starring James Blackwood, Jake Hess, J.D. Sumner, Hovie Lister, the Light Crust Doughboys, the Singing Wills Family, Noel Paul Stookey (of Peter Paul and Mary), Patsy Montana, Nanci Griffith, Leon McAuliffe, and many others. The image above depicts the Masters Five onstage at 1983 festival gospel concert location at First Assembly of God Church in downtown Mesquite. The image below depicts Masters Five members with Mesquite Folk Festival organizers, including First Assembly of God pastor Rev. Hulon Hood.

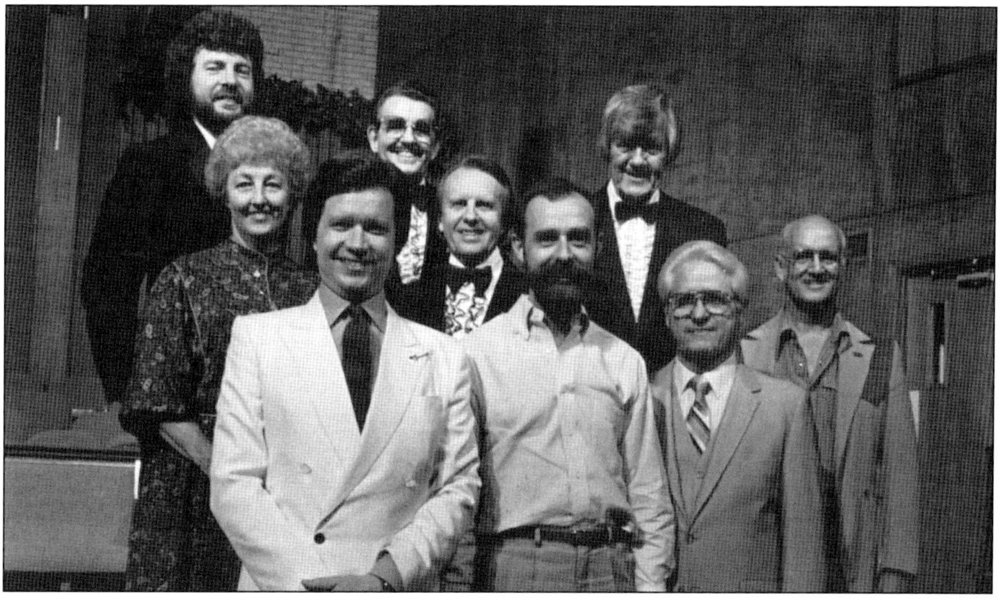

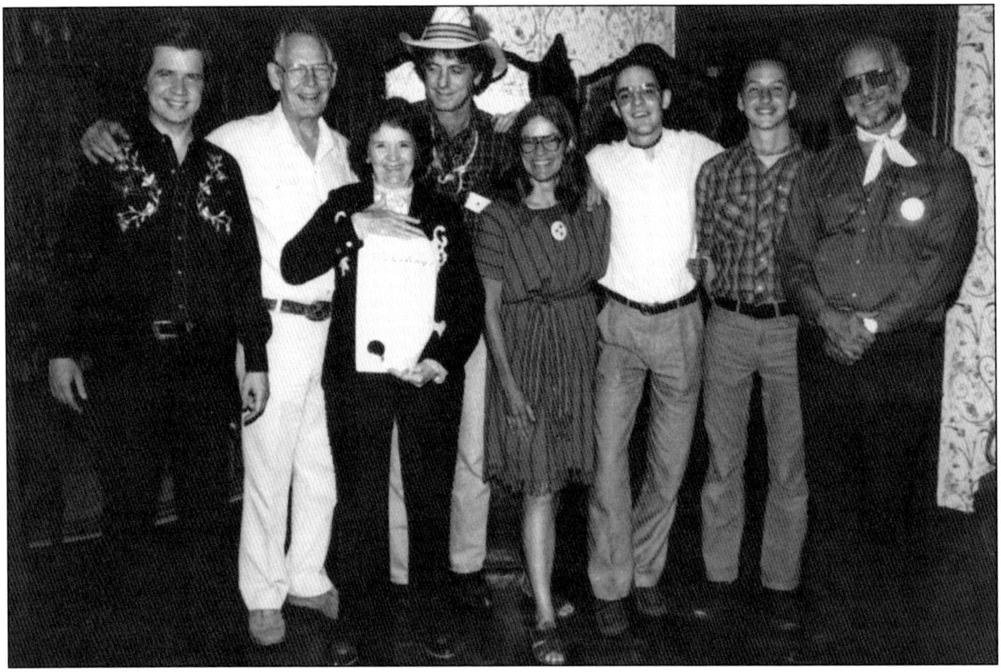

Pictured at a private reception for the Mesquite Folk Festival guest touring artists of 1984 are, from left to right, the author; Leon McAuliffe, world-famous steel guitar player for the Light Crust Doughboys and Texas Playboys; Patsy Montana, the first female country artist to sell a million records (holding Honorary Mayor Proclamation); composer and conductor (in hat) David Amram; Mrs. Rod Kennedy; two caterers from Kalachandji's Restaurant; and folk music promoter (in scarf) Rod Kennedy.

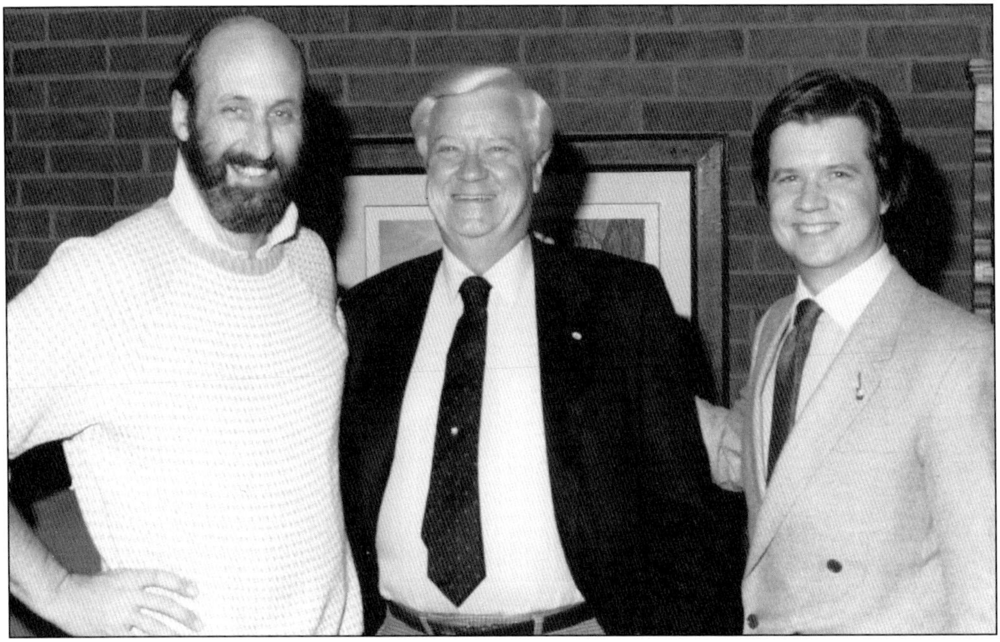

At a Mesquite Folk Festival patron after-party at Eastfield College in 1985, Noel Paul Stookey of Peter Paul and Mary fame (far left) visits with Frank W. Greenhaw and the author.

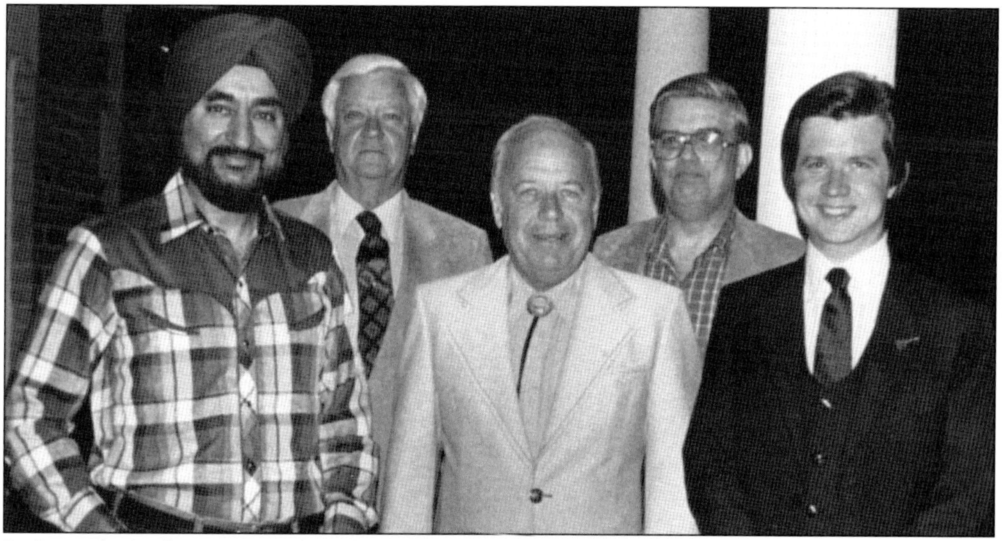

Perhaps the highest-net-worth individual in Mesquite history to rise from middle-class Mesquite origins was Walter "Bitsy" Hailey, pictured at center in a light suit and bolo tie. Hailey acquired control of Lone Star Life Insurance Co. in 1968, developed an insurance marketing system to sell independent grocers group insurance at cooperative rates, and eventually sold his company to Kmart for $78 million. He was a frequent announcer for the Light Crust Doughboys beginning in 1949 and continuing throughout his life. Hailey made an appearance at the 1983 Mesquite Folk Festival as the Doughboys' announcer and is shown here at a reception given in his honor with, from left to right, Ike Sekhon, Frank W. Greenhaw, Gene Shands, and the author.

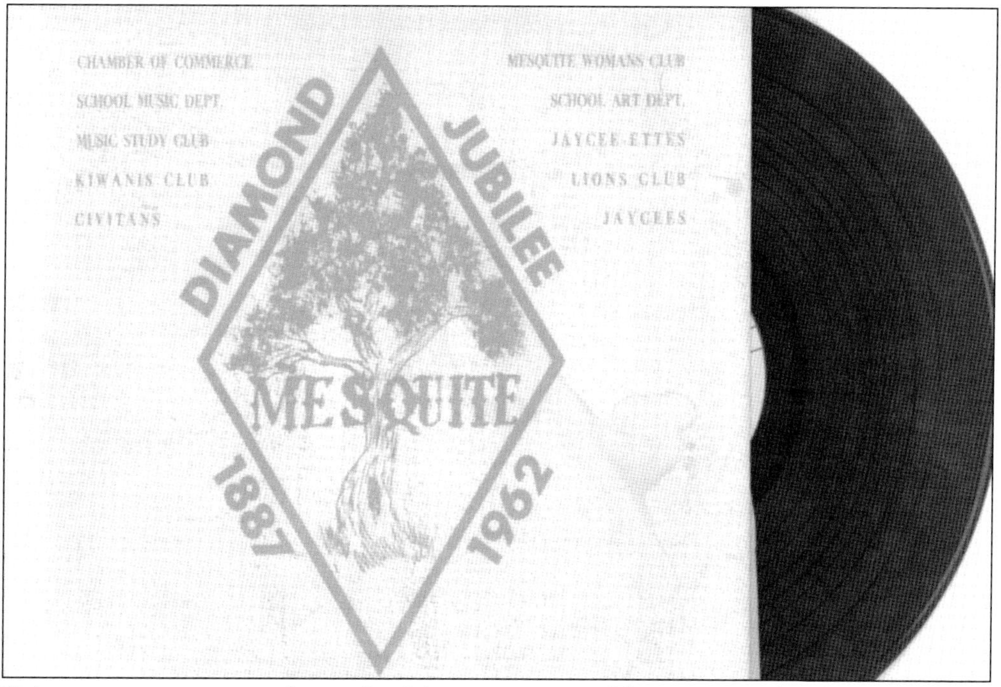

Eight civic organizations and two school departments joined forces to stage the ultimate historical pageant in Mesquite history. Diamond Jubilee was held at the 1962 Skeeter Stadium, and pictured here is the pageant's keepsake record album.

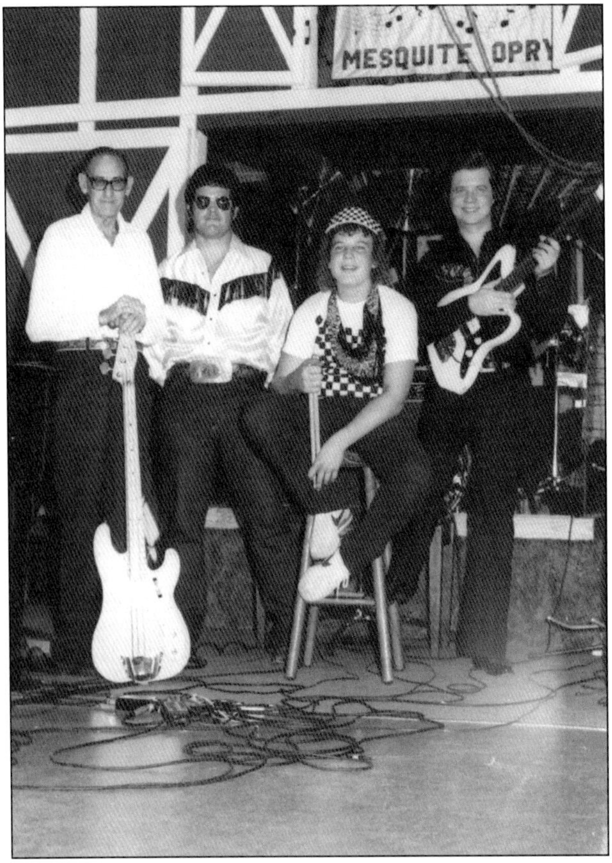

For a period of several years during its glory days in the mid-1980s through mid-1990s, the Mesquite Opry was one of the top-three best-attended country music jamborees in the Dallas–Fort Worth metroplex. The staff musicians, known as the Mesquite Opry Band (in the photograph at left), and the entire cast (seen below) were dedicated to the quality of the shows, and they rehearsed for each upcoming Saturday night performance every Thursday evening and for two hours on Saturdays.

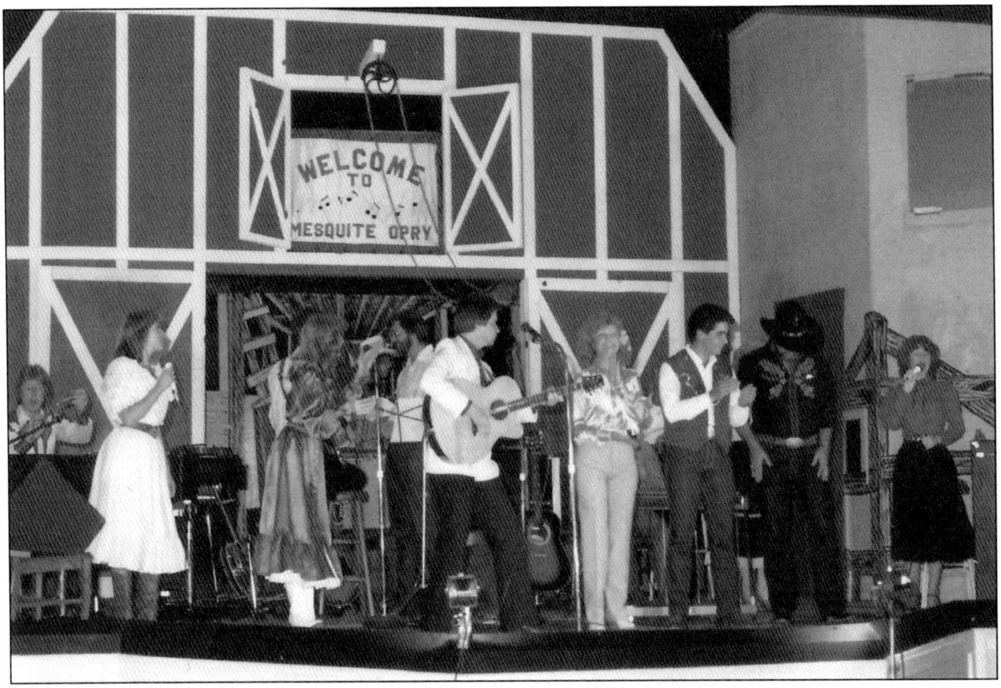

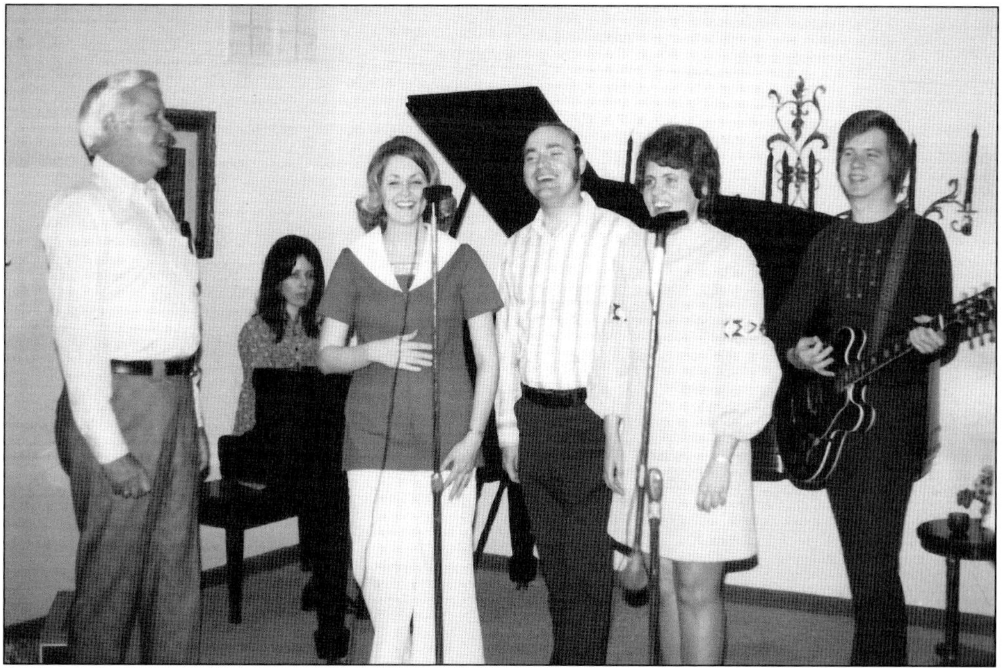

In the slower-paced former Mesquite era of family, flag, and faith, a piano was often found in the living room. In 1972, a small group of Mesquite musicians gathers to play and sing on Galloway Avenue. Pictured are, from left to right, Frank W. Greenhaw, Patsy Bilger at piano, Pat West Root, Rev. Mike Nichols, Judy James, and the author on guitar.

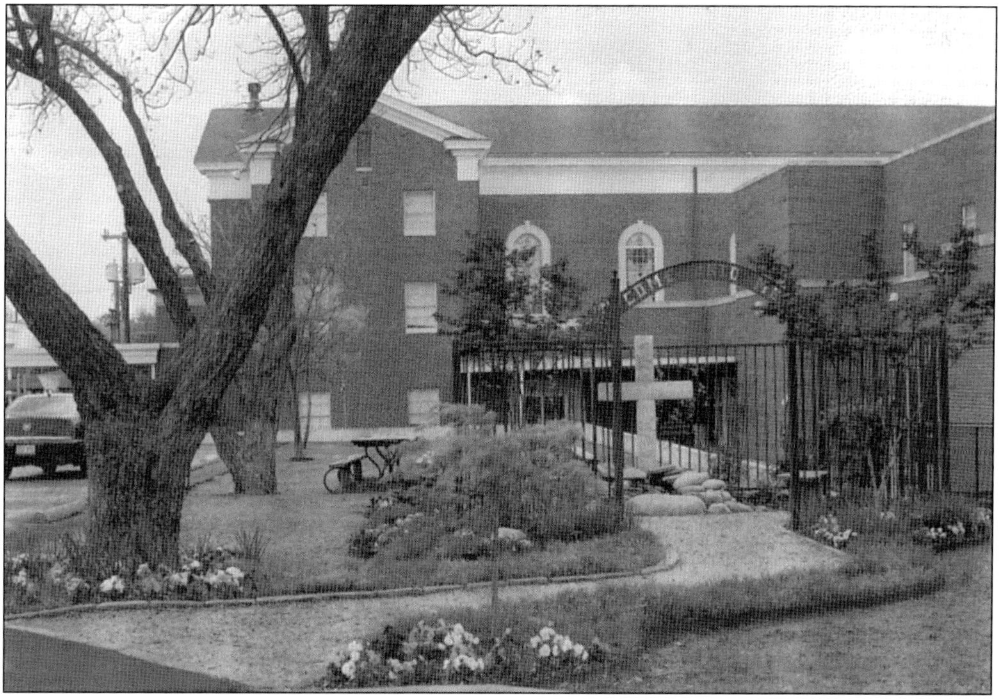

The First United Methodist Church of Mesquite Prayer Garden is an inspiring community landmark developed over the past 20 years. The prayer garden is open to the public 24 hours a day.

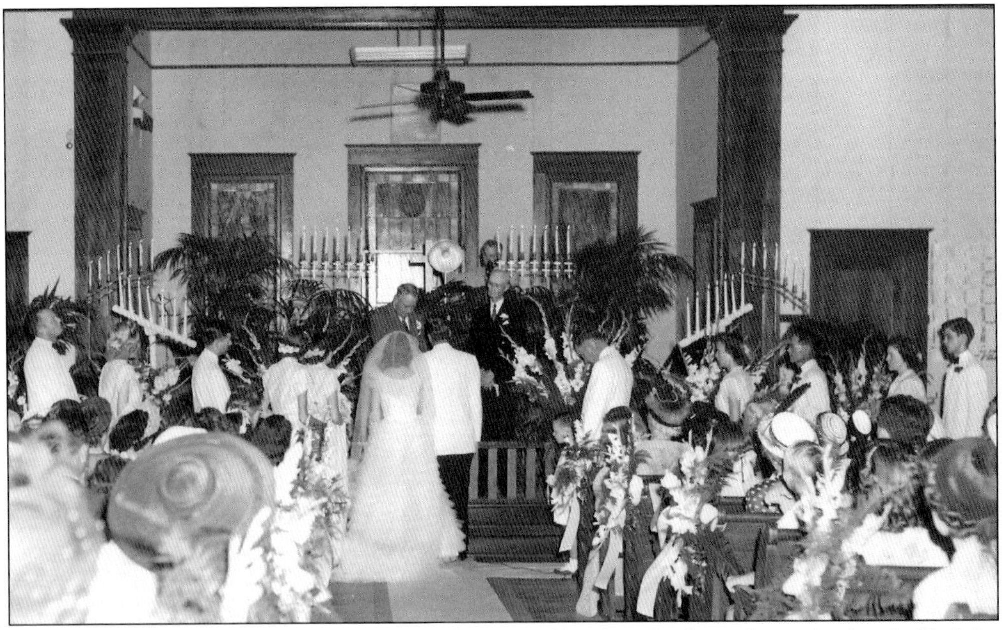

Church interiors adorned like this were architectural landmarks throughout the first half of the 20th century at Mesquite's First Methodist, First Baptist, First Presbyterian, and First Christian churches. First Methodist Church with its beautiful interior, pictured here in 1949, graced North Galloway Street from 1916 until its demolition in 1962.

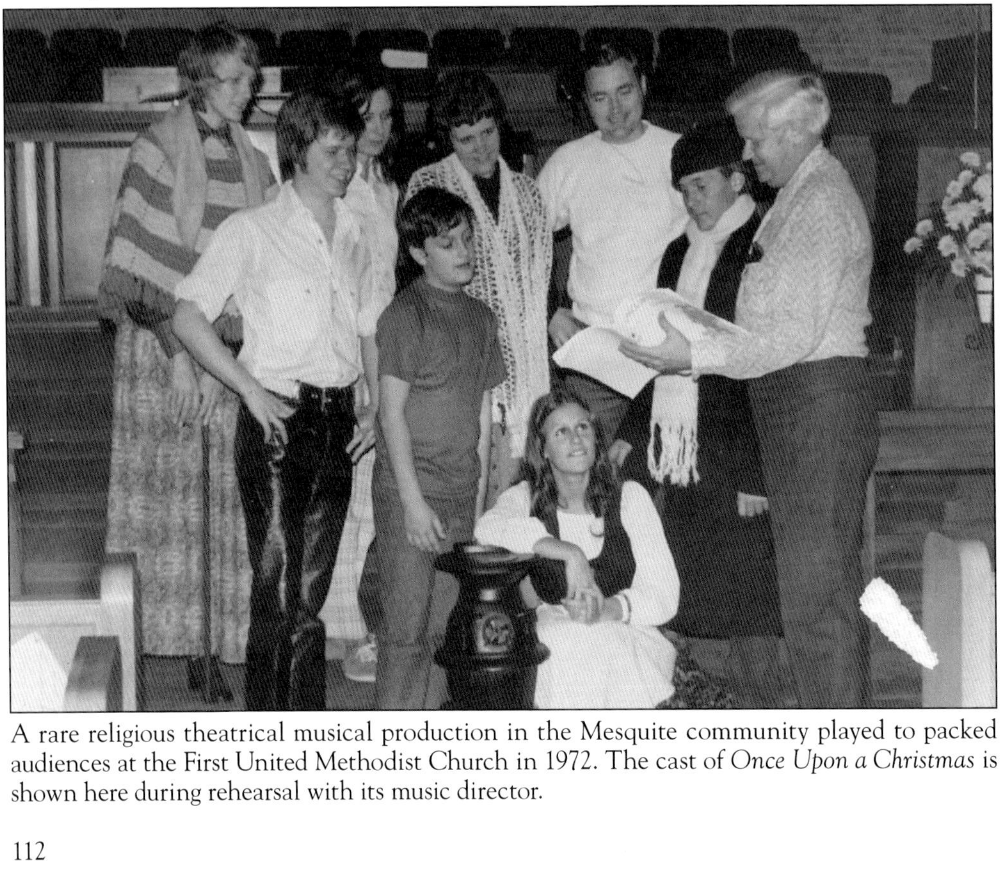

A rare religious theatrical musical production in the Mesquite community played to packed audiences at the First United Methodist Church in 1972. The cast of *Once Upon a Christmas* is shown here during rehearsal with its music director.

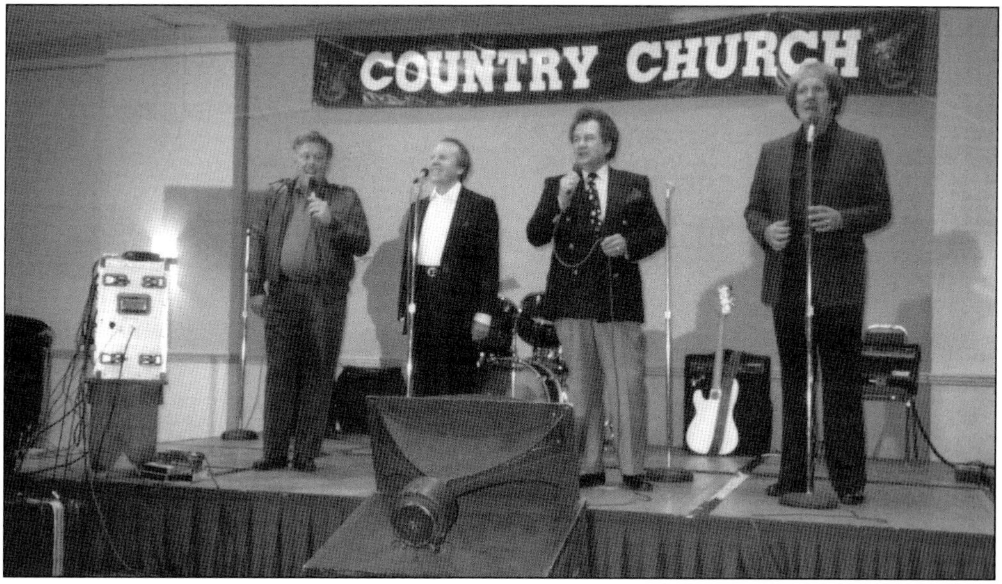

The Country Church, an innovative lifestyle church, was developed in the early 1990s by the Southern Baptist denomination and allowed non-Baptist members from other evangelical Christian denominations to join. Originating in Mesquite, it was the visionary concept of Rev. J.V. Thomas, who conducted organizing meetings at the Mesquite Opry and Western Sizzlin' Steak House. The Country Church was the model the Baptists ultimately used to launch and create the popular "Cowboy Church" congregations now found throughout the country. In the photograph above, the James Blackwood Quartet sings and witnesses. (Country music stars, The Light Crust Doughboys, and a very young Leann Rimes also performed as guest musical artists at Country Church services.) The below photograph shows the hand-painted mural of the Country Church, which was one of the first churches in Mesquite to locate in a strip shopping center.

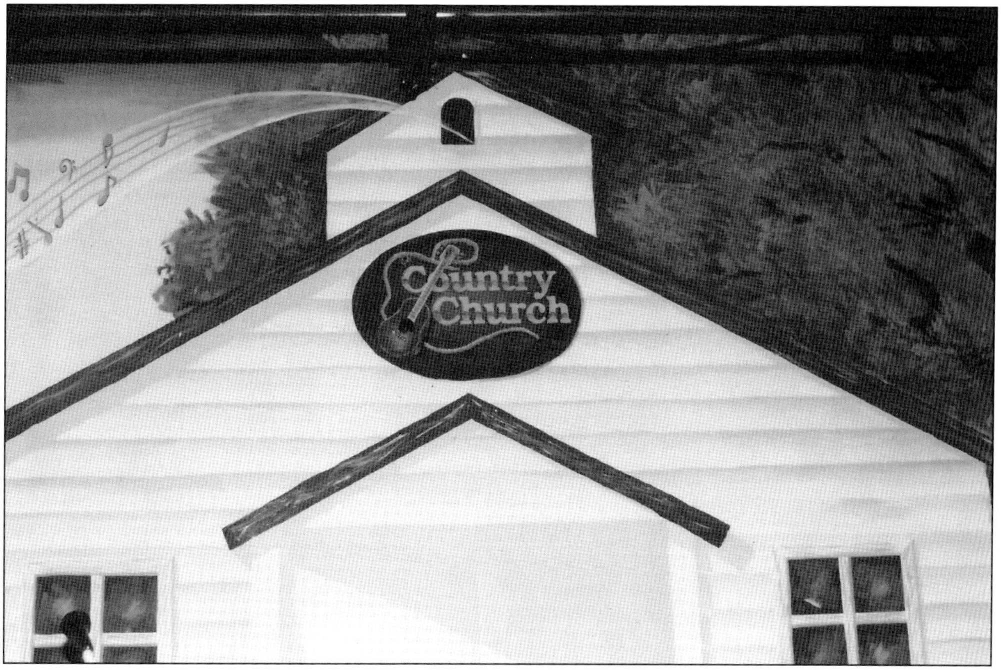

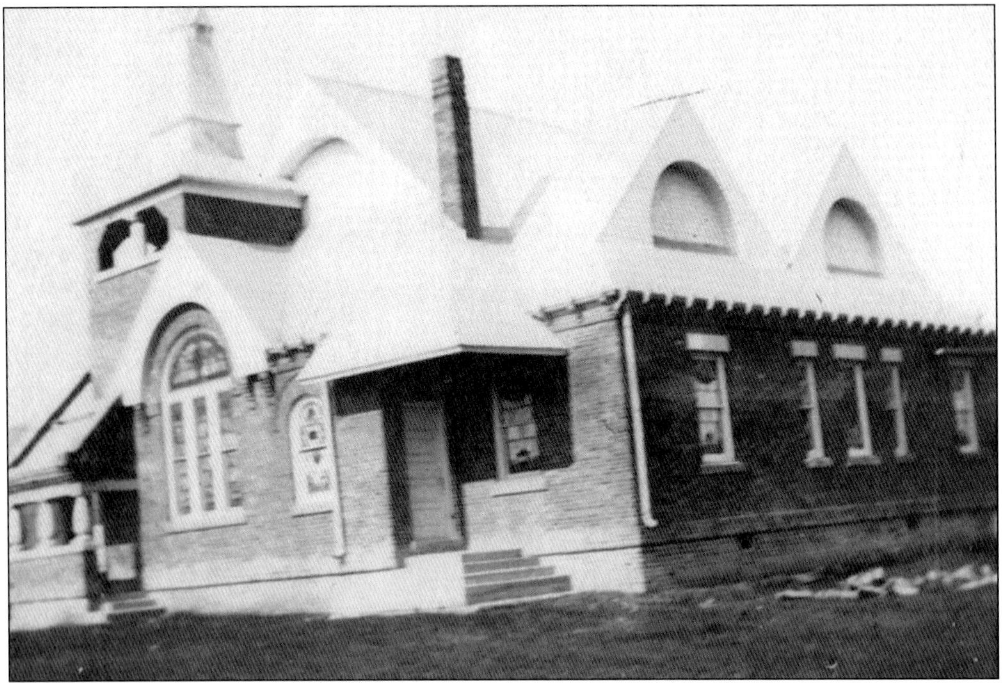

The First Baptist Church of Mesquite building is pictured around 1906. (Courtesy of Historic Mesquite, Inc.)

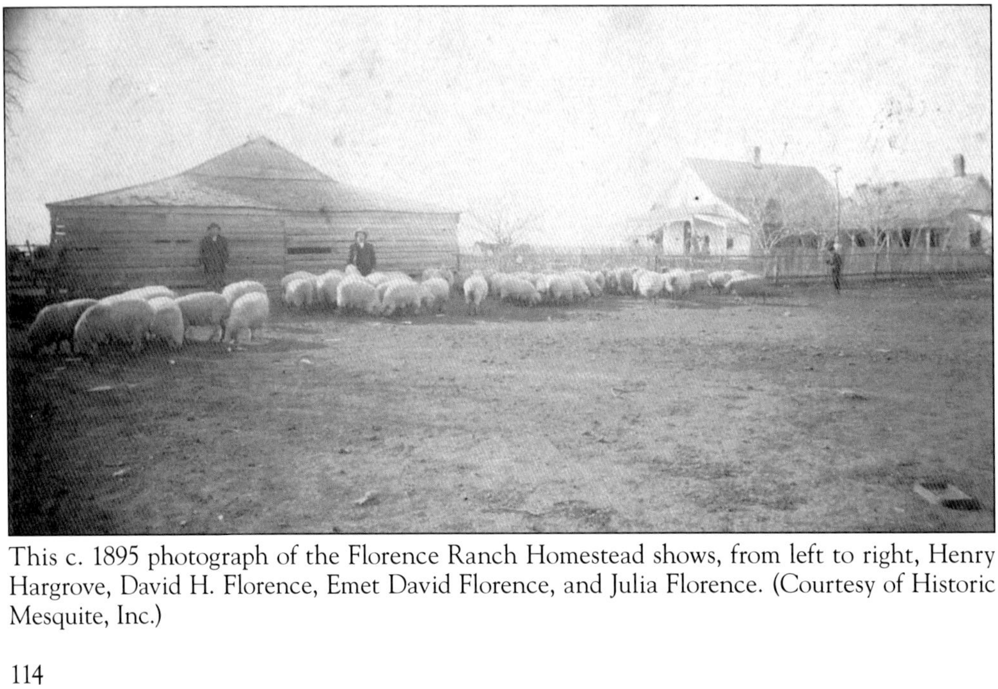

This c. 1895 photograph of the Florence Ranch Homestead shows, from left to right, Henry Hargrove, David H. Florence, Emet David Florence, and Julia Florence. (Courtesy of Historic Mesquite, Inc.)

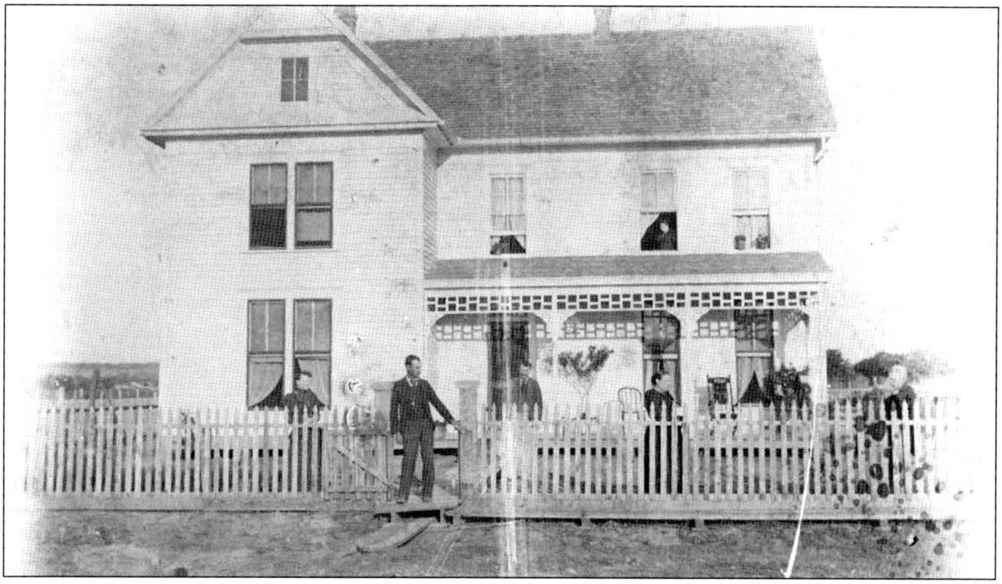

Note the early-20th-century Mesquite residential architecture found in this photograph of the Walker family home place. (Courtesy of Historic Mesquite, Inc.)

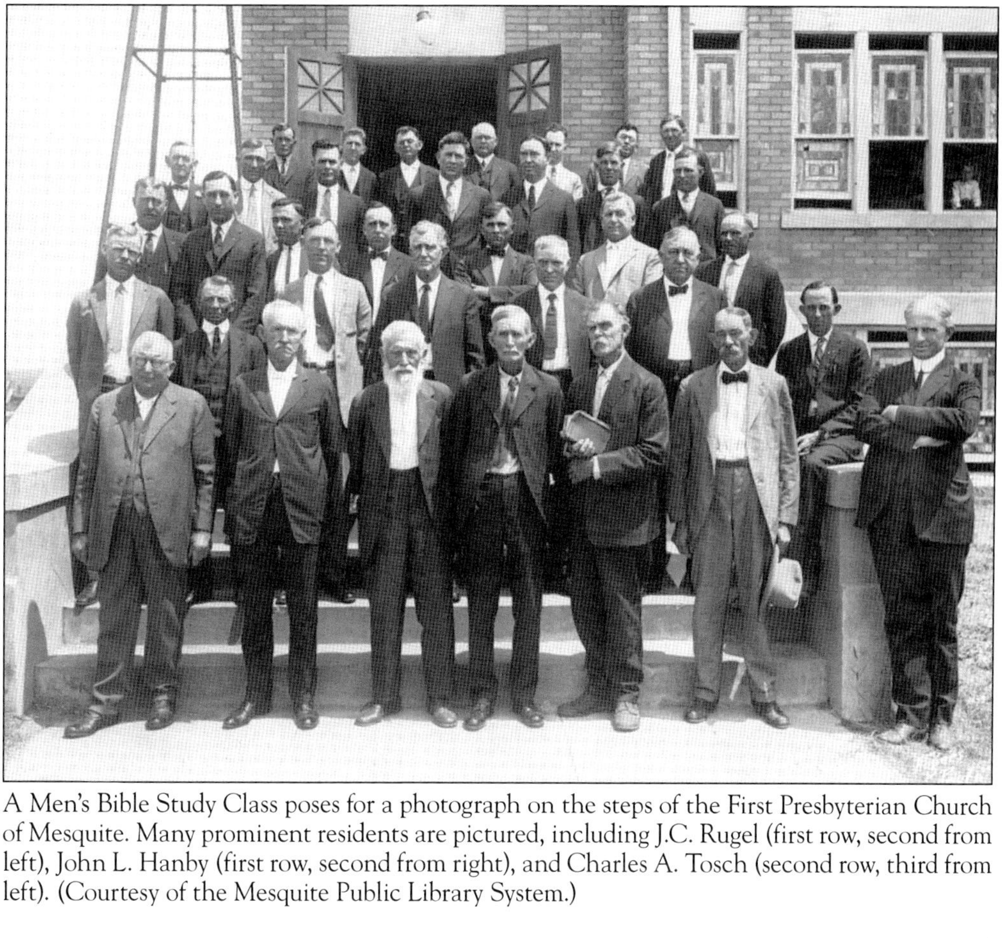

A Men's Bible Study Class poses for a photograph on the steps of the First Presbyterian Church of Mesquite. Many prominent residents are pictured, including J.C. Rugel (first row, second from left), John L. Hanby (first row, second from right), and Charles A. Tosch (second row, third from left). (Courtesy of the Mesquite Public Library System.)

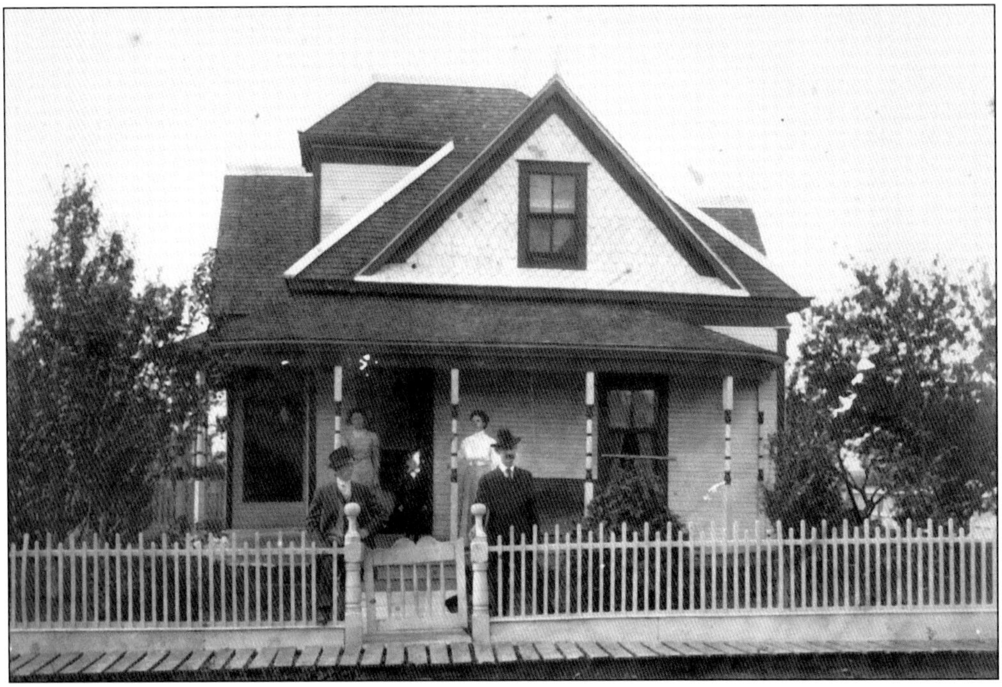

The Paschall family name was one found frequently in Mesquite throughout the 20th century. Photographed here is a very early Paschall family residence. (Courtesy of the Mesquite Public Library System.)

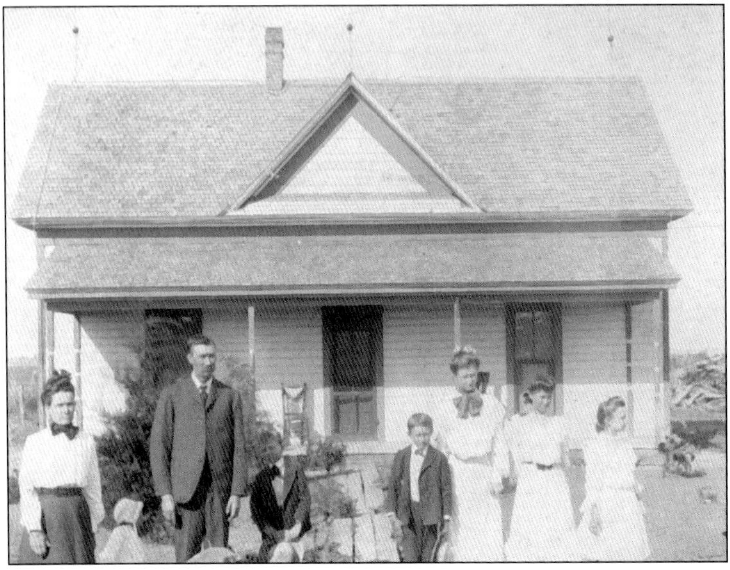

Nathaniel A. Holley's first wife and first-born son died in Mesquite's spotted fever epidemic in 1891. Holley is photographed here with his new family and home place around 1902–1903. Pictured here are, from left to right, "new" family members Adell, baby Eula, Nathaniel, or "Uncle Nat" as he was called by townsfolk, Anson, Raymond, and Elsie, along with two friends of the family.

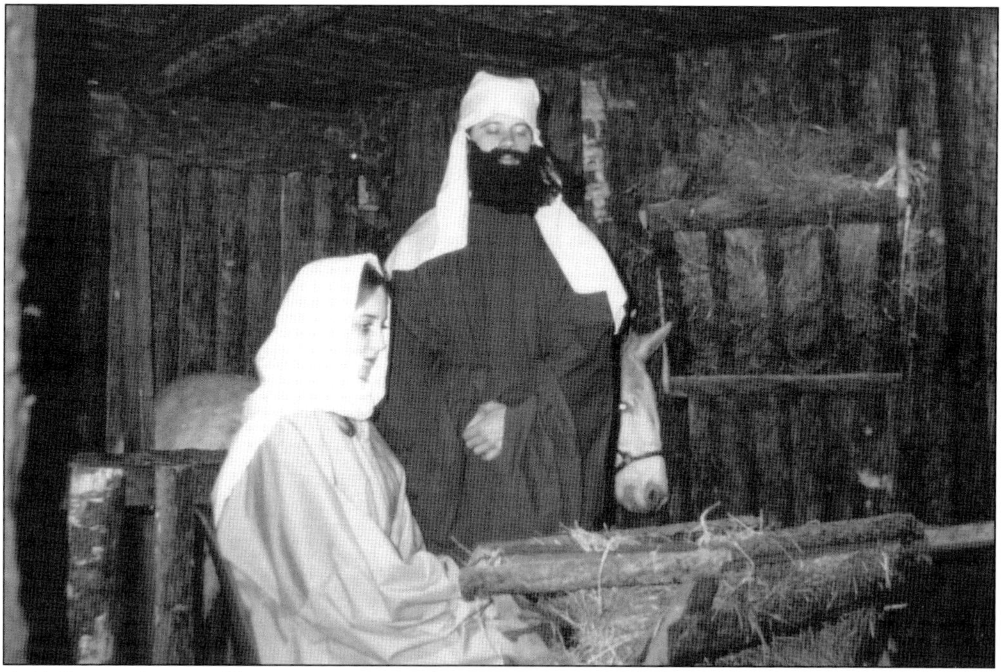

A Galloway Avenue Christmas season milestone since 1963 has been the living nativity scene on the lawn of First Methodist Church. Begun under the pastoral ministry of Rev. Earl Harvey, the reenactment of the first Christmas has involved thousands of church members and participants who stand silently for 30 minutes at a time for two or three shifts throughout the course of December evenings. Pick a member of First Methodist Church in the 1960s or 1970s, and chances are one will find a "shepherd" or a "wise man" actor. In these photographs, Vicki Murdoch portrays Mary, and the author portrays Joseph.

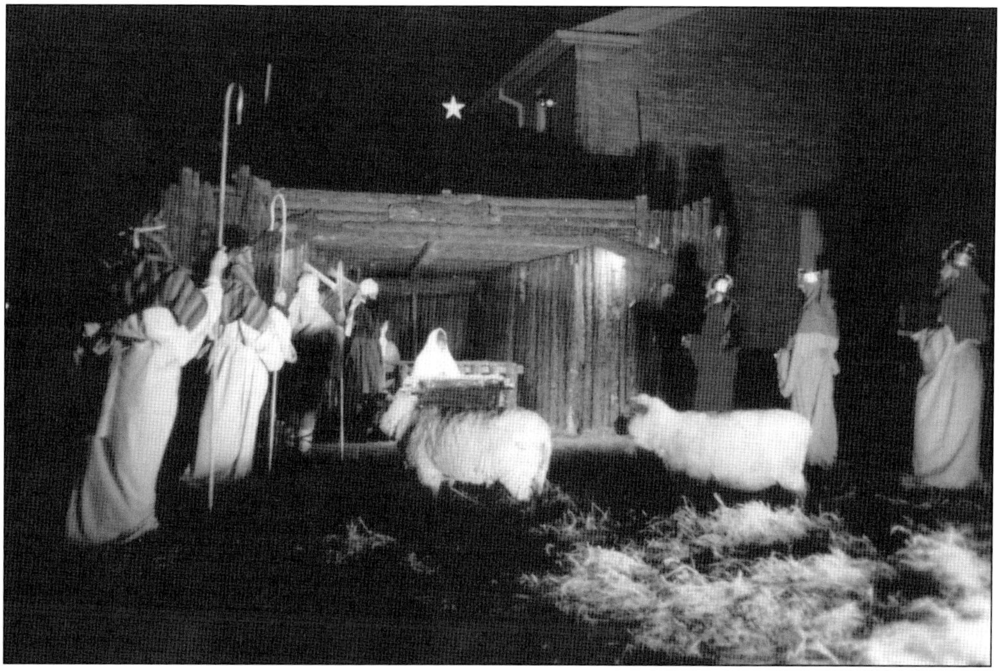

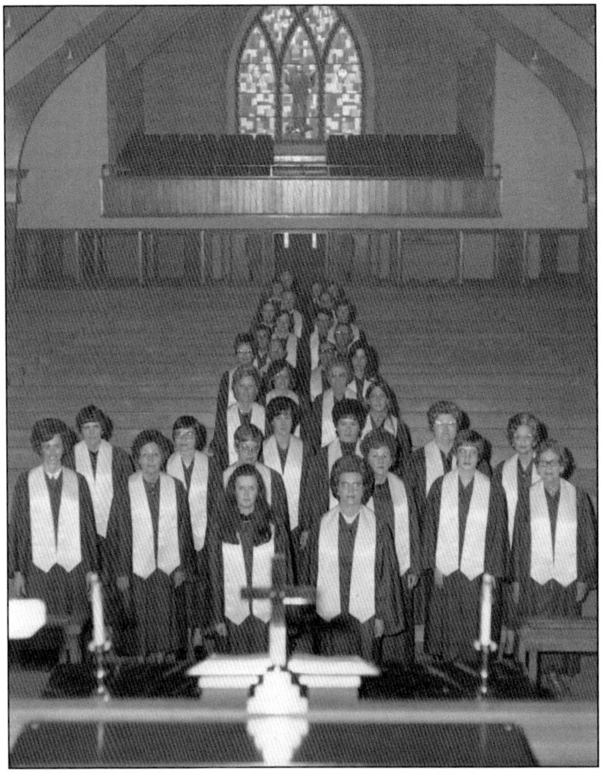

During Boomtown USA Mesquite in the 1950s, several major church sanctuaries were erected, the likes of which have not been equaled since. Pictured here is the magnificent interior of First Methodist Church, in downtown Mesquite, and the landmark stained-glass window titled *Come Unto Me.*

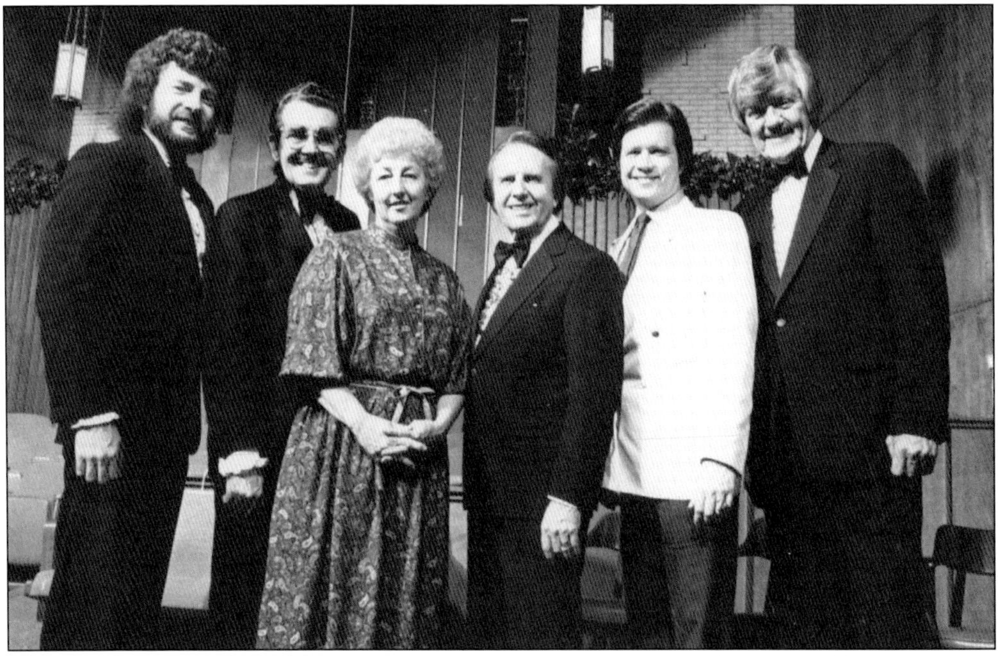

In 1983, the Mesquite Folk Festival production team brought to downtown Mesquite's First Assembly of God Church the most legendary names in 20th-century classic, southern gospel music. Pictured, from left to right, are Sherrill "Shaun" Nielson, Hovie Lister, Joann Cheek, James Blackwood, the author, and J.D. Sumner.

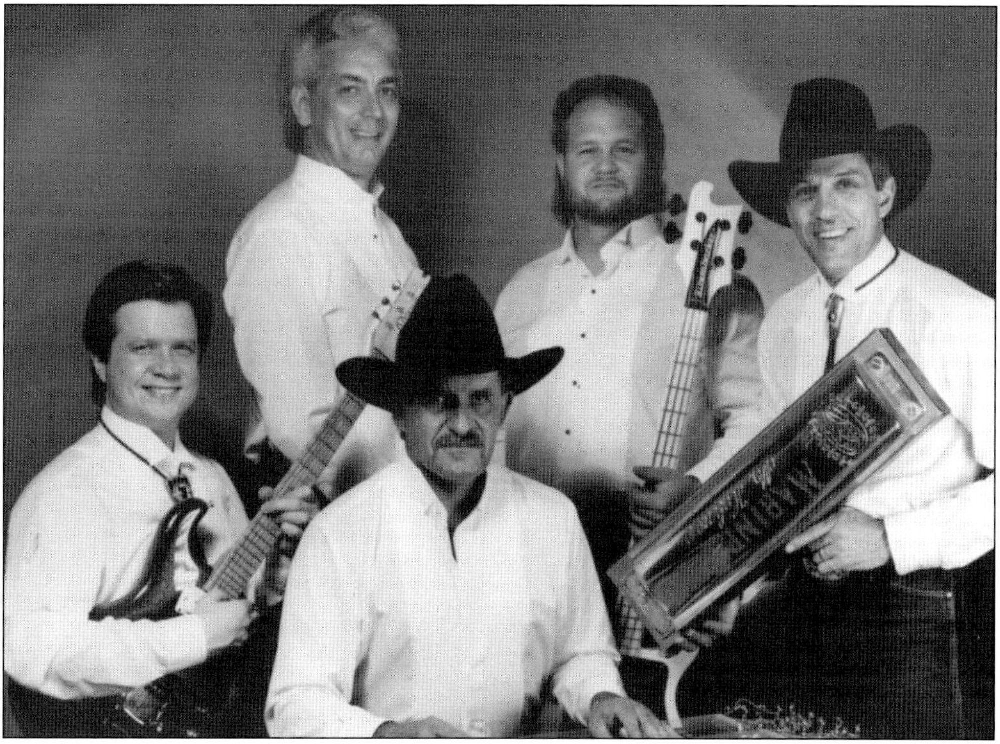

Another incarnation of the popular Mesquite Opry Band from the downtown square poses for Shipman Photography. It includes, from left to right, (seated) the author and Junior Knight, (standing) Paul Polish, Thomas Miller, and Jerl Welch. This particular staff band recorded albums and musically backed opry guest stars including Patsy Montana, Norma Jean, LeAnn Rimes, Johnny Crawford of the Rifleman fame, and others.

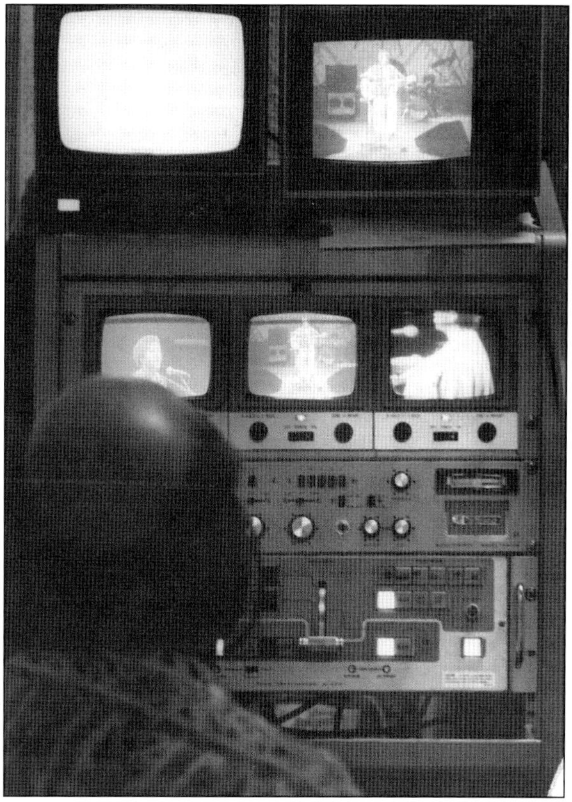

A backstage photograph captures folk legend Odetta on the television screens; she was performing live onstage at the 1982 debut of the annual Mesquite Folk Festival produced in conjunction with Eastfield College, whose president was Eleanor Ott. During this innovative period in Mesquite arts and culture, the City of Mesquite supported, through joint sponsorship with Eastfield College, its very own community television programming named Mesquite Public Access.

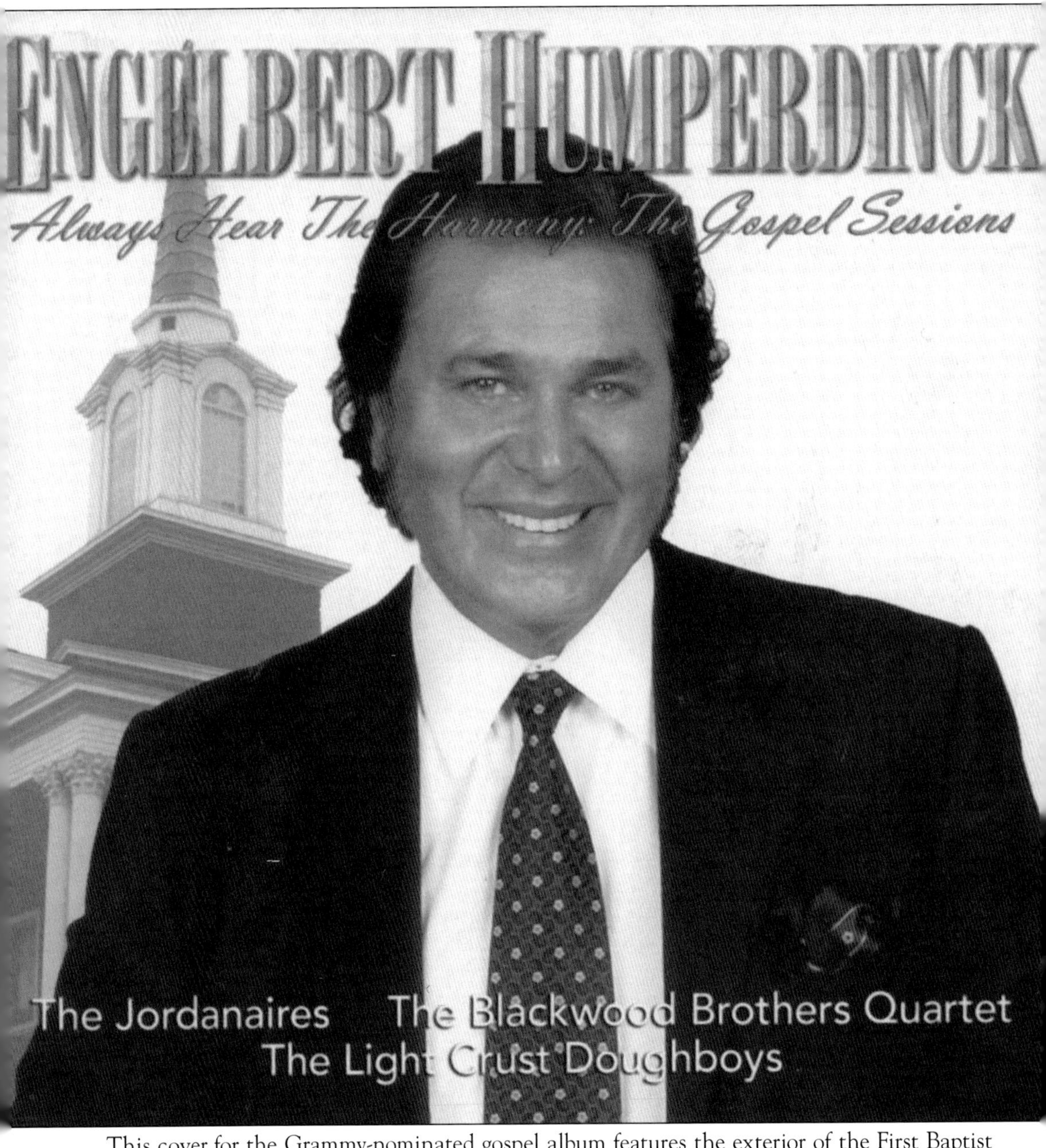

This cover for the Grammy-nominated gospel album features the exterior of the First Baptist Church in downtown Mesquite, Texas, behind music superstar Engelbert Humperdinck. The album was produced and arranged by the author.

A brochure from Mesquite's glory days of arts and culture advertises a Triple Treat Season produced by the City of Mesquite, the Mesquite Arts Council, and Eastfield College that includes the 11th Annual Festival of 20th Century Music, the First Annual Mesquite Folk Festival, and the Eastfield Recital Series.

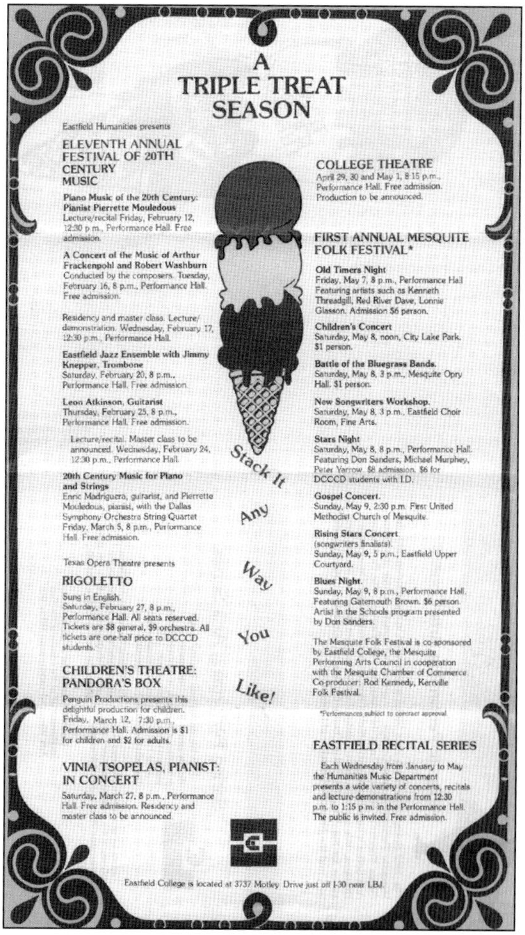

The outside cover of the Triple Treat Season brochure advertises the art and cultural events of the 1982 season in Mesquite, Texas. The combined strength and synergy of the Mesquite Performing Arts Council, Eastfield College, and the City of Mesquite created a powerhouse of culture in the history of Mesquite.

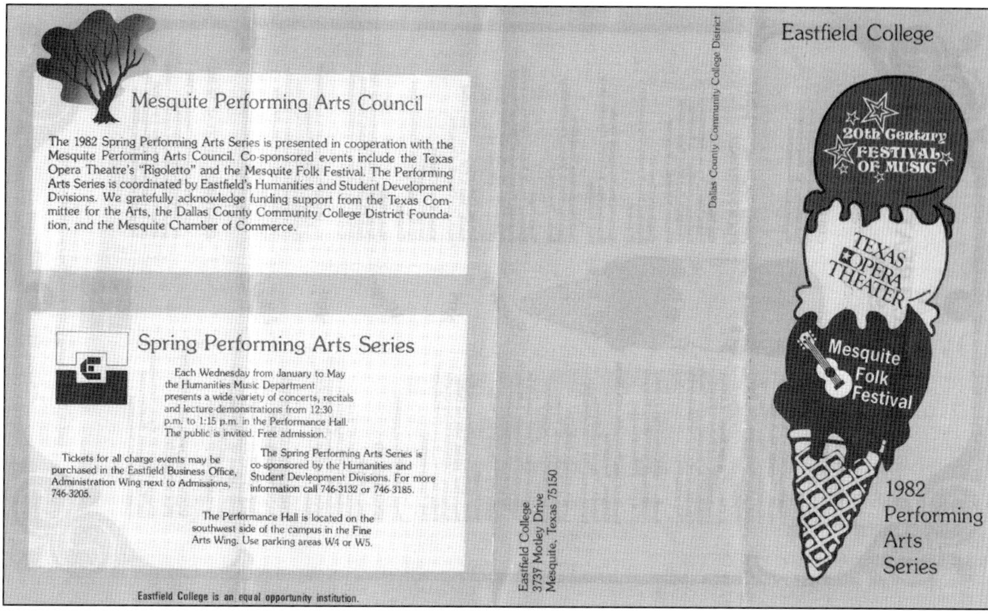

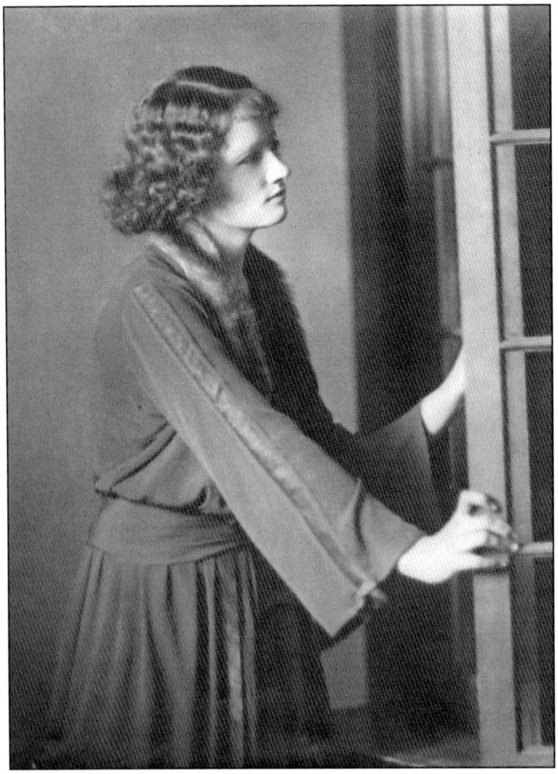

Even in 1920, there was glamour photography and there were girls who could qualify as fashion models or movie stars of the day and age. Character Norma Desmond emphatically states in the film classic *Sunset Boulevard*, "We didn't need dialogue. We had faces!" Like Norma says, this image of young Eula Holley (at left and below, left) needs no words or sound, it has that face! Eula Holley McWhorter lived her entire life from 1901 through 1994 in Mesquite. Along the way, she helped to establish the Mesquite Woman's Club and McWhorter's Furniture-Appliances while homemaking for three generations of her Holley-McWhorter family.

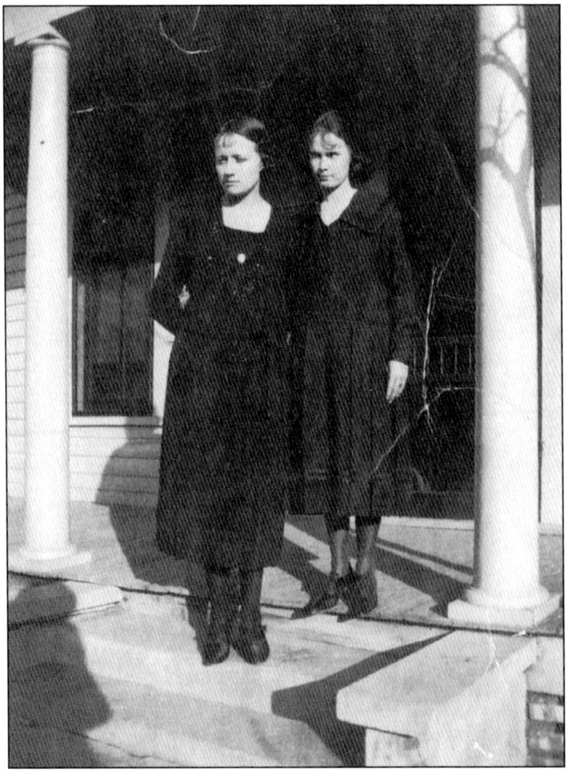

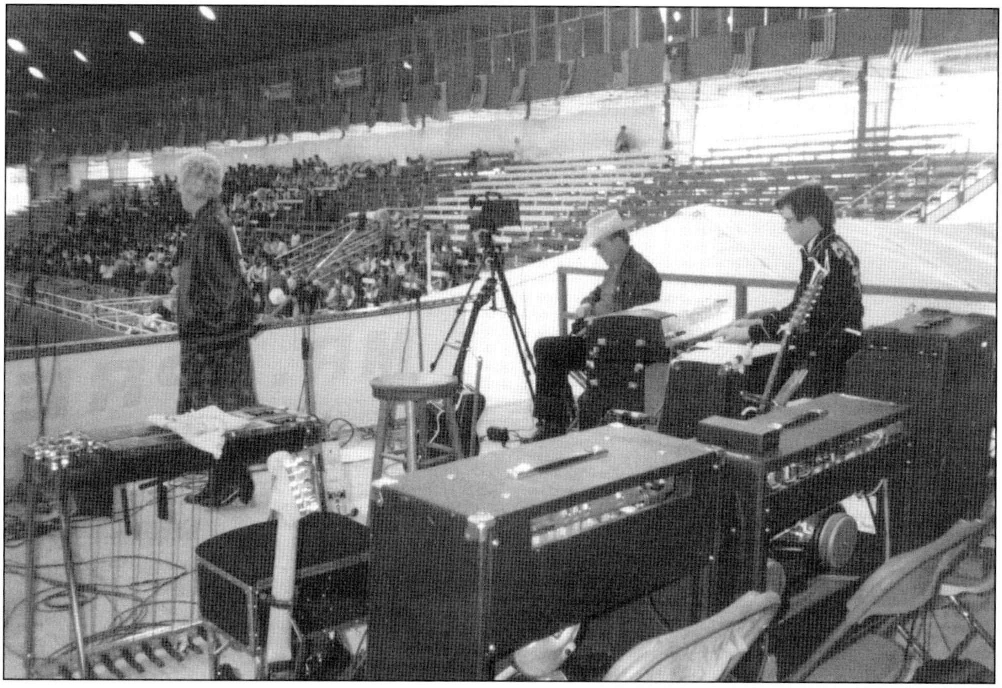

It was indeed a milestone in Mesquite history when sitting president Ronald Reagan made a final campaign stop for George H.W. Bush at the Mesquite Rodeo arena in 1988. The Mesquite Opry Band was tapped to provide musical entertainment, and this photograph depicts, from left to right, opry proprietors Janet and John Ingram and the author setting up the music stage several hours prior to the president's arrival.

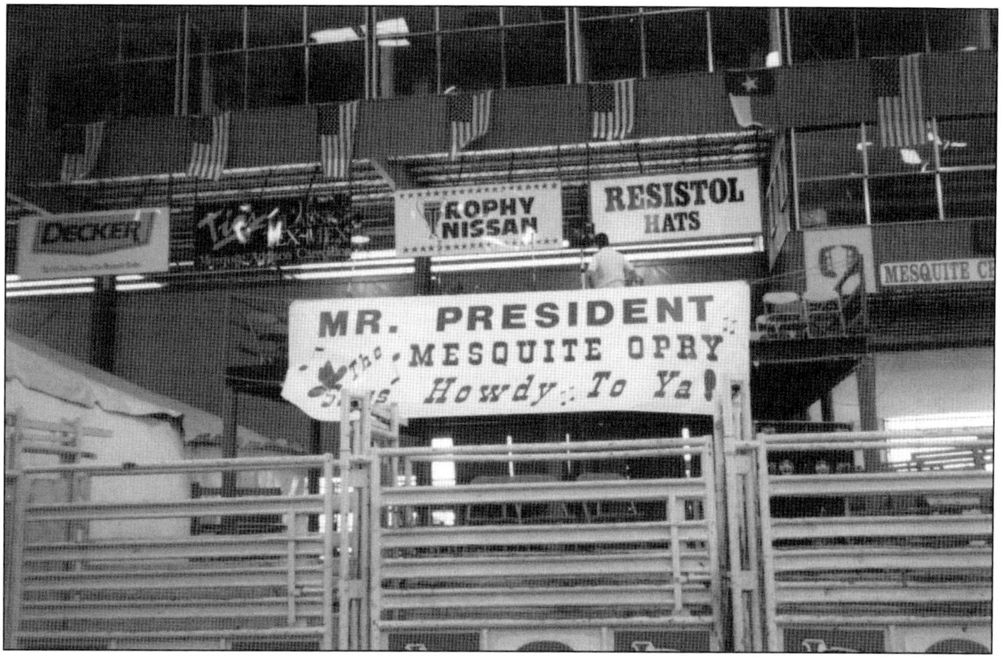

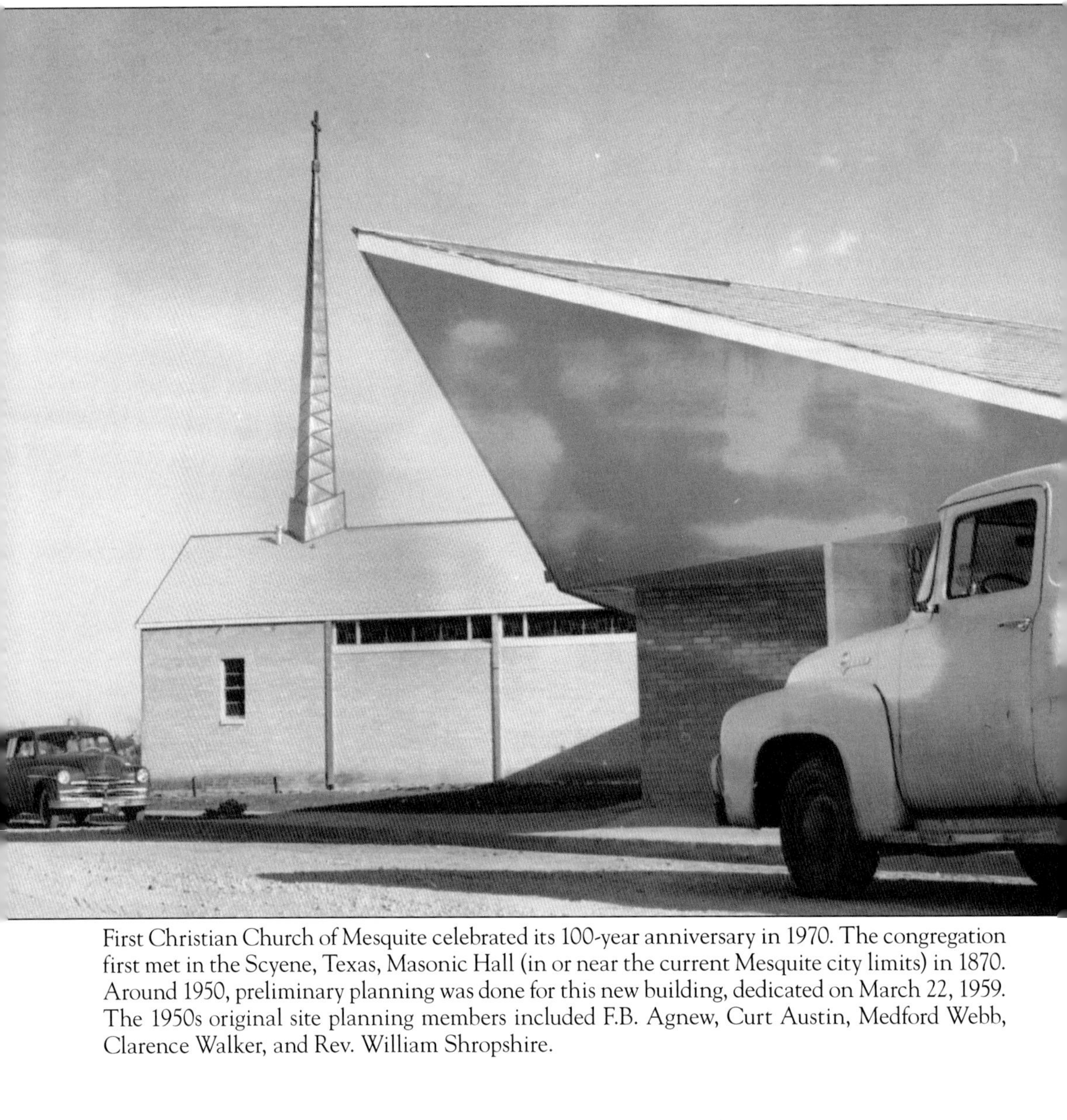

First Christian Church of Mesquite celebrated its 100-year anniversary in 1970. The congregation first met in the Scyene, Texas, Masonic Hall (in or near the current Mesquite city limits) in 1870. Around 1950, preliminary planning was done for this new building, dedicated on March 22, 1959. The 1950s original site planning members included F.B. Agnew, Curt Austin, Medford Webb, Clarence Walker, and Rev. William Shropshire.

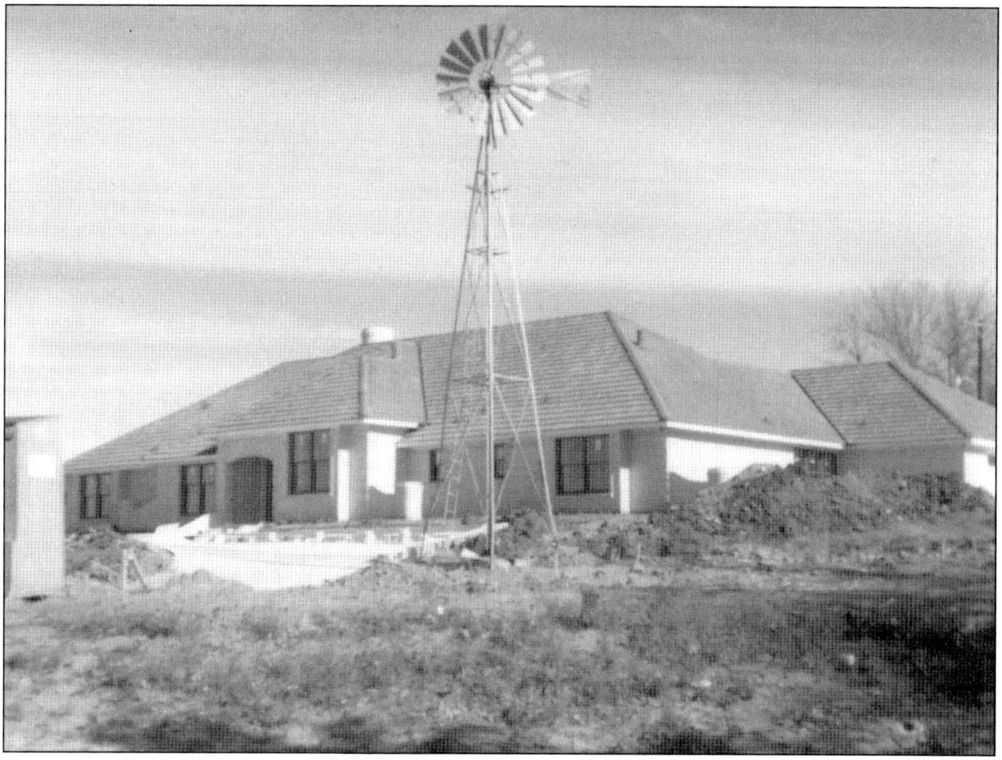

New, upscale, large-lot homebuilding greatly improved Mesquite's housing offerings in the years 1981 through 1986. In this photograph, a magnificent house being built in 1981 by successful cement business owner C.D. Brimer is on its way to becoming a landmark home, inspiring others to also want to invest in premium residential property within the city.

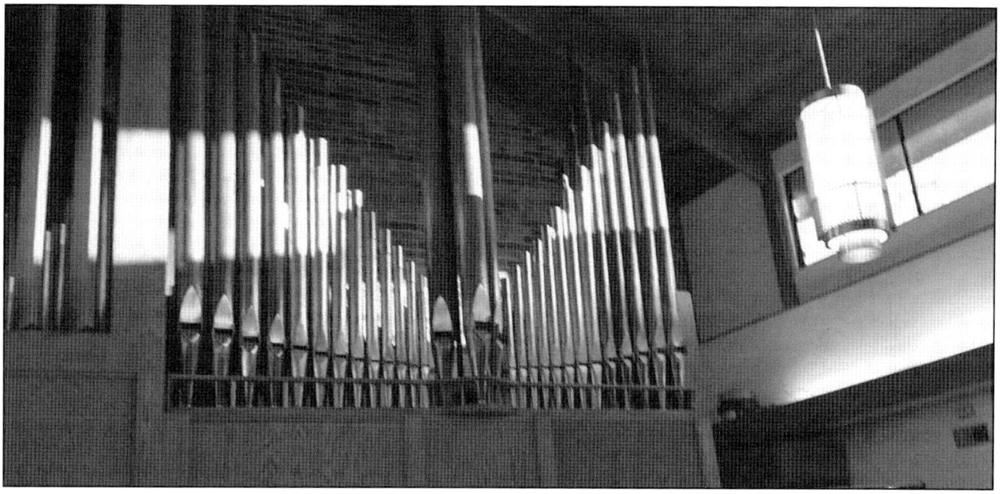

R.M. "Mac" Range of Mesquite was an internationally sought after pipe organ builder. Mac was the son of Rex and Lorene Range and husband to civic leader, arts visionary, and opera singer-teacher Martha Range. Mac's acclaimed work is seen in this photograph of the custom-built Range organ located in Our Savior Lutheran Church in Mesquite. Martha was a key figure in the creation of the Mesquite Symphony and Guild and masterminded the 1986 Mesquite-commissioned comic opera, *The Ransom of Red Chief.* (Courtesy of Caryl Semmler.)

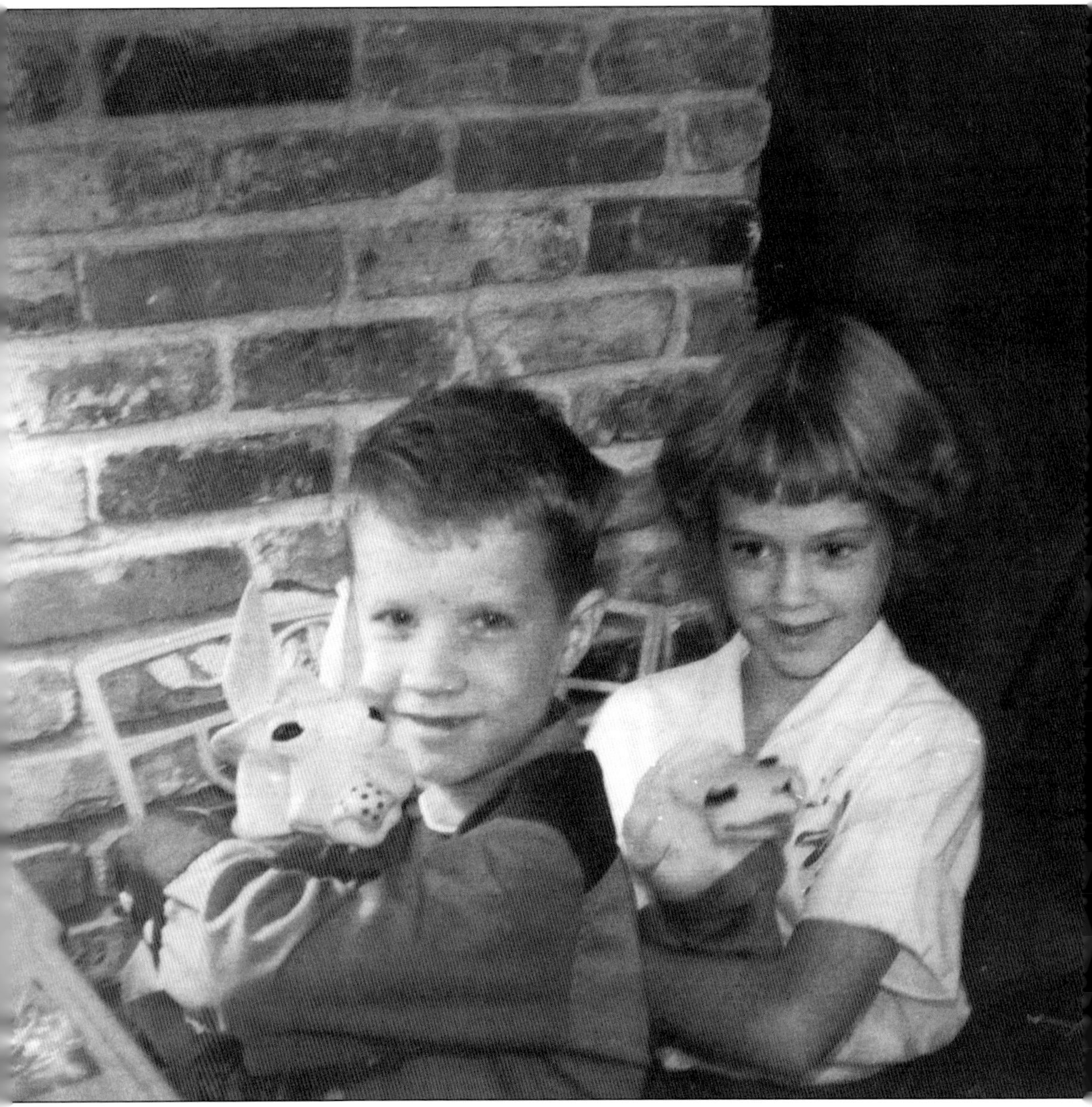

When Mesquite retains its younger and future generations once again to live and work in the city, the best of times will resurface. Pictured here are the author and Carol Anne Poteet, members of the next generation, photographed at the Greenhaw home place.

About the Author

Author Art Greenhaw's Texas and Mesquite roots run deep. He graduated with highest honors from Mesquite High School where he was a National Council of Teachers of English competition award winner and received the *Dallas Morning News* and Zales Corporation Teenage Annual Citizenship Tribute Award. He was the founder of the Mesquite Folk Festival and cofounder of the Mesquite Guitar Festival, served as chairman of the City of Mesquite Planning and Zoning Commission and Environmental Beautification Committee, and was founding president of Mesquite Performing Arts Council. The City of Mesquite awarded both his record label, Art Greenhaw Records, and his band, the Light Crust Doughboys, special proclamation days for national achievements and Grammy recognition. A music producer and real estate developer by vocation, he garnered eight Grammy Award nominations in eight years, winning a Grammy Award in 2003. His avocation is going into all nations and cultures with gospel and Christian music, arts, records, and films.

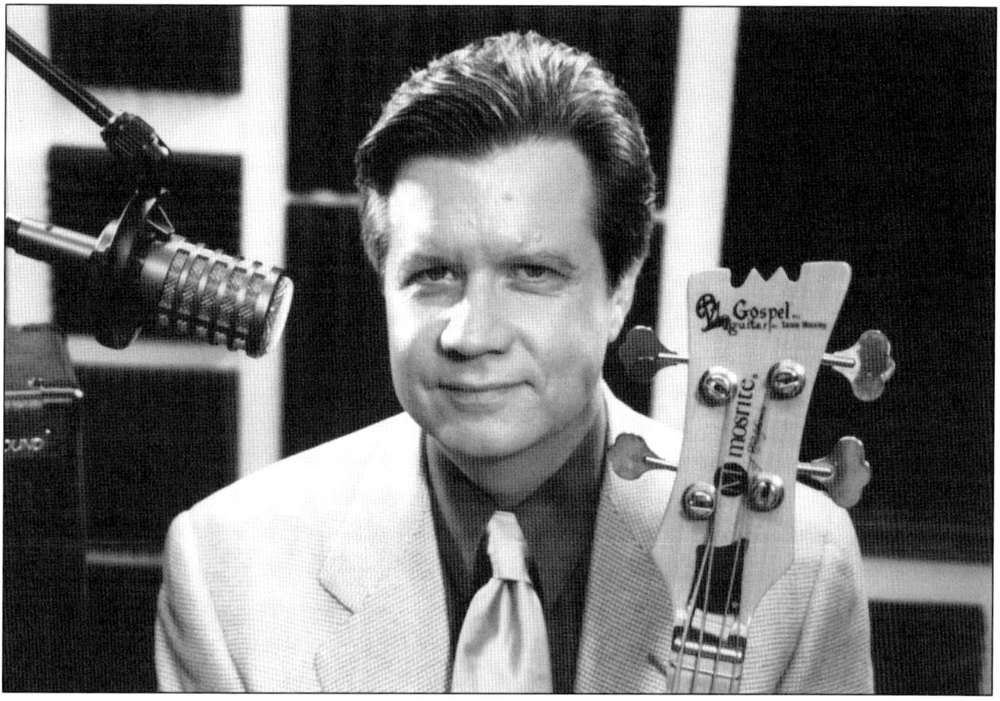